FRANK FURNESS

FRANK

FURNESS

ARCHITECTURE IN THE AGE OF THE GREAT MACHINES

GEORGE E. THOMAS

FOREWORD BY ALAN HESS

PENN

UNIVERSITY OF PENNSYLVANIA PRESS

Philadelphia

A volume in the Haney Foundation Series, established in 1961 with the generous support of Dr. John Louis Haney.

Publication of this book has been aided by a grant from the Wyeth Foundation for American Art Publication Fund of the College Art Association.

Published by
University of Pennsylvania Press
Philadelphia, Pennsylvania 19104–4112
www.upenn.edu/pennpress

Printed in the United States of America on acid-free paper
10 9 8 7 6 5 4 3 2 1

Library of Congress Cataloging-in-Publication Data
Names: Thomas, George E., author. | Hess, Alan, writer of foreword.
Title: Frank Furness : architecture in the age of the great machines / George E. Thomas ; foreword by Alan Hess.
Other titles: Haney Foundation series.
Description: 1st edition. | Philadelphia : University of Pennsylvania Press, [2018] | Series: Haney Foundation series | Includes bibliographical references and index.
Identifiers: LCCN 2017033925 | ISBN 978-0-8122-4952-1 (hardcover : alk. paper)
Subjects: LCSH: Furness, Frank, 1839–1912. | Architecture—United States—History—19th century. | Architecture—United States—History—20th century. | Architecture—Pennsylvania—Philadelphia.
Classification: LCC NA737.F84 T49 2018 | DDC 720.973/09034—dc23
LC record available at https://lccn.loc.gov/2017033925

CONTENTS

THE AMERICAN CREATIVITY
OF FRANK FURNESS

ALAN HESS

As an architectural historian of the American West, I have always been drawn to the exuberance of the region's modern designs that hang from poles, jut out from cliffs, border great highways, and disrupt the narrative of modern architecture as it has been written since the Museum of Modern Art's first exhibit on the International Style in 1932. The West was a region of tremendous growth and innovation in the twentieth century, just as, in the decades following the Civil War, the East had been. It was there, mostly east of the Mississippi River in the realm of the Pennsylvania Railroad, that Frank Furness helped lay the foundation that shapes modern American architecture as we know it today.

What does Frank Furness still mean to us? What were the circumstances that allowed him to see and creatively interpret, free of conventional biases, the forces at work in his day? How did similar approaches devised by other, later architects inspire significant modern architecture after him, even as his own work was largely ignored or misunderstood in the high art and architecture histories? The usual story historians tell about the birth of modern architecture sidetracked Frank Furness long ago. How could they have mistaken such a pivotal figure as a mere curiosity?

Furness grew his modernism not from speculative theories or blue-sky philosophy but from life as the industrial age was creating it all around him. His modern approach was just as much about technical innovations in engineering and construction as it was about the way modern factories and their products were reinventing the lives of people at all levels of society. Baldwin Locomotive Works' thousands of steam engines, manufactured in Philadelphia, and the Pennsylvania Railroad, headquartered and created in Philadelphia, tied the expansive nation together in a way that transformed both corporate commerce and family vacations. A thriving and democratic American economy was creating wealth, enlarging cities, and creating leisure time. Some of the most influential and culturally transformative companies of his day—the Apple, Microsoft, and Google of those times—were in Philadelphia, and their leaders were Furness's clients. Independent of history and disinterested in European fashion, Furness's Philadelphia was still the spiritual home of Ben Franklin, and quite willing to overthrow old traditions, fashions, or theories for a good reason. This was the modernity that Furness captured in his new architecture.

That pragmatic, reality-based spirit would never disappear from the course of modernism, especially in America; but like Furness's career, it wasn't usually reported in the standard histories. The legions of critics and historians documenting the rise of the Bauhaus in Europe in the 1920s favored the European tradition of high art culture wherein academic theory had to underpin any architecture that was to be considered seriously. By the time New York's Museum of Modern Art spotlighted modern architecture's achievements in the 1932 International Style exhibit, the groundwork had been laid for the story of modernism as the province of an elite avant-garde. Even if these historians had heard of Furness (perhaps from reading the memoirs of Louis Sullivan, his one-time employee), his significance was not recognized. Ensconced in New York, Paris, or London, they were unprepared to see how modern life, in all its phases, had developed in unheralded Philadelphia and how its industrial design, technologies, and values had shaped Furness's designs. Reflecting the multiplying power of the commercial economy, the raw power of technology, and the desires and needs of the popular audience, Furness generated forms and solutions that would usually rile the critics as crude, exaggerated, and (from their educated perspective) tasteless. Later critics would have a similar response.

When modernist historians began to look back to find the roots of modernism, Furness appeared to be a fussy historicist Victorian—exactly what modern architecture was meant to overthrow. George Thomas's text correctly identifies Furness as the very embodiment of his modern times. He drew upon the pistons, the raw combination of forms and functions of locomotive designs, the factory skylights, the towering and emblematic smokestacks, and the energetic commercial districts that were as much a part of the Age of Furness as columns and pediments were part of the Age of Pericles.

Furness's approach, incorporating the new materials and the new technologies of his day and making forms to meet specific purposes, would be repeated again and again in the actual course of modern architecture—as it was built and lived in, not just as it was reported in history books and journals—reflecting the symbiotic relationship between modern architecture and modern society that persisted through the next century. The most remarkable results that appeared in commercial buildings and resorts would rarely be noticed, or praised, by critics and historians following the mainstream narrative. They would often be controversial. Yet they are essential to modernism.

Furness's impact on two of his employees, Louis Sullivan and William Price, demonstrated the immediate revolutionary effect of the way he drew on a real, rather than a theoretically idealized, modern life. Sullivan gave shape to the modern office building, a practical architectural tool that improved commerce by combining new steel frame and elevator technologies to create appealing efficiencies and densities. Like Furness, Sullivan saw an artistic expression in this new way of life. Will Price responded to the way Philadelphia's modern industrial economy created wealth and leisure time for a broad cross section of the public by designing magnificent resorts in Atlantic City, where his Traymore Hotel (1914–1915) unleashed the verticality and ahistoricism of so-called American Vertical Style, which Price's firm called the modern style.

The impact of Furness's clear-eyed look at new conditions continued into the next generation. Frank Lloyd Wright, Sullivan's employee, designed suburban homes to reflect a new, more informal way of living that embraced nature, while opening his plans to include the housewife, breaking down old hierarchies and anticipating the future. The suburbs and their lifestyle were a direct consequence of new interurban rail (and later automobile) transportation systems that reshaped American cities as decentralized, multicentered urban areas that demanded their own new architecture—innovations that would continue into the later twentieth century.

Factories for heavy industry, commerce to disperse consumer goods to a middle-class population, suburban decentralization, automobiles: this was modernity as it was being lived. By reintroducing Furness into the narrative, George Thomas expands the history of modernism to allow us to see architecture today through a new set of landmarks, and forces us to reinterpret many of the old familiar landmarks. We can see the power and creativity this approach brought to modernism in the cities where the industrial culture of Philadelphia moved west along the lines of the Pennsylvania Railroad. In their pragmatism, and their creative embrace of technological advances fueled by commercial wealth and social advances, Detroit, Chicago, and Los Angeles followed in Philadelphia's footsteps.

In Detroit, Albert Kahn's factories were designed as carefully as clockworks, but built on an enormous twentieth-century scale that would inspire the young Walter Gropius, Ludwig Mies van der Rohe, and Richard Neutra. As Detroit's vibrant technologies, mass-produced consumer goods, and wealth grew and spread, they created the environment where the modern shopping mall was defined by Victor Gruen, and where Minoru Yamasaki and Eero Saarinen revitalized architecture at midcentury. Los Angeles took modern industry, modern commerce, modern media, and new ways of living to create a multicentered suburban metropolis, its new architecture shaped for automotive living on a mass basis. There, architect Wayne McAllister saw modern life as clearly in the 1930s as had Furness in the 1870s, and was equally unfettered by academic theories when he designed his extraordinary drive-in restaurants. The automobile was now the driving force behind commerce and the shape of the city, as the railroad had been in Furness's time. Automobiles forced a redefinition of urban space to accommodate cars and pedestrians; they demanded a bold architectural scale appropriate to the elongated distance of the commercial strip, and architects responded imaginatively. That scale required an integration of sign and architecture, symbol and meaning that acknowledged architecture's role as a form of urban communication. After 1945, Armét and Davis and other Los Angeles architects would continue this evolution by perfecting the modern coffee shops that served the car-mobile public with startling evocations of the modern age, much as Furness had done in the late nineteenth century in his small commuter rail stations. McAllister would follow Will Price's embrace of an architecture for mass leisure in Atlantic City in the 1910s by designing seminal hotel-casinos in Las Vegas in the 1940s and 1950s.

Like Furness's buildings, these would be either ignored or excoriated by critics as lowbrow. They were seen as undisciplined and exaggerated parodies of the International Style purity that had become mainstream by the mid-twentieth century—or as simulacra of the automobiles that were viewed as wrecking the classic urban downtowns. Outrage was heaped upon Philadelphia architects Robert Venturi, Denise Scott Brown, and Steven Izenour when, in *Learning from Las Vegas*, they dared to acknowledge the profound ideas McAllister introduced in that city. Even well-known architects such as Yamasaki and Saarinen were subjected to similar criticisms. Like Furness, these architects saw the commercial energy and the technological advances of the times, used them to respond to the way the public at large lived, worked, and played—and were vilified or dismissed for it.

By returning Frank Furness to his central position at the birth of modern architecture in America, George Thomas helps us understand the depth of the American roots of modernism. He enables us to see anew a range of building types and interpretations that critics in the intervening years had largely written out of the story: small boathouses as well as monumental rail terminals; branch bank buildings as well as museums and university libraries. High-art critics had dismissed these as commonplace, as not serious, as too commercial, as insufficiently pure in their rendition of architectural theory. They were not the exquisitely spare custom homes, the towering cubic and uninflected skyscrapers, the great temples of high culture that make up the majority of landmarks in the conventional canon of modern buildings, but which remain a tiny portion of the built environment. All of these buildings, whether high culture or popular, need to be part of the story of modernism. All of them are needed as a map for today's architects. Modernism is not one thing, it is many. It is not only minimalist and purist, it is colorful, opulent, ornamented. It is not only exquisitely customized and expensive, but popular and mass produced. It was not just elitist but commercial. It was not just the theoretically pure but the unlimited and exploratory. After all, modern architecture at its heart is an experiment, one that draws on the potency of technology and materials, lifestyles, and imagination.

Creating the very idea of modern architecture required Frank Furness's ability to see culture broadly and with fresh eyes (undoubtedly helped by his family's friendships with Ralph Waldo Emerson and Walt Whitman) and his bulldog determination to pull an entirely new view of architecture from the dynamic and unexpected social and technological forces at work in America after the Civil War. It came from his engagement with—not removal from—those forces. And he certainly did not allow convention, precedent, or elitist taste to blur his view of the raw material of the new culture.

By reclaiming Frank Furness's pivotal role in the development of modern architecture, we can now see the success of that real-world approach in his work, and in the later creative centers of modernity in Atlantic City, Chicago, Detroit, Los Angeles, Miami, and Las Vegas. George Thomas reminds us of how many significant turning points occurred when insights into contemporary life, culture, and technology became a springboard for creative design. His modernism—and Frank Furness's—is not merely a theory but a mirror held up to society. We can only wonder what Furness would have done with the forms of the rocket-styled automobile and the transformative imagination of Walt Disney—but the myriad progeny of his works and those of his students attest to the potency of the industrial age that continues to shape our times.

PROLOGUE

A REVOLUTIONARY GENERATION

We find that a new order of shapes, founded on the uses to which they are to be applied and the nature of the material of which they are made, ha[s] been adopted.

—Coleman Sellers, "American Machines" (1874)

T. S. Eliot tells us that the world ends "not with a bang but a whimper" but, in the modern world, the counterpoint is equally true—it began with a bang. In the nineteenth century, that bang was made by the hammering and pounding of the great machines, powered first by water, later by steam, and eventually by petroleum and electricity, that announced the industrial age and transformed every dimension of life, capturing the imagination of those who were truly alive even as their newness frightened those still ensnared by old knowledge and old cultures. Immersed as we are in the turmoil of our own time, it is easy to underestimate the astonishing transformations that reshaped nineteenth-century America. Frank Furness (1839–1912) lived in momentous times as physical distance was compressed by the iron horse of the railroad and was all but erased by the electric speed of the telegraph; seeing was turned into instant memory first by the daguerreotype and later the photograph and by the 1860s motion was frozen first on individual negatives; at the end of his life movement was captured on film. At the Centennial Exhibition of 1876 in Philadelphia's Fairmount Park, Alexander Graham Bell demonstrated his first telephone and within a year formed the Bell System that would make it possible to speak and hear across vast distances, shrinking first communities, then regions, and, by the end of the century, the nation into the private and personal space of a conversation. In the last decades of Furness's life the automobile had reinvented personal transportation and the first airplanes had flown.

As we will see, though Frank Furness's architecture is clearly and profoundly Victorian in its richness of detail, its delight in textures and contrasts, and its reference to other cultures and times, it also, more than any architecture of the day captured the potency of the present and the future. Where most Victorians concealed the new materials of the industrial age, Furness celebrated them, placing them front stage in his buildings even as he expressed his delight in the possibilities that they represented. From giant steel trusses supporting the side of an art museum and massive steel girders spanning a library reading room to muscular riveted steel columns in the entry lobby and stair of a grand hotel, to his final tour-de-force, the steel beams that form the ceiling of the waiting room in the train station in Wilmington, Delaware, Furness made the "new" integral to his designs. Where his peers were soon to venture into accurately detailed historical revivals, distorting modern life to old forms and spaces, Furness subjected his architecture to the logistical demands of the present, and in the process created a modern response to the great experiment that is at the heart of modern life. In the freshness of his response to the possibilities of his age are the seeds of modern architecture and in a broader sense to modern design—one not constrained by past forms but rather responding to the endless variety of the present. His story begins in the first half of the nineteenth century—just after Samuel F. B. Morse's invention of the telegraph and as the first railroad networks were expanding into the heartland of the nation. Above all Furness connects us to the story that links life and architecture to the possibilities and values of new cultural types of Americans—the inventor, the engineer, and the industrialist. By placing him in the industrial context that encouraged his revolutionary architecture, we see Furness not as an eccentric, but rather as proof that the roots of modern architecture (to borrow a title from Lewis Mumford) came from the experimental culture that flourished in Philadelphia and was extended from east to west along the routes of the Pennsylvania Railroad.

In the late 1860s, emboldened by the wealth created by the city's Civil War–grown industries, the board of Philadelphia's Franklin Institute proposed a world's fair, ostensibly centered on the Centennial of the American Declaration of Independence, but with the actual motive to display to the world the fruits of a second American revolution, this one experimental and aesthetic, which had transformed machine design and architecture in the most industrialized city in the nation. From May 1876, when the fair opened in Philadelphia's Fairmount Park, until it closed six months later, attendees equaling a quarter of the nation's populace, together with visitors from every corner of the earth, saw, heard, and felt the future in vast factorylike exhibition buildings and in the machines that filled those buildings. For those who made their way to the old city to see Independence Hall and the relics of the Revolution, they would have also seen a new and vibrant architecture that included top-lighted, iron-spanned banks within earshot of the old bell of Independence Hall, and across the city, new institutional buildings that made expressive use of iron and steel, an unconventional material that even was used for the exposed flying buttresses on a church in the Rittenhouse Square neighborhood.

The architect of the most interesting buildings of Centennial Philadelphia was Frank Furness. He was singled out for praise in the nation's lone architectural journal, *American Architect and Building News*, albeit with a caution for his originality that hinted at future criticism: "By far the most important element in the recent building in Philadelphia is Mr. Furness's work. Nobody would think of calling it commonplace; and it is so far from being scholastic that a good deal of it is hard to classify."[1] With their hot colors, striking details, bold use of iron and steel as central features of the designs, and logistically conceived and profoundly rational plans, Frank Furness's buildings are one of the instantly recognizable creations of Victorian America, as identifiable as the opening chords of the rock-n-roll hits of the 1950s or the tail fins of a 1950s De Soto. Alternately dazzling and confounding critics from the years when they were built to the present, Furness's buildings now attract fans ranging from contemporary "steampunk" hipsters who see in his designs the expressive energy of the great engines of the Victorian age to others who see in his work the beginnings of the journey that led to modern architecture.[2]

Both views are valid. Furness's buildings drew on the forms of the great engines and machines of his day; training in his office unleashed two generations of students who, following his lead, broke with tradition to take on the possibilities inherent in new technologies and new purposes. Furness's buildings are demonstrations of the core narrative of modern architecture: innovative design arises from innovative cultures. In the second half of the nineteenth century Philadelphia's chief architectural clients were drawn from engineering and industry. The imaginations of these men were shaped not by history but by the new technologies that were transforming modern life. Out of the power of the great machines of the nineteenth century came the modern metaphors expressive of mechanical forces that reach their apotheosis with Le Corbusier's idea of a house as a "machine for living." Frank Furness, working for Philadelphia industrialists, began that process.

Like the counterculture of the 1960s, Frank Furness shared the experience of a revolutionary generation, one that challenged convention and toppled tradition. Both eras were continually disrupted by dramatic innovations in technology. Both were centered on ideological wars, one Civil and fought with cannons, sabers, lances, and bullets, the other cultural and marked by alternative lifestyles, political slogans, music, and protest. Both eras were also marked by artistic revolutions that brought home the meaning of the new age to those open to its new insights. And both eras also ended in dull periods of reaction. The line of American architectural innovation that began after the Civil War was stilled at the end of the century by the white blanket of the Chicago Columbian Exposition's classical spectacle and ensuing Beaux-Arts–based curricula at American design schools that isolated Furness and his most creative students from the cultural mainstream. In our time the commodification of history evident in postmodernism and the historic preservation movement has countered the multifaceted freedom of post–World War II architecture embodied in Edward Durrell Stone's playful modernism, Morris Lapidus's flamboyant Miami hotels, the endlessly amusing California highway-oriented moderns, the vivid representationalism of Louis Kahn and the Philadelphia School, and more recently the ideologically incorrect and heroically generic designs of Robert Venturi and Denise Scott Brown and the programmatic assertions of Rem Koolhaas.[3]

Because he has been pushed to the side in the discussion of the architectural narrative of his time, Frank Furness finds his place in history as a curiosity, both icon and enigma. The meaning and goals of his designs have been lost in the glare of his flamboyant personality and the drama of the presumed conflict between his highly particularized architecture and the conventional, historically based works of his contemporaries. Was his architecture a manifestation of mental distress caused by post-traumatic stress from his service in the Civil War as implied by the title of Michael Lewis's *Frank Furness: Architecture and the Violent Mind*? Was he a "rogue" architect like his British contemporary Enoch Bassett Keeling (1837–1886) or the slightly later Charles Harrison Townsend (1851–1928), both of whom pushed pattern and proportion to extremes, undermining the conventions of the historic styles and middle-class tastes even as they announced the beginnings of art for art's sake?[4] Was he "the Whistler of his craft" as Furness's early twentieth-century champion Albert Kelsey recalled hearing him described, portraying him as an artist who hurled bricks and tiles instead of paint pots at the face of the public?[5] Was he no more than a regional mannerist creating a personal style that had little resonance and modest impact in the future, the Antonio Gaudí of Philadelphia or a Victorian Bruce Goff? Or was he a cutting-edge revolutionary who signaled the beginnings of modern design strategies that continue to affect our world?

Where Furness's works appear as anomalies against the familiar historical narrative, they snap into sharp focus when they are situated in the industrial culture that produced his clients and inspired his architecture. Instead of our seeing him as a rebel mocking convention, a compelling case can be made that he was part of a revolutionary generation of artists turned on by the possibilities of their time. As such he grasped the artist's interpretive role, in Ezra Pound's phrase as the "antenna of the race," to use design to interpret and express the meaning and possibilities of the new technological age. In the same years that Furness was reinventing architecture in the image of the great machines made in Philadelphia, across North America and Europe poets, writers, painters, and sculptors turned away from traditional styles and historical subjects to directly express the new energy and dislocations that underlay contemporary urban life. In the United States, even before the Civil War, Walt Whitman incorporated the cadences of everyday language into a new type of prose poetry that captured daily life with all its commonplaces and tragedies. Later, riverboat pilot and journalist-turned-novelist Samuel Clemens, a.k.a. Mark Twain, grasped the directness of the colloquial to skewer old pomposities and to explicate the inequities of the Gilded Age. Philadelphian Thomas Eakins used the modern tool of the camera and the science of optics to put the viewer of his paintings into a front-row seat at a surgical operation in a medical amphitheater or on the sidelines of a baseball field, or along a river bank at a sculling race. When art took on the themes of modern life, the inherent originality of modernity was made visible.

These innovations were not restricted to the United States. Everywhere modern hyperconnective urbanism transformed life, the arts were reinvented. Joseph Paxton's iron and glass Crystal Palace of 1851 for London's Great Exhibition advanced the possibilities of a new architecture of volume, transparency, and wraithlike delicacy of structure that would spread via train sheds and cast iron storefronts into the great galleries and office buildings of commerce. In 1860s Paris, Edouard Manet caught the freshness of the moment in paintings that froze seemingly offhand glances and moments and immediately relegated the static, pyramidal compositions of the Renaissance and academic tradition to the scrap heap of history. In the next decade the pace of change accelerated as artists, looking at each other's work in shared exhibits in urban centers, first captured "impressions" of contemporary life in glittering daubs of paint that coalesced from individual brushstrokes into understandable images and contrasted with the patiently and laboriously built up layers and glazes of the old academic training. Instead of the conventional view through the picture plane, the modern artist made the viewer's eyes and brain active participants in the process of creating and deciphering while remaking the painted canvas surface as the central focus of the aesthetic experience.

No longer accepting the court artist's role as passive recorder, looking in from the outside, the modern artist—whether Manet, Edgar Degas, or Pierre-Auguste Renoir in Paris, Winslow Homer in New York, or Thomas Eakins in Philadelphia—depicted a world in which they themselves were active participants. Gods and goddesses, portraits of royalty, subjects drawn from history that reified existing hierarchies, heavy-limbed field workers relegated by social distinction to being picturesque objects in a landscape, all gave way to the exuberance of the familiar, the middle-class experiences of modern urban life in bars and parks, sporting events, public avenues, and train stations.[6] A decade later, the post-impressionists took urban values to the countryside and to exotic places, venturing into the psyche and distorting the optics of a scene to vividly express the underlying emotion and the energy of a moment. Cubism and the restless churn of the avant-garde followed, leading to the endlessly varied modes of the twentieth century, all of which were modern in their creators' search for original means of expressing their moment.

Music marched to new beats, joining the voices of nationalism, expressed by merging vernacular musical themes with new compositional forms, while also incorporating the harsh sounds and syncopated rhythms of the industrial age that would lead to the free forms of jazz. The transformative possibilities of futuristic technology were communicated to vast audiences by science-fiction authors H. G. Wells, Edward Bellamy, and Jules Verne, who described travel to distant planets, or far under the ocean, or into future cities made possible by technologies that have largely become reality. In every field of human endeavor during Furness's life, new scientific methods brought knowledge and progress. Medicine was transformed from primitive shamanism to modern science as discoveries about germs and sepsis led to extraordinary developments in public health and healing even as its analytical methods became the investigative tools of Arthur Conan Doyle's Sherlock Holmes.[7] In the great cities of fashion, first in Paris and later in London, New York, and Philadelphia, urban bohemians created new lifestyles that were forms of artistry in their own right and led a multigenerational movement away from academic training and learned forms toward the directness of expression that informs the entrepreneurial counterculture of today. By the end of the nineteenth century the centripetal energy of the industrial cities drew creative artists to their center. There every art was transformed, marking the clear split between traditional and progressive methods, the latter looking forward to our own time, the former now seeming dated, distant, and increasingly irrelevant.

The Industrial Metropolis and Architectural Innovation

In the mid-nineteenth century, architecture was the art that on the surface seemed most resistant to change. Looks were deceiving. By the 1820s architects had begun to incorporate the technics of modern plumbing and heating systems, the veins and arteries that carried fluids and gases through buildings, and by the end of the century they were threading wires through the walls, the equivalent of electronic nerves to ring bells, light interiors, and connect to the world via the telephone. Steam-powered and later electric-motor-powered elevators were the growth hormone that led to ever-taller steel-framed buildings. However, these new systems were typically concealed behind the mask of conventional historical styles that represented the innate conservatism of architecture, reflecting its monetary costs and embedded social and cultural values. As a result, risk-averse clients in most cities chose the familiar over the original. In the century-long run-up to twentieth-century high modernism, architects thumbed their way through the texts of classical design, then the countering Gothic, then turned to the secondary modes, Egyptian, the more neutral Italianate manner, Romanesque, Roman Mannerism, and the Baroque, making the nineteenth and early twentieth centuries a visual compendium of historical styles.

Until Frank Furness burst on the Philadelphia scene in the years after the American Civil War, few architects had clients who demanded representation of their world in the manner of those fortunate painters and sculptors who found patrons outside the salon and the academy.[8] Philadelphia, with its clientele of engineers and industrialists, supported a new architecture, one that would appear over the next generation in similar innovation-centered cities. Architecture shaped by the possible and not by convention followed in Chicago, where it served a clientele conversant in the spatial logistics inherent in modern transportation systems and the managerial revolutions of catalog retailing.[9] It appeared in Charles Rennie Mackintosh's Glasgow, another engineer-dominated center of machine making, shipbuilding, and other heavy industries, and it eventually reached Hector Guimard's Paris, Peter Behrens's Berlin, Otto Wagner's Vienna, William Price's Atlantic City, Josef Gočár's Prague, and Eliel Saarinen's Cranbrook Academy in the orbit of Detroit. After World War II alternate modern strategies continued in Morris Lapidus's Miami and the Hollywood movie culture of Wayne McAllister's and John Lautner's Los Angeles. The earlier Philadelphia and Chicago experiences proved that wherever a critical mass of engineers, industrialists, and, later, media moguls whose training lay outside of classical, history-based systems of traditional education took over the leadership of institutions and government, their cities might become centers of contemporary design.

The hypothesis that modern architecture crossed over from the progressive industrial culture is not new. In *Mechanization Takes Command*, Sigfried Giedion countered the standard narrative of modernism framed by the 1932 Museum of Modern Art exhibit and catalog that defined the so-called International Style.[10] Giedion argued that true modern architecture was more than just a "transient" avant-garde aesthetic challenge to traditional designs and methods; rather it was a "constituent" fact of a radically new culture, differentiated from the past by innovative industrial processes and lifestyles, which incorporated the values, goals, and interests of progressive engineers. Instead of starting from the usual narrative of Euromodernism of the 1920s, Giedion initiated his search for the genesis of modern design at the intersection of people and machines that gave rise to the industrial age. This led him to the late eighteenth-century mechanization of flour milling in Oliver Evans's Red Clay Creek mill in Delaware, just south of Philadelphia; he then continued to the early mechanized slaughterhouses in Cincinnati before returning to Philadelphia's great factories, where he found the innovations of Frederick Winslow Taylor that were later grouped together as "Taylorism," the all-encompassing transformation of work away from its craft origins to industrial process.[11]

But the new industrialists and their values alone did not produce modern architecture. Across the globe, nineteenth-century industrial centers were planned and shaped by engineers who provided water and later steam power for factories, devised water works and sewage systems that improved the health of their communities, established the routes of railroads, and designed revolutionary bridges to span rivers and connect their regions to the hinterlands. Each of these acts contributed to a process that eventually replaced vernacular crafts with modern centralized production systems and methods in new types of communities that were centered on factory work. While engineered experiments advanced machine design, bridge construction, factory planning, and water and steam power systems that served to make work and transportation more efficient, they only rarely crossed over to civic and domestic architecture. As John Coolidge pointed out in his study of Lowell, Massachusetts, the mill owners and their engineers went home to houses that looked like those in the standard pattern books, and their cultural institutions were draped in historical forms.[12] Industrial architecture remained compartmentalized in the water-powered factory districts bounded by Canal Street without crossing over to the commercial fronts of Main Street or the residences of Pleasant Street.

Unlike post–Civil War Philadelphia, none of these early industrial communities, whether Birmingham or Manchester in Great Britain or Lawrence or Lowell in Massachusets, became centers for pioneering architecture beyond the factory districts, and few if any architects or engineers from other early industrial cities transferred the particular characteristics and values of their work culture to public or domestic realms.[13] Factory buildings might be progressive, inventive even, in space planning, in economy of construction and utilization of mass-produced structural elements, as well as in the builder's increasing attention to light and ventilation, but civic and domestic architectural styles in the same towns reflected up-to-date fashions while remaining otherwise conservative. Post–Civil War Philadelphia and a generation later 1880s Chicago were the exceptions to this pattern for an obvious reason. In Philadelphia and later Chicago, industrialists formed a critical mass of community leadership who imposed their values on every type of architecture whether houses, churches, college buildings, or commercial or transportation buildings, all of which came to display the new materials and the new planning typologies of the industrial age.

An Ecological Frame

A central thesis of my explanation of Frank Furness's often astonishing architecture is ecological. Twentieth-century historians' focus on the individual architect has made the monograph the tool of historical investigation and the architect's personality the touchstone of its inquiry. However, it is impossible to fully understand an architect and his works without considering the effects of the regional cultural environment on the architect and his designs. Viewed from the perspective of other fields—botany, biology, or ornithology—the focus on one example of a species without its environment is naive. What naturalist would look at a single subject from within a species, divorced from its environment, its competitors, and its prey? We recognize and understand species not just by their appearance but also by their habitat ranges that reflect the requirements they have for food, temperature tolerance, and the characteristics of their habitual settings, whether woodlands or meadow. Hummingbirds migrate between places where there are continuous blooms of flowers and the tiny bugs that provide protein; ospreys live near places with open waters that provide fish year-round. Critics from other cities, and later historians, who lacked an understanding of the specifics of Philadelphia's culture and its industrial values, could not comprehend the underlying forces behind Furness's designs or those of his contemporary,

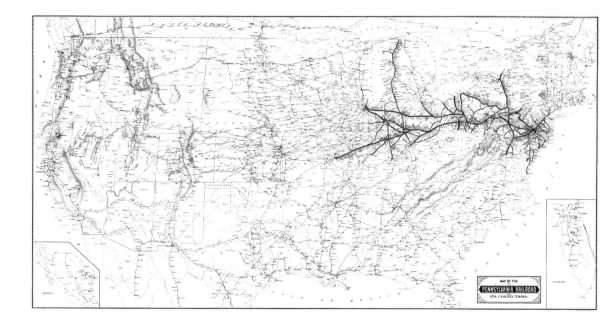

Figure 1 S. C. Patterson, "Map of the Pennsylvania Railroad and Its Connections," Philadelphia, 1889. Courtesy of the Library of Congress.

Joseph Wilson, whose parallel creations confirm the Philadelphia path. As we will see, there was both rhyme and reason in their buildings that are only understood when they are placed in the context in which they were created.

Over the second half of the nineteenth century, when Furness was active, Philadelphia engineers tied American industry to local practices, invented new industrial processes that undid centuries of craft, found a new type of functional beauty expressed in the balance and operative ease of redesigned machines, and explored the potential of new materials in building design, ornament, and construction. The insights and innovations of the city's engineers and industrialists created new wealth that spread across the entire city population, leading to mass consumption and new expressions of mass culture in vast row house districts, in neighborhood clubs and music halls, at professional sporting events, and in the giant amusement parks that surrounded the city. In Philadelphia, these same innovative engineers became the board members of the leading institutions and from their positions commissioned the new architecture that would be built across the city in the last third of the century. In turn the Philadelphia methods spread west through the city's immense hinterland along the lines of the Pennsylvania Railroad (Figure 1) to Chicago and St. Louis, reversing the standard narrative of modern history that makes Chicago the generating center for modern architecture. These engineers chose Frank Furness as their architect.

Like his clients, Furness was an inventor in his own right, taking on industrial design projects for railroad cars and industrial systems, trying color branding to visually unite far-flung corporations, and, on his own account, experimenting with new structural systems and inventing new flooring materials and designs (Figure 2).[14] In these inventions, Furness created the new even as he designed buildings that found their power in the realm that his family and associates referred to as "the poetry of the present."[15] The industrial culture of the city also pervaded Frank's household, shaping the lives of each of his sons. After graduating from Princeton in 1891, his oldest son, Radclyffe (1868–1933), studied at Harvard and became a materials engineer employed at Midvale Steel Company, where he

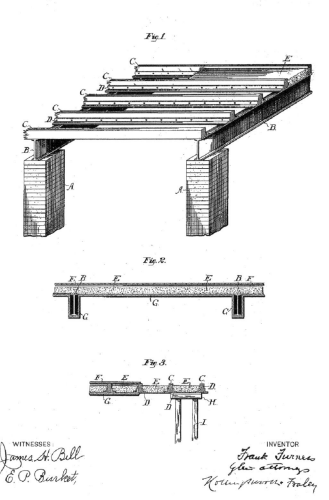

(No Model.)

F. FURNESS.
FLOOR FOR BUILDINGS.

No. 416,907.   Patented Dec. 10, 1889.

WITNESSES :
James H. Bell
E. P. Burket,

INVENTOR
Frank Furness
his attorneys
Hollingsworth Fraley

was in charge of testing that led to significant advances in metallurgy. Theodore (1873–1943) was also a Princeton graduate (1895) with a degree in chemistry that he put to use first with Stephens, Armstrong & Conkling, manufacturers of architectural terra cotta, and later with the Philadelphia Rubber Works, where he continued his father's interest in rubber floor tile patterns with patents of his own. The youngest son, James Wilson Furness (1874–1953), was educated at the Pennsylvania Military College (now Widener University) and became a mining engineer, serving in the Depression under Harold Ickes as the economics branch chief for the Bureau of Mines in the Department of the Interior.[16]

For his Philadelphia clients, Frank Furness took on the role of innovator, like contemporary artists in Paris. Instead of recycling old models that could be repurposed to modern situations, Furness made arresting architectural forms that were conceived to express function, attract attention, and create an identity, even as they provided for future expansion. In industrial Philadelphia, the new was a virtue and Furness gave the city's industrialists the progressive buildings that corresponded to their values. Some artistic revolutions are inexpensive and personal. Others are costly and involve many players. Studio arts require little more than the artist's personal investment in time and the relatively minimal costs of canvas and paint or clay. While their creations could be excluded from the salon and temporarily rendered ridiculous by academic epithets such as "impressionist" or "cubist," still paintings and sculptures that were once viewed as rubbish might end up on museum walls a century later and be more valued than the academic work that had held sway in the exhibitions of the period. A piece of music might have been composed and heard only by the composer; it may even have been booed from the concert hall. Again, a century later, it might be a beloved classic. A novel could be condemned for changing the boundaries of its art and might even have been banned in Boston—but it still exists in the library and is probably now available on the Internet.

Architecture, by contrast, requires access to far greater resources and many more partners. Though design concepts can be understood from drawings and sketches, still, to become architecture the result must be a building. A client must have the need for the new building; an individual or a corporation or a bank must advance the capital to purchase the site and pay for its construction; builders must be able to understand the new aesthetic principles in order to make the building as designed; and a group must coalesce that recognizes the new strategy as representative of its worldview and is willing to commission more such examples to shape the surroundings to match its identity. Above all design revolutions require theories that reveal new possibilities and practices for a new age. In the generation after the Civil War, Philadelphia provided all five ingredients—an expansive industrial economy that required new buildings, a community of shared ideas that was not mired in the past, the desire of a group to express its new status, a stage on which to present its innovative ideas, and a new design theory, one that emerged from the workshops of the city's machine designers, that could be applied to other realms including architecture.

In *The Past Is a Foreign Country*, David Lowenthal reminds us that the historical past is even further removed from our experience than a contemporary place on a distant continent. This gulf requires that we can only begin to understand designs of a century and a half ago by immersing ourselves in the cultural goals and values that produced them.[17] Reyner Banham provided an analogy that applied to the connection between architecture and place. When he emigrated from tradition-bound Great Britain to the Martian landscape of Los Angeles, he quickly realized that in order to understand California's wide-open culture, it was necessary for him to learn its language. Banham observed that Los Angeles architecture and urbanism were united by the "language of movement." Comparing his experience in Los Angeles to "earlier generations of English intellectuals who taught themselves Italian in order to read Dante in the original," he concluded that in the twentieth century, and in the context of Los Angeles, he had to learn to drive an automobile "in order to read Los Angeles in the original."[18] To paraphrase Banham, in order to understand Furness's architecture, we must understand the language of the machine that was spoken in post–Civil War Philadelphia and that differentiated its industrial culture from other places. That language offers clues to understanding the buildings that industrialists commissioned from Frank Furness and his contemporaries.

An Architect's Architect

For nearly a century and a half, Frank Furness has alternately attracted or repelled his fellow architects, critics, and eventually historians, some seeing him as a creative force transforming the possibilities of their profession, others seeing him as a violent destroyer of time-established norms. The facts about Frank Furness were always hiding in plain sight but it has taken half a century of research to clear away the misconceptions that hid his extraordinary innovations that led directly to the beginnings of modern architecture:

The first signpost is Louis Sullivan's bold statement of 1922 in his *Autobiography of an Idea* that he was attracted to the Furness office in 1873 because, unlike other architects who made designs out of books and history, Furness " 'made buildings out of his head.'"[19] Sullivan framed his phrase in quotation marks, hinting that he was recalling an idea either from the office or from another context, perhaps even a lecture or an article by one of the regional machine designers that he could have heard or read during his time in Philadelphia. In any event, Sullivan's phrase about Furness's work method and his aphorism of the 1890s, "Form ever follows function," have added significance as succinct summaries of design strategies that Philadelphia mechanical engineers and industrialists had developed in the decade before Sullivan's time in the Furness office. Their methods revolutionized machine design away from inorganic constructions with applied classical details to purposeful forms that enhanced the work process while their paint schemes changed from gilding and hot colors to a uniform gray that represented the underlying metal. From these industrialists came the core idea that "new purposes needed new forms," and the corollary that "when a thing is right it looks right." Their ideas would spread via Furness from the factory to the civil and domestic architecture that industrialists and engineers commissioned in their city. Because the significance of Furness's Philadelphia context has not been understood, the direct connection between Sullivan's aphorisms and Furness and the innovative architecture that he originated in his native city has been ignored.

Furness's values as expressed in his buildings are a second signpost. These came from the strong foundation of his family, which was led by the Unitarian minister the Reverend William Henry Furness (1802–1896). Both his father and his father's closest friend from childhood and through his life, Ralph Waldo Emerson, were sons of New England and products of the culture that flowed directly from the heroes of the American Revolution and the new streams of American capitalism and individualism (Figure 3). Both were grounded in the peculiarly American version of transcendentalist philosophy that presumed that nature's designs were the outer expression of an inner character, an idea that could be transferred to architectural design. Both men passed on to Frank "inner-directed" values that enabled him to choose against the conventional historical models of his peers. Later the family's friendship with Walt Whitman brought to the family's discussions the idea of a free art, expressed in the common language of the day. The spirits of two great revolutions, the political revolution of 1776 and the revolution in machine design shaped by Philadelphian machine tool makers, together complemented the values of transcendentalism. These values underlay Furness's work and, in turn, were passed on to his students as the scriptures and bywords of American organic design.

The third signpost is found in the culture of Philadelphia, which provided Furness with his clients. Contrary to the city's long-standing reputation for dullness, William Penn conceived Philadelphia as an open city where all who believed in God were invited to live together in harmony and peace.[20] As a result, from its beginning Philadelphia supported a modern hybrid society that juxtaposed experiences and values from the diverse cultures that made up its community and led to a flood of innovations in buildings and machinery. By the mid-nineteenth century, Philadelphia's institutions were led by members of the Franklin Institute, which had become a national and international force for innovation, leading the standardization and scientific management movements to transform industrial production. Better-paid workers made the city an early center of the modern consumer culture, typically owning their own houses and furnishing them from the fourteen department stores on Market Street. It was Frank Furness's and Thomas Eakins's city as well, as both aimed their arts toward the world of the present.

Figure 3 Frederick Gutekunst, "Samuel Bradford, Ralph Waldo Emerson, William Henry Furness," 1875. H[orace] H[oward] F[urness], *Records of a Lifelong Friendship, 1807–1882* (Boston: Houghton Mifflin, 1910).

The fourth signpost is the astonishing volume and endless variety of Furness's architectural portfolio.[21] This alone should have triggered a deeper exploration of the relation of his work to his client base and their city. Instead of designing only the few radical projects for which he was initially known, in fact, in a career of just over forty years, Furness received commissions at the rate of one every three weeks or so (with time off for hunting and fishing in the Rocky Mountains in the summer)—more than 750 projects in all. Unlike Bruce Goff (1904–1982), another American modernist with whom he is frequently compared, whose ideas largely remained on paper, almost all of Furness's designs were constructed. By looking at the national span of Furness's practice from vacation communities on the rugged coast of Maine, west along the routes of the Pennsylvania Railroad to Cincinnati and as far away as St. Paul, Minnesota, and south to the coastal seashore of Georgia, we can trace his clients' activities and interests in a vast arc that marked the range of the railroad empires centered in Philadelphia. The extent of his work alone should have caused a reevaluation of his career if only on the theory that intelligent businessmen, the core of Furness's clients, would not hire an architect who made them look foolish.

The last signpost ties in with the first—Furness's influence on the innovative designers of the future. When the genealogy of modern American architecture is traced, it passes through the Furness office. In Philadelphia, in addition to his influence on his contemporaries, his ideas and theories were passed directly to students, Louis Sullivan (1856–1924), William L. Price (1861–1916), and George Howe (1886–1955), and then indirectly through Howe to Louis Kahn, Mitchell/Giurgola, and Robert Venturi and Denise Scott Brown. The underlying principles that Furness transferred from regional industrial design continued to shape Philadelphia's modern architecture as long as industry and its particularized building typologies shaped the city. Furness's influence reached the Midwest through Louis Sullivan, and via Sullivan extended to his immediate Chicago circle, even reaching the West Coast via Sullivan's draftsman, Irving Gill, who for a time was partnered with William Price's former colleague Frank Mead. From coast to coast, there is an unbroken trail that connects the strains of American modernism back to Furness and to the ideas and sources that circulated between the Furness family and their friends, Ralph Waldo Emerson and later Walt Whitman. Even today, a visit to the Philadelphia suburbs to the Louis Kahn–designed home and workplace of the modern furniture maker and craftsman Wharton Esherick finds the writings of Emerson and Whitman prominently displayed in his library. The genealogy of American architectural innovation and the core idea developed in the industrial culture of Philadelphia, that new circumstances required new forms, have always been critical clues to Furness's achievement.

This study comprises five chapters. The first reintroduces Furness as a member of a generation that transformed all of the arts and as a person uniquely aimed toward his future by his family and their interests, ideas, and values; the second explores the cultural ecology in which Furness operated and analyzes the client group that transformed Philadelphia after the Civil War, who are comparable to the clients who found Frank Lloyd Wright two generations later; the third chapter examines the first critical project, the Pennsylvania Academy of the Fine Arts and compares it to the exactly contemporary Trinity Church in Boston to help understand the impact of the different client groups and different cultures on civic architecture; the fourth lays out the course of Furness's mature career when the architect had mastered his own methods and his clients were most in tune with his goals, enabling the architect to make buildings that were in keeping with the transformative times in which he lived; the last chapter returns to questions raised in the introduction and asks questions about Furness and the historiography of his profession. Throughout the narrative it is Furness who is central to its course.

1 "BUILDINGS OUT OF HIS HEAD"

In the spring of 1873 Louis Sullivan abandoned his boyhood home near Boston to survey his prospects in the emerging architectural profession in the eastern United States. He had just completed a year in the recently formed architectural program at the Massachusetts Institute of Technology, led by William Ware, where he was profoundly disappointed by the methods and the goals of the course of study. Instead of encouraging its students to respond directly to the new conditions and opportunities of the burgeoning industrial age, the Boston version of the Beaux Arts system, like its French model, looked to historical precedents as the basis for contemporary design. Like most sixteen-year-olds, Sullivan was prone to action rather than reflection so he quit his studies and traveled to New York to visit the East Twenty-First Street office of Ware's former teacher, Richard Morris Hunt. Perhaps the source would be purer and stronger than the diluted Boston version. While there, he was shown around by Sidney Stratton (1845–1921), a young architect in Hunt's office. Stratton must have recognized in Sullivan a pilgrim in hot pursuit of a vision that was as yet unformed—or a hot-headed young man who would be trouble in Hunt's already stratified office (Figure 4). Instead, Stratton sent him on to Philadelphia to seek training and work with a former member of the Hunt atelier and office, Frank Furness.[1]

With relatives already living in Philadelphia who could provide housing, Sullivan headed south. But gods don't take orders. Sullivan recounted that when he arrived in Philadelphia, he decided that, rather than pleading his case directly with

Furness, he would look around the city to see for himself if there was any work that warranted his interest. He soon found a remarkable house on South Broad Street that was nearing completion and learned that it was the work of Furness & Hewitt, the very firm that he had been directed to visit. To be sure, after Sullivan had seen Hunt's recent New York work, Furness's Hunt-inspired Neo-Grec detail and inscribed ornament would have been obvious in the sea of red brick early Victorian houses of Civil War–era Philadelphia. But an important part of the traditional narrative of the young pilgrim on his quest is the setting of challenges and the overcoming of hurdles. Sullivan's challenge was to find a master whose vision allied with his own ideas. When he climbed the stairs to the Furness & Hewitt office on the top floor of a modest building at Third and Chestnut Streets, he found a beehive of activity with a small workforce employed on multiple projects that ranged from city and country houses and churches to banks in the financial district and new quarters for some of the largest institutions of the city, including the Pennsylvania Academy of the Fine Arts.[2] Philadelphia's post–Civil War boom was continuing and the young architects were working at breakneck speed.

Half a century later, as he recalled his first meeting with Frank Furness and his ensuing time in the Philadelphia office, Sullivan sketched the principals with the deft precision of a novelist.[3] George Hewitt was "a slender, moustached person, pale and reserved who seldom relaxed from pose" (Figure 5) while Furness

Figure 4 Louis Sullivan, 1876. Ryerson and Burnham Archives, Ryerson and Burnham Libraries, Art Institute of Chicago.

Figure 5 George Wattson Hewitt, c. 1880. Private collection.

Figure 6 Frank Furness, c. 1873. Courtesy of the Architectural Archives, University of Pennsylvania.

was the opposite, "a curious character" who "wore loud plaids, and a scowl and from his face depended fan-like a marvelous red beard, beautiful in tone with each separate hair delicately crinkled from beginning to end" (Figure 6). Sullivan's description set up the dichotomy between the two men with their visually expressed identities that paralleled their opposing approaches to architecture. Hewitt had his nose in books, valuing all things English. It was he who did the "Victorian Gothic in its pantalets, when a church building or something was on the boards." The brash and bold Furness, on the other hand, "'made buildings out of his head.' That suited Louis better." As a corollary to his own original mode of work that he had practiced for nearly half a century, he remembered Furness as a remarkable freehand draftsman who "had Sullivan hypnotized, especially when he drew and swore at the same time." When he left the Furness office late in the fall of 1873, in the depths of the financial crash brought on by Jay Cooke's railroad speculations, Sullivan had learned a new method of design and received inspiration that would guide him for the next half century in his groundbreaking Chicago and mid-American buildings.

Sullivan's story checks out to a remarkable degree, attesting to his own powers of observation as well as the indelible impact of his encounter with Furness. His recollection of the house on South Broad Street led later historians to rediscover the Bloomfield Moore mansion. His characterizations of the office and its location in Philadelphia's old business district were exact. More telling was Sullivan's partition of the office into Hewitt's zone of influence with its historical, English-based sources, each element grasped delicately with "pincers" and placed on a drawing as one might pin a butterfly in a collection, and the contrasting free manner and innovative work of his mentor, Frank Furness. In the scheme of Sullivan's *Autobiography of an Idea*, the detailed description of the Furness office and the opposing principals served as a foil to his own career. Hewitt's historical sources and European models led to the "decorous sublimities of inanity" that inexorably pulled the profession toward the historicism of the Chicago Fair, which undermined Sullivan's course toward a free American architecture.[4] Against the Beaux Arts system of historical models, Sullivan posed his own process of working from analysis of a problem to a direct solution—the method he had first learned from Furness.

Sullivan's *Autobiography* framed critical questions that had been debated by architects in the half century between his entry into his chosen profession in the 1870s and his death in 1924 and that continue to be relevant today. Would architects look forward, exploring and utilizing the new technologies and materials created by modern science and incorporating the ever-evolving systems of the modern world into an original architecture worthy of their time? Would they be freed by a new culture rooted in science and rationalism to shape new types of spaces and new forms that both fitted and gave aesthetic expression to modern life? And would they be empowered by a new type of client, one with the new knowledge of the age who could become a collaborator on a design, providing ideas as well as money and a site? Or would they continue to rely on historical models that forced contemporary life into the straitjacket of the past? Sullivan's texts and buildings and the texts and designs of his pupil Frank Lloyd Wright both looked forward and as a consequence have been incorporated by later historians as key progressive American contributions to modern architecture. Frank Furness, apart from his bit role as the critical catalyst in the Sullivan narrative, disappeared.

Because Sullivan's *Autobiography* remains an essential part of the literary canon of American architecture, his praise for Furness has never been forgotten, though later historians such as Henry Russell Hitchcock scoffed at it.[5] After all, to paraphrase Hitchcock, writing in 1936 with the goal of connecting Henry Hobson Richardson to the narrative of modern architecture, how could Sullivan, who mattered to the modernists, have learned anything from the Philadelphia oddball? There were additional roadblocks to understanding Furness and his work. By the 1950s, when Furness was being rediscovered by a new generation of scholars and architects, the outlines of modern architectural history had already been delineated and Furness and, for that matter, post–Civil War Philadelphia, were largely excluded from the story. Formulating their histories to make a connection between American architecture and the reigning European International Style modernism, architectural historians traced a genealogy from the Germans who had trained in Peter Behrens's shop, Walter Gropius and Ludwig Mies van der Rohe, and the Swiss Charles-Édouard Jeanneret (Le Corbusier) back to Chicago and Frank Lloyd Wright, and from Wright to his master

Sullivan, finding connections via visual motifs that were more a matter of tangency (a chance similarity) than congruency (an invariant and internal consistency). But in the United States, the historical narrative diverged, in part because of earlier Sullivan essays, first published in 1901 and 1902, and collected in book form in 1918 as *Kindergarten Chats*. There, in an early essay entitled "An Oasis," Sullivan had praised what he had learned not from Furness but from his contemporary Henry Hobson Richardson (1839–1886) of Boston, whose Marshall Field Wholesale Store in Chicago was personified in a piling up of words nearly as massive as the building: "Here is a man for you to look at. A man that walks on two legs instead of four, has active muscles, lungs and other viscera; a man that lives and breathes, that has red blood; a real man; a virile force—broad, vigorous and with a whelm of energy. . . . Four-square and brown, it stands, in physical fact, a monument to trade, to the organized commercial spirit, to the power and progress of our age, to the strength and resonance of individuality and the force of character."[6]

Sullivan's image was compelling, though it was at odds both with the delicacy of much of his own mature work and the actuality of the Richardson building, which was U-shaped in plan, brick red in color, and conventional in construction.[7] This is not to say that Richardson's later works in Chicago, the Glessner house and the Marshall Field Wholesale Store, had no role in Sullivan's evolution as a designer or for that matter in the large, simplified forms of post–World War II corporate modernism. The monumental, arcuated, giantism and coloristic unity of the Wholesale Store affected all of Chicago architecture and in Sullivan's case caused him to turn from the small-scale, piecemeal designs such as the Jewelers Building (Figure 7), or his north Chicago townhouses that characterized his earliest Furness-influenced work, toward the greater simplicity demanded by the vastly larger scale of modern high-rise buildings. In its impact on Sullivan's Auditorium Building and his later masterpieces such as the Wainwright Building in St. Louis and the Guaranty Building in Buffalo, Richardson's broadly scaled mode was vital, but as Sullivan later realized, the historical allusions and primitive masonry construction were contrary to his own expression of the new means of steel-frame construction and out of place in the new times that formed the setting for his work. Instead, Sullivan's method, whether for high-rise office buildings or sprawling department stores or his late, brilliantly detailed, small-town banks, focused on finding direct solutions using contemporary technics and self-created detail. Where Richardson relied on historical sources, in a method learned at the École des Beaux Arts in Paris and sanctioned by the architectural profession, Sullivan's approach, learned in Frank Furness's

office, began with the logistics of use and movement expressed in plan and fenestration, to which were added the efficiency and elegance of new construction materials to produce architecture that aimed toward the specifics of a task and a forceful expression of purpose.

Figure 7 Adler & Sullivan, Jewelers Building, Chicago, 1881. Photograph by George E. Thomas, 2008.

Sullivan's *Autobiography* was written at the end of the first quarter of the twentieth century, a generation after his profession had turned from Victorian individualism to historicism and Beaux Arts groupthink, leaving Sullivan, like his mentor Furness, outside the mainstream. Ironically, after participating in the creation of the steel-framed, modern office building in the city most identified with its design and with his career in decline, Sullivan was left with a niche market for brilliant jewel-like banks that were scattered in small Midwest towns (Figure 8). Their sites, far from the urban centers, enabled him to conceive original, nonhistoric, billboard-like façades that stood out on the street and demanded attention. In their color, their concentrated and original ornament, their personal intensity, and their brilliantly lighted spaces, they recalled the banks that Furness was designing in 1873 when Sullivan was in his office (Figure 9). Sullivan's late projects explain the particular focus of his narra-

Figure 8 Louis Sullivan, Merchants'
National Bank, Grinnell, Iowa, 1914.
Photograph by Robert Thall, 1977.
Courtesy of the Library of Congress,
Prints & Photographs Division,
HABS, HABS IOWA, 79-GRIN, 1–1.

Figure 9 Furness & Hewitt,
Guarantee Trust & Safe Deposit
Company, 1873. Building now
demolished. Courtesy of the
Historical Society of Pennsylvania.

tive about his time in Furness's office, which ignored the Pennsylvania Academy of the Fine Arts and the Jewish Hospital, focusing instead on projects on which he had worked such as the "Savings Institution that was to be erected on Chestnut Street."[8]

The Chicagoan's recall of the exuberant and individualistic banks by Furness and the obvious link between these buildings and his own late works forms yet another bridge between the two men. In any event Furness's reputation owes a great debt to Sullivan. The *Autobiography of an Idea* kept the memory of Furness

Figure 10 Frank Furness, c. 1890. Collection of George Wood Furness.

alive even as his early twentieth-century midwestern banks countered the dull repetitiveness of the standard Beaux Arts banks that dotted most towns. Fortunately, Sullivan's banks were recognized as works of genius and have survived, while with few exceptions, Furness's banks in Philadelphia and its suburbs have been demolished, their DNA surviving in their descendant Midwest buildings. But the critical point of Sullivan's commentary was that Furness was not looking in books, or journals, or history, or to other sources outside the present, but rather was directly making new buildings suited to purpose and to his own time "'out of his head.'"

Despite Sullivan's praise, it would take another long generation for historians to rediscover Furness. When he resurfaced it was in the profoundly different cultural frame of European international modernism as the dominant theory of the nation's architecture schools and histories. In Sullivan's narrative, Furness was important for finding a method that correlated with modernity. In the 1950s, in reaction to the gray-flannel-suit conformism of international modernism as it was playing out in American cities, young historians and architects portrayed Furness as a counter to corporate modernism. In that role he was depicted as a Nietzschean hero, or its counter, an irascible rogue outsider, a tragic and misunderstood figure, in short a genius, for whom there is no rational accounting (Figure 10).[9] The rejected artist, reformer of his craft who creates the new while being spurned by all around him, fits into the metanarrative of the modern artist created in the 1930s by the Museum of Modern Art's Alfred H. Barr, Jr.[10] In this role Furness is like a colorful meteor blazing across the darkened Victorian sky, trailing sparks that flashed for a moment, but unlike Whistler, who eventually achieved considerable influence, the Philadelphian apparently signified little, an aberration within the history of architecture.

Furness himself aided and abetted the scorned artist narrative as he invented the model for an architectural personality type that still resonates today—that of the brash individualist, asserting his own beliefs rather than looking to the herd of his fellow architects. Where Charles Dickens skewered the eclecticism of Victorian architecture when he caricatured his architect Seth Pecksniff as "a direction-post, which is always telling the way to a place, and never goes there," Furness's self-created and continuously evolving identity was the corollary to his aggressive design strategies.[11] A virile activist and former cavalry officer, who was described by his former student Albert Kelsey as "striding through life with a free-swinging soldierly stride and a devil-may-care attitude," he hunted and fished across the Rocky Mountains with Theodore Roosevelt, the son of one client, and Owen Wister, the nephew of his sister and the inventor of the literary form of the American western.[12] Furness's smoking room, modeled on a Wyoming hunting camp, brought the rugged life of the Rockies to the rear of his conventional brick Philadelphia row house (Figure 11), while his garb, remembered by Louis Sullivan for its loud plaids, was as identifiable as the façades of his Chestnut Street banks.

Figure 11 "Mr. Frank Furness's Smoking-Room," modeled after a Wyoming hunting camp, was tucked away in the rear of his brick Philadelphia row house. George Sheldon, *Artistic Houses* 2 (New York: D. Appleton, 1884).

In focusing on the most flamboyant aspects of Furness's architecture and allying it with his colorful personality, historians have missed a far more telling story—that of how nineteenth-century Philadelphia industrialists, engineers, and businessmen, together with their chosen architect, Furness, shaped the great ongoing experiment that underlies modern architecture. Telling the story of Furness independent of the culture that sustained him would be like leaving the Renaissance princes and popes out of the biography of Michelangelo. The setting matters. During his life Philadelphia was transformed by the tectonic plate movements of modernity as the new knowledge, systems, and experimental culture of the industrial age intersected with the life of the city. For all his originality, Frank Furness was a product of his place and time. Rather than repeating by rote the memorized odes of the historic tradition, Furness was among the first architects, in the phrase of family friend Walt Whitman, to grasp "the pulse of the life," drawing on the energy of his own time in a way that connected architecture with the values and goals of his clients.[13]

Making Frank Furness: New England Culture, New York Training, Philadelphia Experience

The experiences and acculturation that freed Furness to strike out in such original directions began in a three-and-a-half-story red brick row house at 1426 Pine Street, on the edge of Philadelphia's burgeoning Rittenhouse Square neighborhood. As noted earlier, Frank was the son of the minister of the city's First Unitarian congregation, the Reverend William Henry Furness, who gained fame, even notoriety, for his support of abolition.[14] His father's New England roots and lifelong friendship with Ralph Waldo Emerson (1803–1882) put Frank in the center of the intellectual whirlwind of ideas and values that created America's independent culture and distinguished it from old Europe.[15] The elder Furness's strongly held beliefs were articulated in the sermons he addressed to the congregation of the Unitarian church each Sunday. No doubt these ideas and phrases were tested and sharpened in conversation at the dinner table. Frank would have been fifteen when he listened to his father's sermon "The Sources of False Doctrine" with its observation that "another great source of error [is] the undue fondness for authority." This idea led to his conclusion that "the generality of men are afraid to think each for himself." Dr. Furness continued: "We are commanded to judge each for himself what is right, to prove all things and hold fast that which is good, to be fully persuaded in his own mind. But we are afraid to think for ourselves, especially if we have any reason to fear that we may be led to differ from others, and forsake the sympathy and countenance of the multitude. We dare not run the hazard of going counter to popular opinions."[16]

To borrow a phrase from sociologist David Riesman, the future architect was a member of a family in which "inner-directedness"—essentially guidance by an internal compass of hard-won values—was a core characteristic.[17] With this background, Furness would think for himself, often differing from his professional peers in his planning and expressive strategies, and as a consequence he would run the hazard of going against popular opinion. His father's advocacy of self-honesty and his life among strong individuals gave Frank the backbone to take risks for his beliefs, first on the battlefields of the Civil War and later in his practice.

As noted, the American philosopher Ralph Waldo Emerson was another central figure in the life of the future architect. Emerson and Frank's father were best friends from nursery school through Harvard College and on until Emerson's death in 1882. Emerson was a frequent guest in the family's Pine Street home and they in turn visited the philosopher in New England.[18] Emerson's aphorism "self-trust is the first secret of success" might be taken as the motto of the Furness family.[19] Emerson's ideas spoken in lectures, "The American Scholar," read to the Phi Beta Kappa Society of 1837 at Cambridge, and "Young America," addressed to the Mercantile Library Association in 1844, were essential to the future architect. In both lectures, Emerson challenged Americans to live up to the revolutionary values of their free and open society and to demand arts that would reject the forms and values of old Europe. Instead Americans should incorporate the power of the democratizing forces of their culture—the energy of the railroads, growing scientific knowledge, and the infinitely varied expressions and inner logic of nature.[20] These ideas also were the theme of William Henry Furness's address to the nascent American Institute of Architects at its meeting in Philadelphia in 1870. Dr. Furness's lecture was a model of nineteenth-century elocution, rooted in historical knowledge, but its conclusion was revolutionary when he demanded "a new order of architecture" that reflected "Universal Liberty, now no longer a dream but a fact, a component of the heart's blood of forty millions of people."[21] Instead of adapting past forms from Europe, Furness's father reasoned, the new American civilization deserved an architecture reflecting the universal liberty implied in the national founding documents drafted in Philadelphia a century before, but with his challenge came a warning: "It is an adventurous thing . . . to set before us anything of which we cannot at once tell what to think. We resent it . . . and take satisfaction—the law of taste—into our own hands and condemn it."[22]

Accepting the challenge of his father, Frank Furness worked in an adventurous manner for an adventurous clientele. As was usually the case in the nineteenth century, his clients with few exceptions were men. Several had been members of his Civil War unit, the Sixth Pennsylvania Cavalry; others directed large businesses; many were trained in the sciences and engineering. Most shared a fundamental characteristic of working in the industrial culture of Philadelphia. The unrelenting flood of their commissions ensured that there was nothing tragic about Furness's career as he went from triumph to triumph. No other architect in the nation could lay claim to having shaped the identity of three of the nation's largest corporations: first, in the 1870s, the Philadelphia and Reading Railroad; second, in the 1880s, the famed high-speed Royal Blue Line of the Baltimore and Ohio Railroad; and finally, after 1890, the world's greatest railroad, the Pennsylvania.[23] In an age when architects were beginning to specialize, some for churches, some for houses, some for commercial buildings, Furness tried his hand at every building type. His commercial façades were the biggest, boldest signs on their street. The strategies that he invented for commerce also carried over to the civic realm, to the billboard-like façade of the Pennsylvania Academy of the Fine Arts, to the astonishing tower entrance of the church and parish house for the First Unitarian Church, and to the boiled-lobster-red, towered exterior of the University of Pennsylvania Library. His best houses, whether in the city or suburb, were portraits of their owners, asserting their individuality and describing their aspirations and lifestyles in their room sizes and shapes, their façades and their fenestration. His institutional buildings, for client boards led by engineers and industrialists, were manifestations of the new knowledge that characterized the modern sciences, incorporating ventilation systems overlaid on a framework of logistical planning and energized by architectural forms from industry. As the extraordinary record of Furness's career makes clear, more than simply being shocking or amusing, he must also have been persuasive, perhaps learning from his father lines of reasoning.[24] In the mid-1890s, when Frank's brother Horace remonstrated with the University of Pennsylvania's recently appointed provost, Charles Harrison, for not hiring Furness to design the university's new dormitory complex, the provost countered with the tantalizing observation that Furness was "intensely interested in his own architectural views."[25] Unfortunately we have only a few texts by Furness laying out these views that might give us insight into his ability to persuade and little written evidence from his clients, though their loyalty is telling. What we do have are his buildings as the best testimony to his intent as an architect inventing the future.

Architecture thrives on metaphor and finds new metaphors to reflect the changing possibilities of the moment, as witness the streamlining of machines and then architecture in the 1930s, or the rocket-modern imagery of the automobile in trademarks such as Oldsmobile's "Rocket 88," which led to the Googie and futuristic architecture in California in the 1950s.[26] Where his peers were mining history, Furness's unique training and clientele enabled him to incorporate into architecture metaphors from the giant machines and engines that were the driving force of nineteenth-century industry. Transcendentalist philosophy informed and focused the ongoing conversations, both written and spoken, that continued between the Furness and Emerson families. A central idea, that nature's design was purposeful and not arbitrary and that innate essences were made visible in the creatures and plants of the world, would inform Furness's architecture. Parallel ideas reappeared in the Philadelphia School nearly a century later when its members, Louis Kahn, Romaldo Giurgola, and Robert Venturi, "unpacked" the box of 1950s corporate modernism by applying the Philadelphia presumption, carried forward from its industrial culture, that every design decision should be based on and expressive of the facts of a program, the materials and methods of the construction, and the implications of a site. The constituent elements of Furness's art, the intent to correlate architecture with the power and imagery of the machine, the appreciation of the new forces of industry as an appropriate cultural frame for design, the never-ending delight in natural beauty, and above all the principle that every act required thought to find its appropriate expression, all were shaped by the family circle.

Other American architects such as Furness's near contemporary William Ralph Emerson (1833–1917) were certainly exposed to many of the same ideas and values that passed through the Furness household but none made the leap away from tradition achieved by the Philadelphian. Emerson was a nephew of the philosopher and practiced in Boston in the same years that Furness practiced in Philadelphia. Yet the Bostonian's buildings, scattered throughout New England from Massachusetts to Maine, remained firmly rooted in traditional forms and materials and standard details of historicizing Boston, only reaching toward independence in resort houses and chapels in the relatively free mode of the shingle style.[27] While it is obvious that the two architects must have been different in personality, the principal causes of the differences in their output were surely the settings of their careers and the interests and goals of their clients.

The Furness family's townhouse was an outpost of New England's intellectual culture but it was set in William Penn's culturally open city that attracted Benjamin Franklin at the beginning of the eighteenth century and others, including the British scientist and radical philosopher Joseph Priestley, at the same century's end.[28] Armed with the philosophy of Emerson and with the shield of his father's belief in the virtues of individual responsibility and self-trust, but growing up with major industrial districts a few blocks to the north, west, and south of his home, the future architect was immersed in a city that was focused on actions and facts rather than theories, history, and Europe. In the midst of the great round of technological revolutions that would turn the United States into the world's premier industrial power, there was no better place than Philadelphia for a young American architect to mature.

Education

A central factor of the future architect's life was the family's New England–born belief in the value of higher education. The second oldest of Frank's brothers, Horace (1833–1912), who showed an interest in academic studies, was sent to his father's alma mater, Harvard College. After graduation and the requisite tour of Europe, he read law in a Philadelphia office, preparing him for the profession he practiced until deafness made its pursuit impractical. William (1828–1867), the eldest and the namesake of the father, was initially placed in "a counting house" but his talent in drawing caused him to be sent to Dusseldorf, to the academy where so many of the Hudson River School artists had trained.[29] Sister Annis Lee (1830–1908) was home-educated and furthered her father's love of words in a career of translations and poetry.[30] Frank, who had shown an interest in architecture, was first placed in the local office of John Fraser (1825–1906), who taught the would-be architect "the use of the instruments."[31] When that experience proved successful, he was sent as a late teenager to the New York atelier of Richard Morris Hunt (1827–1895).[32]

Hunt had recently returned from study at the École des Beaux Arts in Paris and a period of professional practice in the Parisian office of Hector Lefuel.[33] He met Frank's brother William in Paris and, apparently at his invitation, visited the family on his way to Washington, D.C. Hunt's visit made a strong impression on the then-sixteen-year-old Frank. When Hunt returned to New York and established his office he was quickly approached by several of Horace's Harvard classmates to teach a course in architecture. This in turn led Horace to report back to Philadelphia about the success of Hunt's teaching, leading to Frank being sent to New York to study with Hunt. There, he was the youngest of the group that would shape the next generation of American architecture.

Horace's Harvard classmates Charles Gambrill (1832–1880, the future partner of Henry Hobson Richardson) and Henry Van Brunt (1832–1903) were already present. They were soon joined by Van Brunt's future partner, William Robert Ware (1832–1915), later the first professor of architecture at the Massachusetts Institute of Technology and eventually professor of architecture at Columbia College. The last to arrive was the future corporate architect George B. Post (1837–1913), who was just two years older than Frank Furness.

Furness entered Hunt's atelier as an impressionable seventeen-year-old, arriving, as he recalled, immediately after the opening of the Tenth Street Studio building. Hunt had designed the building as a workplace for artists, with giant studio windows on its main front representing the interior uses of space. Its overall effect was to re-create in miniature the bohemian environment that Hunt had experienced in midcentury Paris. In its prime studio spaces and its skylighted top-floor communal gallery, the building brought together the leading lights of the New York art scene, Albert Bierstadt, John La Farge, Frederick Church, Winslow Homer, and Sanford Gifford, among others, creating a community where art and architecture could be discussed and where the gargantuan canvases of the first age of excess could be created.[34] Here Furness was exposed to an idea, foreign to Philadelphia, that art was a vital component of successful urban places. Outside on the bustling and energized streets of New York, he also would have experienced that city's trendiness through its businesses that imported current fashions from Europe and its focus on mutability and the moment, which contrasted with the durable architectural forms of Philadelphia. Certainly he must have grasped Gotham's appreciation of art as an expression of its time. Instead of being a frill separate from the consequential aspects of business and commerce, art was both an organizing principle and a business and therefore a worthy subject for a life's work. Above all, the Hunt experience gave Furness a rich exposure to the rising energy of cities and in particular the commercial orientation of New York, which offset his Philadelphia and New England experiences.[35] In Hunt as a teacher Furness also found a kindred spirit and a model for the assertive, masculine personality type that was passed on to Louis Sullivan during his time in Furness's office and eventually via Sullivan to Frank Lloyd Wright.[36]

Little is known about Furness's life in New York beyond his own account of his studies with Hunt, although family photographs capture an increasingly dapper young man, looking very much the New York flaneur (Figure 12). An interesting tidbit comes from the 1860 U.S. census, which reported a group of Hunt's protégés and several young artists living together in a rooming house in the vicinity of Washington Square. Among the denizens were Van Brunt, Emlen

Figure 12 Frank Furness, c. 1857. Collection of George Wood Furness.

Figure 13 Lieutenant Frank Furness, c. 1861. Collection of George Wood Furness.

Littell (misspelled as some variant of Emily), Gambrill, Edmund Quincy (who returned to New England and the ministry instead of practicing architecture), and "Frank Furnace," the standard phonic misspelling of the family name. Like his housemates Furness was listed as an architect, indicating that he was no longer a student but, as he recalled, an employee in Hunt's office.[37] Friendships made in the studio and after, in Hunt's office, survived the Civil War. In 1866 Gambrill and Littell would nominate Furness for membership in the New York chapter of the American Institute of Architects, and in the same meeting Henry Hobson Richardson would also be nominated.

Civil War: Cavalry Officer

The opening salvos of the Civil War stopped much of the business of architecture across the nation and caused Furness to return home to Philadelphia. There, in support of his father's commitment to abolition, he enlisted in Rush's Lancers, which became one of the nation's most decorated volunteer cavalry regiments.[38] Nothing in his past could have prepared the twenty-one-year-old for the next three years. He left home as the callowest of youths, hair slicked down, as it doubtless had been from childhood (Figure 13). A daguerreotype taken of Frank at the time of his enlistment, swimming in his overly large uniform with a cavalry saber that nearly rivaled him in size, was soon supplanted by Mathew Brady's photograph of the Sixth Pennsylvania Cavalry, known as the Lancers, in camp with their lances standing in a cluster, and Lieutenant Furness reclining on his elbow in the center of a group of soldiers, a man at ease with his fellow troopers and comfortable in the adventure of war.[39]

Over the next three years Furness and his regiment participated in the most dangerous actions of the eastern theater of the war, beginning with their first charge, medieval lances in hand, into a defended fencerow in Virginia.[40] In early July 1863, his battle-hardened regiment helped take control of the Gettysburg battlefield, which ended with Furness engaged in the skirmish at the South Cavalry Field, near the site of the monument that he would later design to mark his regiment's service at Gettysburg. He remained in service until the fall of 1864 as the war turned toward the finish—a season that was marked by a series of brutal battles as General Ulysses S. Grant's forces hammered at Richmond. Fortunately for American architecture, Furness survived the largest cavalry engagements of the war, first at Brandy Station, Virginia, in the lead-up to Gettysburg and then in the Battle of Trevilian Station in the summer before he was discharged. At the height of the Trevilian Station battle, Furness, by then the captain of his regiment, volunteered to carry ammunition across an open field to an exposed outpost, an act for which, many years later, he was awarded the Medal of Honor for conspicuous valor.[41] When he returned to Hunt's New York office after his enlistment, he was in his words, "proverbially a dragoon," a former cavalry officer, his face crossed by a mustache that linked to his sideburns and framed his bare chin and nearly shaved head (Figure 14).

Figure 14 Frank Furness, c. 1867. Collection of George Wood Furness.

Architect After the Civil War

The impact of war on the survivors is an oft-told tale. We can only wonder what its long-term effects were on Furness, but it is clear that he had become a man's man, as comfortable in the saddle as at a drafting board and with the ability to communicate directly and forcefully with the industrialists who would become his clients. He was ready to get on with his life. After a brief reentry into Hunt's New York office, in which he recalled that the verbal skills he'd gained in the cavalry were put to good use in dealing with contractors, he returned to Philadelphia, married Frances (Fanny) T. Fassitt in a Unitarian ceremony presided over by his father on March 8, 1866, and set up a practice. With a commission for a small Unitarian church in Germantown in hand, he initially worked on his own before forming a partnership with his former instructor, the politically connected John Fraser. Eventually, they invited George Wattson Hewitt (1841–1916), another well-connected young architect, into their practice under the revised name of Fraser, Furness & Hewitt. In their first years together, they received an array of commissions, some reflecting Fraser's Republican, Union League associations, others coming from the cross-cultural connections of the Reverend Furness, whose links to the Jewish community brought the young firm important projects including the largest synagogue in the city (Figure 15) and the Jewish Hospital. Hewitt had trained in the office of John Notman (1810–1865), which had received the principal Episcopalian commissions in Philadelphia for a generation. He brought to the office the project for the tower for Holy Trinity Church on Rittenhouse Square, the Church of the Holy Apostles in South Philadelphia, and St. Peter's Episcopal Church in Germantown, as well as several center city houses.

The city to which Furness returned after nearly a decade of study and soldiering was in the midst of an extraordinary transformation as railroads and industry overran its riverfronts and tore through its neighborhoods, even reaching into its center with tracks running along Market Street and through Penn Square to a freight terminal at Thirteenth Street. While the core of the city remained in its old location along the Delaware River and on Chestnut and Walnut Streets, the Civil War had accelerated the city's industrialization, making it into a vast agglomeration of invention, manufacturing, and transportation aligned along the railroad's rivers of steel. In every direction, giant chimneys belched smoke from coal-fired furnaces, outnumbering the church steeples that had been the focus of the skyline of eighteenth-century Philadelphia. These cylindrical towers with their plumes of smoke augured larger changes across the city. In 1870 the decision was made to move the city government to the intersection of Broad and Market Streets, where the nation's largest and most architecturally ambitious public building would be constructed.[42] This act was precipitated not by a fire or other catastrophe but by the rational foresight of engineers who saw the need for a larger downtown that would rise around the new city hall.

Figure 15 Fraser, Furness & Hewitt, Rodef Shalom Synagogue, Philadelphia, 1869. Benjamin Linfoot, lithographer. Building now demolished. Courtesy of the Historical Society of Pennsylvania.

One by one, Philadelphia's institutions were also being transformed as well. The city's boards still included lawyers and representatives of the finance, shipping, and retail worlds, the sources of wealth in the first half of the century, but they were joined by the engineers and industrialists who were actively engaged in building the Victorian city.[43] Instead of looking to history and precedent, as graduates of Boston Latin and Harvard College did, Philadelphia's new board members were products of a new kind of training, one that relied on the continuous experimentation and innovation that typifies the progressive industrial and

engineering world. They demanded continuous refinement of processes, greater productivity, the capacity to see and shape new markets, and eventually the means to enforce industrial discipline in ways that benefited their core region. In this culture, innovation was a virtue and change was expected and not feared.

In the course of their own careers, the industrialists commissioned factories that incorporated new plan types, new materials, and innovative construction systems that made their workplaces more efficient. When the inventors of the industrial culture were brought onto institutional boards, none of these men ever thought to demand that a building reflect the style of Leon Alberti or Claude Perrault; instead they were comfortable asking their architects to use the materials and methods that they applied in their workplaces. Nikolaus Pevsner's mid-twentieth-century attack on the late Victorian architect Charles Townsend for his "reckless repudiation of tradition" tellingly captures British cultural conservatism that persisted well into the twentieth century, freezing architectural innovation in Britain until after World War II.[44] Over the two generations in which they controlled and shaped Philadelphia, innovative engineers and industrialists ignored tradition in every aspect of the built environment of the city from their homes to their offices, to the institutions on whose boards they sat. Architectural historians tend to focus on their immediate subjects—architects and their designs—but most projects are at least as much the consequence of the client who initially assesses the need for a new building and then, by choosing the architect, sets the course of the project. Understanding the interests and values of the client broadens our insights into the ecological setting of an architectural practice, as well as explaining the reasons that an architect was given a commission and the type of design that was produced. Like Frank Lloyd Wright's clients two generations later, who as Leonard Eaton discovered were mostly "manufacturers or directly involved in industrial processes," Frank Furness's clients came out of the industrial cultural ecology of Philadelphia that flourished in the generation on either side of the Centennial.[45] To understand Furness, then, it is first necessary to understand his clients, their values, and the impact of those values on the city that nurtured them.

THE PHILADELPHIA CLIENT

INDUSTRY AND THE FUTURE

The future is already here—it's just not

very evenly distributed.

—William Gibson

William Gibson, the "noir prophet" of the cyber age, reminds us that the future, like the ocean tides, arrives unevenly, reaching some places ahead of others. As the Civil War loomed, few Americans would have imagined that Philadelphia, the supposedly staid Quaker city, was being impelled forward on a wave of industrial innovation to become what Englishman Arthur Shadwell would later term the "greatest manufacturing city in the world."[1] The idea of Philadelphia as a place where the future arrived early runs counter to long-standing narratives of the city. We see what we know. For most of the twentieth century, Philadelphia's reputation for stodgy conservatism has been served up in novels from Theodore Dreiser's *The Financier* and *The Titan* to Hollywood movies such as *Kitty Foyle*, *The Philadelphia Story*, and, more recently, *Rocky* and *Trading Places*. Even academic studies such as Robert A. M. Stern's otherwise illuminating biography of George Howe have adhered to the standard urban legend of Philadelphia as "hidebound by strict conventions in architectural taste as in everything else."[2] Similarly by focusing on his thesis of the failure of the descendants of the Quaker founders to provide institutional and cultural leadership in the nineteenth century, sociologist E. Digby Baltzell missed the engineers and industrialists who were the actual movers and shakers of the post–Civil War city.[3] Twentieth-century historians, only seeing what they expected to see, overlooked nineteenth-century Philadelphia's remarkable creativity in industrial practices, which through the agency of engineers and industrialists as clients spread to architecture and the arts, while shaping the region's distinctive culture.

Philadelphia had taken its own original course from its beginnings in 1682 when it was founded as a place of religious liberty and human rights that attracted a diverse population from all of Europe and the Americas. By the end of the eighteenth century the city stood at the fall line of a torrent of medical, industrial, and engineering revolutions that set it apart from its peer American cities.[4] Long before the well-known example of Benjamin Latrobe's steam-powered waterworks on the city's Center Square, Philadelphians had made machines a focus of their interests. In the 1780s, local engineer Oliver Evans (1755–1819) had harnessed waterpower to run every task of a grain mill so that a single operator could raise grain to the top of the mill by an Archimedean screw, move the grain into hoppers that led to mechanical winnowing devices that removed the chaff, and then pass the grain through the great stones that ground it into flour, finally conveying the flour into barrels for distribution. When Dr. James Mease published *Philadelphia as It Is in 1811*, he recommended a visit to a mill designed by our "self-taught genius," Evans, along with the standard tour of the business district and historical sights of the city.[5]

Popular images of the city confirm the story. A full generation before the Civil War, it was obvious that Philadelphia's industrial culture had spread from the factory to commercial and institutional buildings and on to civic and domestic architecture, marking a distinctly different course from that of Boston and New York. George Lehman's aquatint of the *New Suspension Bridge at Fairmount, Philadelphia* (1842) anticipated the city's future, celebrating the proximity of a public enterprise, the waterworks, with Charles Ellet's cable-suspension bridge, which springs lightly across the Schuylkill River from one riverbank to the other. A restaurant atop the waterworks turned a feat of engineering into a mass-culture attraction. Just as visitors to the Centennial Exhibition would later gape at George Corliss's giant engine, so pre–Civil

Figure 16 *Philadelphia Times* banner, December 2, 1885. The banner illustration depicts aspects of Philadelphia's industrial identity. Private collection.

PHILADELPHIA, WEDNESDAY MORNING, DECEMBER 2, 1885

War Philadelphians thrilled at the chance to see turbines impelling water uphill, creating a reservoir where the Philadelphia Museum of Art now stands, whose pressure could force aloft a towering fountain that cooled the glade behind the waterworks. Similarly the post–Civil War front page banner of the *Philadelphia Times* was an affirmation of the city's identity (Figure 16). Instead of choosing Independence Hall as its icon, it portrayed Philadelphia as an industrial power of factories, smokestacks, locomotives, and towering cranes.

By the mid-nineteenth century, Philadelphia was the home of the recently founded engineering program at the University of Pennsylvania together with the nation's largest and most scientifically based manufacturing and transportation businesses, the Baldwin Locomotive Works and the Pennsylvania Railroad, and the critical technical businesses of the day led by the nation's premier machine tool maker, William Sellers & Co.[6] These industries and a dozen related businesses were located just north of Philadelphia's center city, forming America's steam- and machine-age equivalent of today's Silicon Valley. As the Civil War neared its end, the city's engineers and its inventors were grappling with the problem that locally based industrial systems limited connectivity across the nation. Spurred by the Pennsylvania Railroad's vast expansion west to St. Louis and Chicago, Philadelphia engineers and industrialists realized that machines made in Philadelphia needed to be repairable in other cities along their routes. Mid-nineteenth-century shop practices, based on craft systems, made such universality impossible because each factory produced its own formulae for everything from the angles of screw threads to the gauges of metal. Anyone who has attempted to assemble an early nineteenth-century bed frame, held together with giant bolts and nuts, is aware that there can be differences within a set so that there is only one correct nut for each bolt. But with Philadelphia's Baldwin Locomotive Works aiming to supply the world with locomotives and the Pennsylvania Railroad linking the cities of the nation in what it would later term "an Assembly Line 26,000 Miles Long," connectivity became crucial to expansion and to success.[7]

In 1864, Philadelphia engineer and machine tool maker William Sellers (1824–1905), in his role as president of the Franklin Institute, proposed a national standard for the design of the screw, the fundamental unit of industrial connectivity.[8] He initiated the process by personally designing a standardized system of screw threads that had the advantage of simplifying manufacturing because the threads were set at readily determined angles based on an isosceles triangle.[9] In line with Sellers's corporate goals of efficiency and ease of production, his new system could be accomplished with greater precision by less skilled workmen, thereby reducing costs while producing higher-quality work. The U.S. Navy quickly adopted the

Sellers system, but the Tenth Amendment to the Constitution prohibited federal enforcement of national standards. The leaders of the Pennsylvania Railroad grasped the challenge, announcing that they would demand such standards. Over the next decade the railroad established in-house chemical and engineering laboratories, taking on the role of setting material and track gauges that reified its asserted status as "the Standard Railroad of the world."[10]

Because few businesses could risk losing sales to the nation's largest corporation, by the 1870s, standardized screw threads became the norm and other standards, from metal thicknesses to track gauges that supported the railroad's agenda, quickly followed.[11] The Pennsylvania Railroad's corporate strategy of standardization had the benefit of tying American production to Philadelphia systems, which in turn favored the region's factories. At the end of the century Philadelphia industrialists further strengthened their hold on the standardization movement by forming the American Society for Testing Materials (commonly known as the ASTM) as a joint venture of the Franklin Institute and the University of Pennsylvania's Engineering Department. It was funded every year by a grant from the Pennsylvania Railroad.[12] Long after World War II, Philadelphians controlled the industrial culture of the nation through the institutions and systems that they created.

In the generation after the Centennial, working in the same environment and for the same industries, Philadelphia engineer Frederick Winslow Taylor (1856–1915) devised the principles and practices of scientific management, applying the rigor of scientific measurement and ergonomic logic to remake work practices from the happenstance of craft into a component of modern industrial process. His experiments, many undertaken in factories controlled by William Sellers, led to dramatic increases in productivity, which, in turn, supported higher wages that transformed the lifestyle of the entire city.[13] The increase in wages produced by Taylorism made Philadelphia's factory workers into consumers. By the 1880s, in contrast to the mean tenement districts of New York and the triple-deckers of New England, a Philadelphia factory worker typically owned his own two-story, three-bedroom, brownstone-trimmed, brick home in the vast tracts of row houses that surrounded his workplace. Taylorism shortened work hours and paid higher wages, providing leisure time that could be spent in the amusement parks that sprang up at the rural ends of trolley lines or at the mass resorts, accessible by railroad, that sprouted along the New Jersey shore.

From the middle of the nineteenth century until the beginning of the twentieth century, Philadelphia institutions were led by a unique cohort of industrialists and scientists who contrasted with the tradition-oriented British elite, the history-oriented New England elite, and the commercial and fashion-oriented New Yorker. In these circumstances successful Philadelphia architects were quick to create new architectural forms, many of which were derived from the new practices in industrial buildings, and woe to those who resisted the new trends. Even today a walk through Philadelphia's Rittenhouse neighborhood finds steel beams spanning entrances to grand houses and carriage houses, as well as monumental stairs of iron and steel in public buildings, while industrially scaled chimneys enlivened the silhouettes of houses and institutions alike. Iron even found its way into the parlors of city mansions, when Furness used it to ornament mantles framing fireplaces. Where British and most American architects in their native cities rarely used iron in a public manner, in Philadelphia, iron was a component of Victorian buildings of all classes and types. In their widespread use of iron, their original architectural vocabulary, and their functional plans, the architects of the city created an industrial identity that was as confounding to high-architectural critics as it was natural to the industrial clients.

The architects of Philadelphia were not the only artists who responded to the aesthetic possibilities of the new age. After the Civil War, Thomas Eakins, Thomas Anshutz, Colin Campbell Cooper, and at the end of the century Joseph Pennell and Charles Sheeler, as well as the principal figures of what was later called the "Ashcan school," William Glackens, Robert Henri, George Luks, Everett Shinn, and John Sloan, all got their start in Philadelphia, many in its newspapers, where their drawings communicated a story before the photogravure replaced the artist's sketch. They found their subjects in Elizabeth Johns's subtitle for her study of *Thomas Eakins: The Heroism of Modern Life* (1983), itself borrowed from Charles Baudelaire who had demanded that art address "the heroism of modern life."[14] These Philadelphians captured on canvas and paper the daring of medicine, the majesty and power of industry, the energy of mass sporting events, and the freedoms of the new leisure. Clearly the arts in Philadelphia were different although the how and why of their distinctiveness were usually ascribed to causes that missed the actual reason.

The Quaker Question: Antipathy to the Arts or Early Moderns?

The usual late nineteenth-century explanation of Philadelphia's peculiarities and more specifically of Furness's original design strategies held that the Religious Society of Friends, pejoratively and later familiarly known as "Quakers," was hostile to the arts. The Friends' seventeenth-century rejection of finery and fashion to express their revulsion against class distinction was extrapolated into the unfounded idea that they rejected all things aesthetic and further that they continued their rejection of the arts well into the nineteenth century. This idea even found a place in Frank Furness's father's address to the American Institute of Architects in its 1870 annual meeting held in Philadelphia when he warned that new architecture in his home city was held back by local custom: "With all our freedom, we do not tolerate oddness. We insist, in this country, upon everything's being cut to one pattern. Only think what a long day of it one particular style (the Quaker Style—marble steps and wooden shutters) has had here in Philadelphia."[15] In a more gruesome simile, an editor for the *American Architect and Building News*, wrapping up the year's focus on Philadelphia and the Centennial, concluded that in the Quaker city, the arts, like a defective newborn child, were "quietly smothered."[16]

Philadelphia Quakers' anti-art reputation held for generations, continuing into the early twentieth century when Boston Brahmin and high-church architect Ralph Adams Cram wrote a series of articles on the generation of young Philadelphia architects, Frank Miles Day, Cope & Stewardson, and Horace Trumbauer. The subtext of his articles was to welcome Philadelphia architects back into the fold of traditional design, which Cram contrasted with the "Furnissic [*sic*] revolt" of the Quaker city. Elsewhere in the same article he provided a thumbnail history of Philadelphia design that ascribed to the city's pre–Civil War designers a "stolid stupidity almost unparalleled." These men were followed, according to Cram, by "a group of abundant vitality but the very worst taste ever recorded in art," clearly referring to the Furness generation.[17] With no understanding of the underlying regional industrial culture that formed the basis for Philadelphia's architecture, Cram could only complain about the lack of a public taste and compare the situation to other innate and therefore "incurable failings on the order of birth defects."[18]

The arts in Philadelphia were indeed different than in other American cities, but as will become obvious below, while Quaker values nurtured individualism, they were not the chief agents of the new architecture. This is not to say that Quakers had no role in shaping the city's aesthetic. In commissioned furniture, for example, Quakers had arrived at an aesthetic of materiality—one that celebrated beautiful woods rather than superficial detail. Furniture focused on the natural beauty of the material has persisted into the twentieth century in the regional craft work of Wharton Esherick and later George Nakashima. In the late seventeenth and early eighteenth centuries, Quakers grappled with the modern problem of differentiating their identity from that of the Church of England by purposefully distinguishing their meetinghouses from churches. In their first half century in Pennsylvania, Quaker meetings were identifiable by a variety of plan types that ranged from square to hexagonal, by the absence of steeples, by the elimination of the standard altars, pulpits, and box pews of church buildings, and by orienting their buildings to the south in the manner of houses. Nonhierarchical seating and the absence of a pulpit architecturally expressed their core belief in personal revelation.[19] Later in the early nineteenth century, when church architects in Great Britain and the United States reverted to traditional forms based in the Middle Ages, Quaker meetings remained rooted in the proportions and details of the late Georgian manner that flourished when Quakers created a separate identity in Pennsylvania. Contrary to the standard narrative that they were not interested in artistic expression, Quakers used design with pointed sophistication. By highlighting beautiful materials rather than by following the dictates of transitory fashion, and by creating buildings that expressed their religious practices and beliefs, Quakers established a long-lasting aesthetic and in turn provided fertile ground for the new values of the rising industrial culture.

Another value that gave Philadelphians backbone lay in a central component of the Quaker religion, that truth is discovered by the individual rather than imposed from above by a religious leader or transmitted by doctrine. This essential belief underlies the Quaker worship in which individual witness, spoken aloud and framed by silence, replaces the usual rituals and sermons delivered by a select leader. Quakers' religious practices promoted a unique willingness to speak out and to hold to personal counsel even when it was contrary to the views of the broader community. Furness's Unitarian background had obvious parallels to Quaker values. Like Quakers, Unitarians were relatively creedless in their beliefs and they also shared with Quakers worship in a relatively egalitarian space that contrasted with the elongated, hierarchical Episcopal ecclesiastical plans of the Gothic revival. William Strickland's square plan for the Unitarian church at Tenth and Locust Streets, built for the Reverend Furness's growing congregation, was certainly influenced by the plans of early Quaker meetings. Half a century later, Furness's plan for the next building for his father's congregation would utilize giant trusses to create a column-free nave in which all shared a common space, lighted by a skylight that ran along the central axis of the interior.[20]

Lifestyle choices further distinguished Quaker families from other American regional elites.[21] Where the upper classes in other cities aimed their children at professional positions in finance, academia, and the church, elite nineteenth-century Philadelphians more often than not found their life's work in industry and science, usually forgoing the New England elite standard of a college education for on-the-job training. In *Albion's Seed: Four British Folkways in America*, David Hackett Fischer found that the settlers of the mid-Atlantic region, who largely came from the English midlands, valued the practical over the theoretical in education in contrast to New England, whose settlers from East Anglia valued philosophical and theory-oriented higher education.[22] British historian Arthur Raistrick has made the further connection between the Quakers' absence of antiscientific dogma in their theology, which left them open to modern sciences and industry.[23] Historian of science Arnold Thackray cited Élie Halévy's thesis that the new scientific value system arose in the "Nonconformist England, the England excluded from the national Universities," which was widespread in the region of origin of the Quaker and Universalist groups who settled in Philadelphia. Thackray then quoted J. F. Bernal, who "in his *Social Function of Science* . . . argued that '. . . it was in Leeds, Manchester, Birmingham, Glasgow and Philadelphia, rather than Oxford, Cambridge and London, that the science of the Industrial Revolution took root.'"[24] University of Pennsylvania historian Thomas Cochran made a similar point when he described his region: "We have not been a people essentially political, literary, metaphysical, or religious. Our habits and folkways have not been formed only by voting, reading, logic-chopping, or prayer. Our manners are not simply those of conventions, lyceums, schools, and churches. We have been primarily a business people, and business has been most important in our lives."[25]

Furness was freed to work in a new manner by his Philadelphia clientele who operated from Quaker egalitarian values and were free from the determinant of historical precedent, but his particular direction was catalyzed by the new values of the industrial culture. While the Quaker heritage provided a supportive setting, it was the industrial culture's aim toward progressive innovation that provided the foundation for the strategies that set the city apart from its northeast peers. These strategies were determined by a new institution, the Franklin Institute of the State of Pennsylvania for the Promotion of the Mechanical Arts.

The Franklin Institute and Nineteenth-Century Philadelphia

At the end of the eighteenth century Philadelphia had suffered the loss of both the state and federal governments and its citizens were casting about for a new role in the evolving nation. Though the city retained the federally chartered

Bank of the United States, which enabled it to shape the nation's finances, its inland location far up the Delaware River was days farther from Europe than the ports of New York and Boston, making it a secondary port for shipping. Simultaneously it lost its access to the nation's center via overland roads that it had built in the eighteenth century to New York's Erie Canal. Philadelphia had advantages in the sciences and the related chemical industries that were allied with the University of Pennsylvania's medical course, but these were of minor import compared to its losses. As the new century began Philadelphians had to reinvent the focus of their city, though what it would become was not immediately obvious.

Philadelphia's engineering-led community found its focus in the winter of 1824, in the second floor gallery of Independence Hall, with the formation of the Franklin Institute of the State of Pennsylvania for the Promotion of the Mechanical Arts.[26] Its founders exemplified the city's future. One was Samuel Vaughan Merrick (1801–1870), an engine builder and later founder and first president of the board of the Pennsylvania Railroad. Another was William H. Keating (1799–1840), the professor of chemistry at the University of Pennsylvania and afterward a mining engineer and later manager (the term for president) of the Philadelphia and Reading Railroad.[27] Their interests tied their transformative institution, the Franklin Institute, to the core regional industries of iron manufacturing, engine building, and railroads.[28] The convergence of Merrick and Keating in Philadelphia was the beginning of an agglomeration of young men from around the world who were devoted to the modern sciences and their practical application and who over the next century gave the city its nickname, the "workshop of the world." The Institute that they envisioned was to be inclusive rather than exclusive, admitting anyone to its classes and its discussions in the expectation that those who came would stay and build their community, while those who returned to their hometowns would retain a loyalty to the city that had given them training. Just as in the final third of the twentieth century Silicon Valley attracted the geeks of the computer age to the open cubicles and interconnectivity of northern California, the Franklin Institute made nineteenth-century Philadelphia a magnet for those with curiosity, drive, and talent in the mechanical and industrial arts.

The Franklin Institute's remarkable open membership policy attracted would-be professionals and amateurs alike to the severely classical building on Seventh Street that had been designed by the institute's second architectural instructor, John Haviland. In the latter category, both William Henry Furness, Sr., and his son, the future artist, William, Jr., took drawing courses, sharing the classroom with the young William Sellers.[29] Frank, though apparently never a student in the institute's courses or later a member, was, as previously noted, caught up in the same creative wave as an industrial designer, patenting a variety of building systems, testing materials for wear rates, and inventing rubber floor tile systems as well as their patterns. Membership in the institute as well as access to all its classes was open to women, making the institute a peculiarly Philadelphia version of the education-focused mechanics' institutes that would be formed around the nation.[30] Unlike traditional elite learned societies such as Benjamin Franklin's eighteenth-century creation, the American Philosophical Society, which only admitted mature scholars and scientists to their ranks, the Institute gathered its members from all social classes and levels of training. William Sellers, who had served as president of the Institute from 1864 to 1866, explained the value of this practice in an 1874 lecture marking the Institute's first half century:

> Our Franklin Institute was from the beginning a Mechanics Institute in one sense of the word. It taught by lectures and sometimes by classes but it was always more than was contemplated by the societies abroad. If I may so express myself, it was and is a democratic learned society; it is not exclusive. No well-behaved person is excluded from its membership. All who desire to reap its benefits or to aid it in its great work of promoting the mechanic arts can join it. This is not so with the so called learned societies of this and other lands. They select their members from among those who have already distinguished themselves in the arts or sciences or are likely so to distinguish themselves, hence their membership is confined solely to the learned of the land. Now mark the difference in our case. Learned men join our society and in its hall come in contact with those who may be unlearned so far as books are concerned but better informed in some special art or trade. Theory and practice are brought together and each helps the other.[31]

In addition to bridging the entire Philadelphia community from factory workers to academic theorists, the institute's members were drawn from New England to California, thereby gathering and disseminating information from and to every corner of the nation.[32] By the end of its first half century, the Franklin Institute and its journal provided a national forum in such diverse fields as industrial production, applied and basic sciences, civil and mechanical engineering, architecture, and education. Training at the institute created an elite workforce and leadership cadre that benefited Philadelphia industries. Its library provided a central resource for industrial research that was accessible to the entire membership.[33] Further, by bringing together academics and workmen, the institute shortened the time between conception, testing, and general application of new practices. In the nineteenth century Philadelphia's Franklin Institute was the equivalent of the Bell Labs or modern think tanks in the creation of a shared conversation across the region.

The Ecology of Innovation: Philadelphia's Liquid Networks

In his 2010 book-length essay *Where Good Ideas Come From: The Natural History of Innovation*, Steven Johnson offered several general models for the origins of innovation that are applicable to Frank Furness's Philadelphia.[34] Because of its open society, eighteenth-century Philadelphia attracted freethinkers from Benjamin Franklin to Joseph Priestley. The contrast between Britain's Birmingham, where mobs had burned Priestley's home and laboratory, and Philadelphia, which welcomed him, is obvious. Open communities, particularly those freed from religious intolerance, were critical to invention. At the end of the eighteenth century some cities were moving from chance connectivity of ideas— what Johnson terms the "adjacent possible," a condition in which individuals working in general isolation might connect by happenstance—to being networked and strongly interlinked. This new form, catalyzed in Philadelphia first by Franklin's American Philosophical Society and the University of Pennsylvania's medical school and, after 1824, by the Franklin Institute, led to a new level of connectivity, forming what Johnson terms "liquid networks" that offered intentional interactions in structured meetings and activities such as exhibits that exponentially increased the rate of innovation.[35]

The liquid networks of the Franklin Institute linked the city's industrial and professional offices, which became centers for discussion and innovation. Furness's architectural innovations were part of this discussion but he was not alone. The workshops and offices of the Pennsylvania Railroad produced the team of engineers and architects, led by Joseph M. Wilson, drafted to design the main buildings for the Centennial Exhibition, which introduced the nation to the Philadelphia industrialist's perspective. In the January before the Centennial, this team left the railroad to found the architectural and engineering firm of Wilson Brothers & Co. Its principal contribution was to rethink architectural design from the dual perspectives of engineering and material science.[36] These innovations confirm Johnson's theory that communities characterized by interconnected institutional networks, like Philadelphia when it was shaped by the Franklin Institute, the Pennsylvania Railroad, and the industrial cluster around the Baldwin Locomotive Works, were supportive of new design strategies, encouraging their spread into other dimensions of modern life.[37]

Just as some environments produce a greater variety of life—a jungle swamp sustains more variety than a desert—so too a community's potential for innovation is determined by its overall intellectual ecology. In mid-nineteenth-century Philadelphia, engineers formed a technologically sophisticated group of professionals that paralleled the earlier group of medical professionals who had led the city's many medical schools and hospitals and occupied many board seats in the early nineteenth century.[38] Together, they provided a unique reservoir of progressive values embodied in scientific insights and training that differentiated Philadelphia from every other city in the country, and with few exceptions such as Glasgow and later Berlin in the world. It was Philadelphia's meritocracy and its new institutions led by the Franklin Institute that formed the ecological niche in which Frank Furness and his cohort worked.

The Posthistorical Client: The Engineer-Industrialist

The founding and growth of the Franklin Institute in Philadelphia coincided with the consolidation of the American engineering profession. Engineers earned public credibility by their personal problem-solving creativity, tempered by the absolute laws of physics, and by developing a professional culture of individual responsibility.[39] In time, credentials gained in schools and institutes were affirmed by licensing examinations by peer boards.[40] With its focus on progress and aimed at the present and the future, engineering as a profession offered a strong and powerful antidote to a culture heretofore trained to look for precedent and historical sources. Unlike the inherited aristocracies of New England's Cabots and Lowells or the New York Four Hundred, Philadelphia's new engineering and industrial meritocracy faced the future rather than the past and by the 1860s was busily engaged in creating an efficient industrial metropolis. What was remarkable, however, was the extent to which the goals and values of industrialists crossed over from the factory district to the downtown, shaping both the city's institutions and the buildings that housed them.[41] So long as historians' investigations of Philadelphia architecture were focused on the Revolution and the Athens of America narrative, the multiple tides of industrial influences that passed from engineering to architecture across the city were overlooked.

In Philadelphia, connections between progressive engineering values and the arts were far more widespread than we have been led to expect. Beginning in the 1850s, directly coinciding with the years when engineers and industrialists were brought onto city boards, examples of the connection between the new engineering culture and architecture became widespread. For example, the booklet published in 1857 to mark the completion of the American Academy of Music on South Broad Street described the proscenium arch supported by "two iron arches, each cast in a single piece measuring 70 feet across the curve" while the great dome was suspended from a lattice of "wrought iron ribs."[42] Of the Academy of Music's six-member building committee, two were engineers and Institute members, Frederick Graff (1817–1890) and the young Fairman Rogers (1833–1900). Graff had continued his father's engineering service to the city as the director of the waterworks while Rogers, then in his midtwenties, had just completed his studies in civil engineering at the university.

Simultaneously with the construction of the Academy of Music, John Myers Gries (1828–1862), also an architect and a board member of the Franklin Institute, devised a method of fire-proof construction for the Farmers' and Mechanics' Bank on the 400 block of Chestnut Street. Steel beams capable of spanning large spaces had yet to be manufactured, leading Gries to resort to a system of trusses using readily available cast iron instead of the usual timbers to span the banking floor. But cast iron is brittle and is only effective in compression. To solve this problem, Gries placed the bottom chord of the truss in compression by the use of tensioned steel cables of the sort that were being produced in John Roebling's nearby Trenton plant.[43]

Elite domestic architecture was subject to the same forces. In the early 1850s engineer Joseph Harrison commissioned Samuel Sloan, a fellow member of the Franklin Institute, to design his mansion and art gallery on the east side of Philadelphia's Rittenhouse Square. In an aside in his obituary for Harrison (1875), Coleman Sellers, mechanical engineer and at the time the president of the Franklin Institute, departed from his biographical sketch to comment on Harrison's application of his engineering knowledge to his mansion: "Of interest it may be to mechanics only, . . . hidden under the plaster of that house are very many ingenious devices to insure stability and to economize space by the use of iron in forms and shapes not commonly known to architects at that time. These were special adaptations suggested by a mind fertile in resources, familiar with the use of iron and possessed of knowledge of how to form it and use it to good advantage."[44] The Harrison house represents the type of overlap between architecture and engineering that one would expect to find in an engineering-centered city and that began to appear with considerable frequency across Philadelphia before the Civil War. The iron elements in the Academy of Music and in Harrison's house and the cast iron trusses of John Gries's bank were concealed under plaster with no visible architectural role, but they were intrinsic to the new scale of construction, the new types of space, and the idea, if not the actuality, of fire-proof construction.[45]

In the previous generation Philadelphia architects had given visible expression to the new materials and the new technology of the industrial age. In the 1840s, Thomas Ustick Walter used cast iron plates ornamented with egg and dart moldings to infill the ceiling within the colonnade of Girard College, while cast iron balusters supported the wood railings on the cantilevered stone stairs of its entrance halls. In 1851, Stephen Decatur Button, following the model of John Haviland's use of iron plates to simulate ashlar masonry on the façade of the Miners Bank in Pottsville (1829), applied cast iron plates to the base of the façade of the Spring Garden Institute (demolished), an early technical institute at Broad and Spring Garden Streets. By 1860 Walter's imposing cast iron-clad dome of the U.S. Capitol, constructed on an armature of wrought iron trusses, was under construction in Washington, D.C. (Figure 17). Both Walter and his engineer, Montgomery C. Meigs, traced their lineage through Philadelphia's professional genealogy, Walter through his teacher William Strickland and Meigs through studies at the University of Pennsylvania before study at the engineering program at the U.S. Military Academy.[46]

Another example of the flood of technology that left its mark on Philadelphia architecture is to be found in City Hall. Designed by John McArthur in consultation with Walter, it usually has been interpreted as a vast and traditional masonry building with a marble skin cladding its load-bearing brick walls. In fact the exterior envelope of load-bearing masonry masks the materials of the new industrial age that are plainly visible throughout the building. In its corridor ceilings, exposed steel beams carry shallow brick vaults in an early version of fireproof construction, while the doorway portals and many of the decorative elements are of cast iron in lieu of hand-carved and flammable wood.[47] During its construction, McArthur redesigned the tower several times, each time aiming higher to surpass a rival structure. Eventually the weight of the ever-taller tower exceeded the limits of the foundations that had been constructed to carry the much shorter earlier scheme. To solve the problem of load, the final sections of the tower including its clocks and its crowning dome were redesigned in steel and iron by a Philadelphia engineer, C. R. (Carl Robert) Grimm, of the Tacony Iron and Metal Company.[48]

Figure 17 Thomas Ustick Walter, "Section Through United States Capitol Dome," 1859. Courtesy of the Library of Congress.

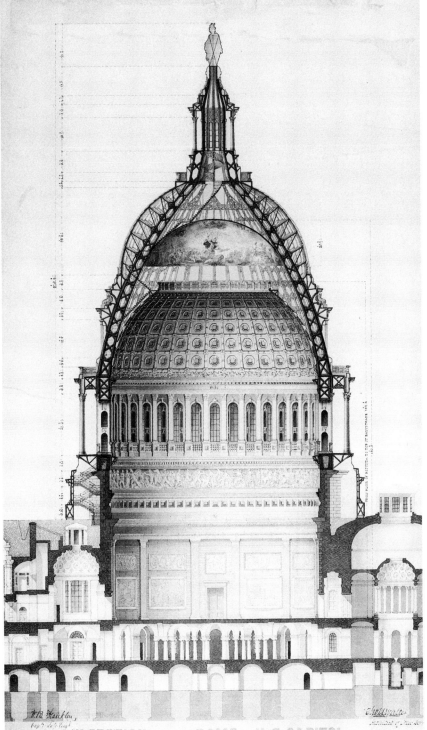

SECTION THROUGH DOME OF U.S. CAPITOL

Grimm was certainly aware of the problems of cast iron as a façade material because the dome of the U.S. Capitol required repainting every seven to ten years.[49] This difficulty was even greater because the cast-iron-clad structure that Grimm designed was to be constructed atop a stone tower, nearly five hundred feet in the air. Copper plating could protect iron from rusting but it weathered to green oxide, which would stain the marble of the lower levels of the tower. In the previous decade, a Philadelphia manufacturer, William Frishmuth, provided an aluminum pyramidal cap and lightning rod that crowned the Washington Monument. Its silver-gray metal weathered to a white powder that left the marble blocks of the obelisk unmarred by streaks of iron rust or copper verdigris. With the Washington Monument as a model, Grimm proposed to electroplate the iron plates of the upper levels of City Hall's tower with aluminum, at the time a semiprecious metal, over a base of copper plating. Aluminum would weather to gray that would blend in with the marble, making it possible to avoid the future expense of painting the iron while also not staining the stone.[50] Beginning with the Franklin Institute's original architectural instructors, William Strickland and John Haviland, who as early as the 1820s incorporated iron columns, railings, and façade facings into their buildings, the materials of the industrial future pervaded Philadelphia architecture.

Building Modern Institutions:
Industrialists on Philadelphia Boards

Even as industrial materials and systems were crossing into high design for Philadelphia's architecture, its institutions were being similarly transformed. The University of Pennsylvania's tilt away from history and high learning toward applied sciences was emblematic of Philadelphia's transformation under the new engineering culture. Prior to the 1860s, the path to Penn's board was through social status, so that a list of the university's board of trustees read like the markers in the graveyard at St. Peter's Episcopal Church at Third and Pine Streets. After the Civil War, however, while ministers of the principal Protestant denominations remained on the board, they were a minority with a largely honorific role.[51] William Sellers, then president of the Franklin Institute, was appointed to the board in 1866 and was made chairman of the committee that supervised the university's strongest program, the Department of Agriculture, Mines, Arts, and Mechanic Arts. Three years later he was joined on the board by Fairman Rogers, who had been the university's professor of civil engineering and a board member of the institute. In 1868 instead of choosing an Episcopal clergyman of the sort who had led Penn since the 1780s, the university trustees selected as its new provost Charles Stillé, a public historian active in Civil War politics, as well as a progressive educator. With a secular provost leading Penn, the board was also transformed. On the eve of the Centennial in 1875 Penn's leadership included engineer John C. Cresson; iron manufacturer J. Vaughan Merrick, whose father, Samuel, cofounded both the Pennsylvania Railroad and the Franklin Institute; John Henry Towne, a son of the former partner of Samuel Merrick and himself a partner in J. P. Morris, Towne & Co., an engine manufacturing business (later, his donation would fund the engineering school); Richard Wood, who headed iron industries in Millville, New Jersey, and would later found the Wawa Dairy, which persists to this day as the Wawa Markets; Franklin Institute members merchant John Welsh, attorney Peter McCall, and financier Frederick Fraley; and three medical professionals.[52]

The industrialist-led board determined in 1870 to abandon the university's former campus in the downtown, choosing a site that would provide for expansion in new purpose-built structures. Behind their Victorian Gothic façades, designed by Thomas W. Richards, Penn's buildings incorporated the materials of the industrial age, giving them aesthetic as well as functional roles. Cast iron columns supported beams that spanned large lecture rooms, and stairs incorporated rolled steel stair stringers and risers, cast iron newels, and wrought iron railings. Interior ventilation systems, signaled by a roofscape of stacks, ensured a healthful flow of fresh air even in winter, distinguishing Penn's new buildings from the houselike structures of the previous campus. Each of these features linked the new campus to the industrial culture of the city. In 1881, when Stillé was forced out as provost, the board, still led by Sellers, focused its selection criteria on candidates from the modern sciences, first proposing civil engineer and board member Fairman Rogers, and when he refused, choosing William Pepper, a scientist and medical doctor. Pepper would lead the university between 1881 and 1894, vastly enlarging its research and science facilities.[53] Under Pepper the university maintained its course away from the conventional classical education to adhere to Franklin's vision of education aimed at the contemporary world.[54]

In the 1880s, with William Pepper as provost, William Sellers chairing the board, and Frank Furness nominally the campus architect, the designers of the next round of buildings abandoned the Victorian Gothic and green serpentine stone designs of the first generation of buildings for industrial Philadelphia's hard red brick, windows sized and positioned according to usage, and direct architectural expression of separate functions in the manner of nearby mills.

Penn's new buildings included a utilitarian biology building that looked like a factory's office building (1884); a highly specific veterinary hospital by Furness & Evans (1885) (Figure 18); a mortuary and maternity ward, also by the Furness firm, located near the hospital south of Spruce Street (1887); the Furness-designed university library, facing the Lea Institute across Thirty-Fourth Street (1887–1891); an engineering school and attached power plant with an immense industrial chimney (Figure 19), both by Wilson Brothers, situated adjacent to the new library at the prominent corner site of Thirty-Fourth and Spruce Streets (1888); a factorylike school of public health and hygiene by Collins & Autenrieth (1890); and the Wistar Institute for medical research, designed by Hewitt Brothers, with most of its volume a steel-framed loftlike structure for expandable laboratories juxtaposed with a small office wing (1892–1894). In their shared brick façades, their expression of purpose through their forms and fenestration, and their use of the new materials of the industrial age, Penn's second-generation buildings

Figure 18 Furness and Evans, University of Pennsylvania Veterinary Hospital, Philadelphia, 1883. Building now demolished. Courtesy of the Architectural Archives, University of Pennsylvania.

were representations of the culture of the industrial city. Indeed, the public health school by Collins & Autenrieth was virtually indistinguishable in architectural detail and character from a dental factory a few blocks to the north by the same architects.[55] Together the engineering school, power plant, public health school, and university library dominated the prominent intersection of Thirty-Fourth and Spruce Streets, giving the university a visual identity more akin to a giant factory complex than the traditional Gothic-styled and ivy-draped college.

Under Sellers's leadership, the University of Pennsylvania had been remade in the image of industrial Philadelphia. In 1905, the year of his death, engineering remained the university's largest department, as it had been since its founding half a century before. After a fire destroyed its Wilson Brothers–designed engineering school adjacent to the power plant, a new building, named for engineer John Henry Towne, would open in 1906. Despite Cope & Stewardson's medievalizing façade, a Sellers-type machine shop occupied the skylighted core of its main floor in the center of

Figure 19 Wilson Brothers & Co., University of Pennsylvania power plant and engineering school, 1888. Courtesy of the University of Pennsylvania Archives.

which was a Sellers-made planing machine. Under a new provost, Charles Harrison, the architectural identity of the campus turned toward English late medieval modes but the soul of the university would remain with the sciences and the medical school.[56]

The University of Pennsylvania was not unique. Its future neighbor, the Drexel Institute of Technology, was conceived and then planned and designed by engineer, architect, and Franklin Institute president Joseph M. Wilson. In 1887, Wilson was sent by financier A. J. Drexel to Europe to study technological institutes. When he returned, he was asked to design a curriculum and then to design the building, which was erected in the early 1890s. Wilson's plan adapted the systems approach that he had exploited in the Centennial Main Exhibition Building and the Machinery Hall—a grid of iron columns and beams surrounded by a rationalized masonry skin with the added delight of a vast skylighted hall at the center made possible by steel trusses.

A survey of Philadelphia institutions from the Philadelphia Museum School, founded at the time of the Centennial, to the newly energized Zoological Society with its new buildings (many by Furness & Hewitt), Fairmount Park, and others of similarly diverse purposes finds them led by boards dominated by medical and engineering professionals. In the previous half century, Franklin Institute–led industries and their directors had transformed the city's economy, created a consumer lifestyle that spread across every stratum and neighborhood of the city, and reshaped the city's identity. By any measure, including its profound influence across industrial America, the wealth shared by all levels of its community, and, perhaps most tellingly, its ability to attract outsiders with knowledge, capital and energy, post–Civil War Philadelphia was thriving, throwing off wealth in the way boomtowns have always done.[57]

In the first half of his career, through 1890, most of Furness's clients outside his immediate family circle were drawn from the city's industrialists: machine tool maker William Sellers, locomotive designer William Henszey, iron makers George and Edward Brooke and Edward Burd Grubb, paper manufacturer Bloomfield Moore, and engineers Fairman Rogers, Alexander Cassatt, Thomas Scott, and George Brooke Roberts, as well as numerous members of the medical profession. Hospitals became a particular Furness specialty beginning with the Jewish Hospital, then the factorylike hospital for the Jefferson Medical College, followed by the tuberculosis hospital of the Good Shepherd in Chestnut Hill, the Bryn Mawr Hospital, and other hospitals as far away as Reading, Pennsylvania. Together with nearly 200 railroad commissions beginning with 125 designs for the Philadelphia and Reading Railroad, then another 35 for the Baltimore and Ohio, and finally a dozen ferryboats and more than a dozen buildings for the Pennsylvania Railroad, Philadelphia's industrialists were the heart of the Furness practice.[58] Two generations later, Frank Lloyd Wright would find a similar clientele who also thought in "mechanical terms" and were not wedded to historical styles.[59]

"Regardless of Precedents": Philadelphia Machine Design

In addition to the necessary new clientele, the new fortunes, and the booming economy, Philadelphia's industrialists also devised a new design strategy for machines and engines that was applicable beyond the factory. Well before the Civil War, Philadelphia-designed machines were distinguishable from those of the rest of the nation so that knowledgeable professionals could visually distinguish them from those manufactured in other parts of the country. Philip Scranton quotes a New England tool maker who, when asked to summarize the differences between the machines made by his peers and those made in Philadelphia, responded: "Our New England tool makers are all the time trying [*sic*] how cheap they can make tools [but] in Philadelphia the tool makers try how well they can make tools."[60] A more nuanced perspective was offered by Philadelphian Edwin Freedley in *Philadelphia and Its Manufactures* (1859). He described the particular characteristics that set Philadelphia-designed machinery apart from those of the remainder of the nation and the world: "The machine work executed in the leading establishments in Philadelphia ... is distinguished by certain characteristics which enable a competent judge to ... detect a Philadelphia-made machine by its 'earmarks.' Excellence of material, solidity, an admirable fitting of the joints, a just proportion and arrangement of the parts, and a certain thoroughness and genuineness, are qualities that pervade the machine work executed in Philadelphia and distinguish it from all other American-made machinery."[61]

To Freedley, more than simply manifesting quality, machines made in Philadelphia were visually identifiable because of design attitudes that were reflected not just in their materials, strength, and the carefully fitted parts but also in perceptible aesthetic characteristics signaled by "a just proportion and arrangement of the parts" and "a certain thoroughness and genuineness." In other words, the Philadelphia-made machines were identifiable at a distance without reading the maker's plate. Similar qualities were described in the reviews of the machines manufactured by William Sellers & Co. that were displayed at the French Exhibition of 1867 and the Vienna International Exhibition of 1873. These reviews were quoted at length in the *Philadelphia Public Ledger* on October 4, beginning with a particularly effusive account entitled "Motors, Machines and Machine Apparatus," written by Professor Franz Reuleaux, director of the Industrial Academy of Berlin:

> In the first direction Sellers & Co., of America [Philadelphia], have accomplished the most. They are distinguished from us [European manufacturers] by more direct and rapid conception. The American aims straightways for the needed construction, using the means that appear to him the simplest and most effective whether new or old. Our historically heaped up material and the cautious character of the German are so inseparably interwoven that among the number of known means we often forget to ask whether they are the simplest or whether new ones might not be better. The American [meaning Sellers and the Philadelphians] constructs in accordance with the severest theoretical abstraction; observing on the one side a distinctly marked out aim, weighing on the other the already available means or creating new ones, and then proceeding regardless of precedents, as straight as possible for the object.[62]

The *Ledger* then continued with a passage from the British journal *Engineering*, referencing the Vienna exhibition, again singling out Sellers's machines in particular for "an individuality which shows it to be the special design of its maker" and concluding that Sellers's methods were being copied across Europe.[63]

Sellers and the Philadelphia Design Strategy

In 1874, to celebrate its fiftieth anniversary, the Franklin Institute previewed the coming Centennial Exhibition with an exhibit of Philadelphia-made machines in the former Pennsylvania Railroad freight station at Thirteenth and Market Streets.[64] At the conclusion of the exhibition, Coleman Sellers delivered a lecture on the machines that were the focus of the exhibit. As he was the president of the institute, a nephew and partner of William Sellers, and an important machine designer in his own right, there was no one better than he to put into words the design strategies of the region's industrial designers.[65] He outlined the evolution of machines and explained the new principles by which Philadelphians shaped them:

I would gladly trace the progress in the arts during the past fifty years, could it be done in the limited time I dare address you, but I would be derelict in my duty were I to fail to do so in one particular instance, because it seems to me great principles are involved. The machine display in this room is unquestionably very fine, and when one glances over that broad expanse of iron servants of man's will, and peers through the forest of belts that give motion to these machines, one cannot but be struck by the remarkable uniformity in color there shown, and doubtless may think the dark gray tint, the absence of all gay colors indicative of our Quaker tastes and habits. Ladies and gentlemen, there is to the student of a nation's art progress, more in that quiet color than can be traced to any such reason. The lesson it teaches is worth learning.

* * *

When machine making became a trade, man still seeking to satisfy his innate longing for the beautiful, borrowed from other arts, regardless of fitness, forms and colors of acknowledged beauty. He called to his aid every type of architecture and decked his Gothic or Corinthian steam engine with all the gorgeous hues a painter's palette could offer him. As man's taste develops by culture he learns that beauty cannot be separated from fitness, that the most graceful forms, the most lovely colors fail to satisfy the eye when transported from their proper sphere or inharmoniously blended. It is an uneducated taste that finds satisfaction in brilliant colors only or seeks to beautify uncouth forms by gorgeous paints, while a higher culture fashions forms to suit the purpose for which they are designed, and colors them in subordination to their uses and surroundings. The grotesque architectural machinery of not many years ago is now seldom seen; conventional forms beautiful enough for some purposes when wrought in wood or stone have been abandoned, so that now, looking over this typical collection of machines for so many varied uses, we find that a new order of shapes, founded on the uses to which they are to be applied and the nature of the material of which they are made, have been adopted and the flaunting colors, the gaudy stripes, and glittering gilding has been replaced by this one tint, the color of the iron upon which it is painted.

That sombre tint is no indication of any Quakerish objection to bright colors but indicative of a higher culture and more refined taste.

In place of the standard Quaker-hostility-to-art narrative that Reverend William Henry Furness had raised four years earlier and that the "Correspondence" author of the *American Architect and Building News* would presume when framing his discussion of the arts in Philadelphia in 1877, Coleman Sellers made the case that these machine designs and their gray paint marked a purposeful aesthetic that had been developed by Philadelphia engineers independent of any thought of Quaker heritage. Sellers had been exploring these ideas for some time, as for example when he lectured on "Transmission of Power" at the Stevens Institute of Technology in 1872. There, Sellers summarized his aesthetic views: "In machinery, as in nature, fitness to intended purposes has much to do with our ideas of beauty."[66] Instead of adhering to old biases, historical forms, and out-of-date models, his firm and its fellow Philadelphia machine makers intended to express purpose through design that would lead to "a new order of shapes, founded on the uses to which they are to be applied and the nature of the material of which they are made." In clear contrast with John Ruskin's contemporary definition of architecture as the addition of "otherwise unnecessary" features on construction, Sellers argued that sound design principles were inherent to the creative process; in the case of his firm's machines, their principles were reductive toward an essence, expressive of uses, and appropriate to the materials. These principles could be applied to any design realm from machines to architecture.[67]

A decade before, Ralph Waldo Emerson had drawn a similar correlation between directness of form, purpose, and aesthetics, asserting that "all beauty must be organic; that outside embellishment is deformity."[68] Rather than being the result of the addition of "otherwise unnecessary" components, such as columns, beads, and bright colors, good design, Sellers, in line with Emerson, believed, resulted when "higher culture fashions forms to suit the purpose for which they are designed." Sellers's theory provides a succinct and rational strategy that better explains Furness's architectural goals and values than four decades of recent scholarship have offered. By "proceeding regardless of precedents, as straight as possible for the object," as Reuleaux had phrased it, such a method would enable a designer to break with historical sources and to find a new type of expression that could represent modern means and modern ends.

Instead of the backward craft-based or biblically sourced theories of John Ruskin, Sellers in Philadelphia pointed the way toward modern design. Parallels can be found between Sellers's design strategies and Charles Darwin's theory of a generation earlier that posited that present-day biological species were the result of a process of continuous change in response to their environment through "natural selection" rather than arriving complete on the earth as the result of divine intervention. Though constructs of humanity, Philadelphia machines

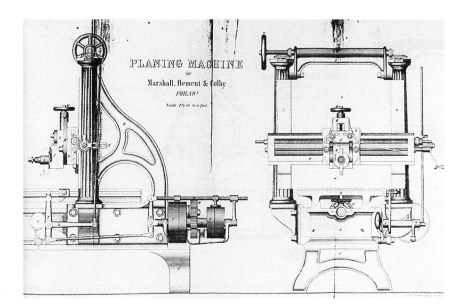

were designed in an analogous process of functional and visual refinement toward ever more effective use and economy of construction and material while also aiming toward closer tolerances that could be produced by less skilled workmen (Figure 20). Because they were developed in the liquid networks of Philadelphia and the Franklin Institute, the resulting machines, whether designed by the Sellers's firm or by other businesses in the Philadelphia orbit, were instantly identifiable as the product of one culture and place.

Figure 20 Marshall, Bement & Colby, planing machine, c. 1855. http://www.practicalmachinist .com/vb/antique-machinery-and -history/looking-william-sellers -co-info-190737/ (Accessed May 2017).

As Philadelphia machine makers' cohesive strategies for machine design proved, the new theories reflected their city's unique cultural and intellectual environment that produced the great machines. Whether Sellers and his cohorts consciously integrated Darwin's theory into their method or whether it was a concept in the air that crossed, via engineering values, into the design of ships, machines, bridges, buildings, and every other major construct of the day is not important.[69] What is clear is that in Philadelphia around the end of the Civil War, a design strategy had been codified, one that could cross boundaries into all fields and was an open invitation to express the inherent potency of contemporary life in new architectural forms. And just as animals were graced with spots, stripes, manes, and tails, together with brightly colored feathered wing patterns, the iridescence of beetles, or the lace of ferns, ornament could be inferred as a part of natural design insofar as it was expressive of purpose and function.

The special attributes of Philadelphia industrial design were reiterated in 1876 by British judges who evaluated the machines exhibited at the Centennial Exhibition. Once again they were dazzled by the achievement of the Philadelphia machine makers, as evidenced by their justification for the gold medal for the machines created by William Sellers & Co. And again, by presuming that Philadelphians represented the entire nation, the European judges missed the distinctive regional voice. The British judges described Sellers's work as

> remarkable . . . for the large amount of originality that is shown in the numerous new devices that are introduced, [Sellers's collection] is probably without a parallel in the past history of international exhibitions and taken as a whole it is worthy of the highest honor that can be conferred. Besides, it is thoroughly national in its characteristics, and preeminently worthy of the United States. . . . The whole of these machines are characterized by extreme refinement in every detail, by the superior quality of material employed in their construction, by first-class workmanship, both in regard to nice fitting and precision and the mathematical accuracy of all the parts; by the beautiful outlines that are imparted to each structure; by the correct proportions that have been worked out in the determining of strength and form, and the disposal of material to take full share of duty.[70]

The review continued with praise "for the scientific skill displayed in the application of mechanical force; for the daring shown in fearlessly breaking through the trammels of the past by introducing variously constructed devices and arrangements of gearing for the transmission of power in more direct course to the point of action, yet maintaining correct construction mechanically and without departure from true principles." The judges' report concluded by stating the impossibility of realizing in words the "full measure of such refined, mechanical, scientific, and artistic merit."

Against the cultural bias of architectural critics toward a norm based on history, the engineering judges were open to originality and approved the idea that distinctive design qualities were based on the formal expression of the particular functions of the machine rather than the application of historically derived details rooted in traditional design. The Philadelphians' strategy exemplified a new type of organic beauty not unlike that which another New England transcendentalist-influenced theoretician, Horatio Greenough, had described in his midcentury essays. After World War II, cultural historian John Kouwenhoven reintroduced Greenough's essays on aesthetics as an American source for organic and modern design:

Looking at the skeletons and skins of animals, birds, and fish, he [Greenough] found a variety and a beauty which led him to observe that there is "no arbitrary law of proportion, no unbending model of form in them. It is neither the presence nor the absence of this or that part or shape or color that wins our eye in natural objects; it is the consistency and harmony of the parts juxtaposed, the subordination of details to masses, and of masses to the whole." And from these direct, unborrowed observations of the world around him he deduced a theory which anticipates— even in its phrasing—the famous theory of which Louis Sullivan became the apostle a half century later: "If there be any principle of structure more plainly inculcated in the works of the Creator than all others, it is the principle of unflinching adaptation of forms to function."[71]

Boston, ruled by history and tradition, and New York, looking to current fashion derived from London and Paris, were inhospitable to these ideas. Philadelphia, with its new leadership drawn from industry and engineering, was open to innovative designs based on industrial theory. In the Centennial decade, the seeds of the ideas of machine designers would bear fruit in the expressive architecture of Frank Furness and the less inflected but equally original systems designs of Wilson Brothers. Their ideas spread into the work of many other architects working in Philadelphia and its cultural hinterland so that the influence of the Philadelphia-centered industrial culture is visible in Reading, Lancaster, Wilmington, Delaware, west to Pittsburgh, and on to Chicago.[72]

Unlike Sellers's gray machines, Furness's buildings initially were multihued and overlaid with reconceived details from the past—though his trend in the 1880s toward a unified red hue, indicative of their brick and terra cotta construction, may represent a parallel course to the unified metallic color advocated by the great machine designer. In the Victorian age buildings existed in a different social context than machines. Ornament was one of the architect's tools in suggesting purpose and calling for attention in the commercial marketplace. Nonetheless, a comparison of the dynamic asymmetry of Seller's great planing machine and the similarly purposeful asymmetry of the library for the University of Pennsylvania demonstrates what Furness had learned from the machine designers (Figures 21 and 22). Instead of borrowing from history, Furness in Philadelphia was free to break "through the trammels of the past" to fashion "forms to suit the purpose for which they are designed." In a competitive marketplace there was a role for the feral forces of identity as well as the expression of purpose, and Furness was comfortable with both.

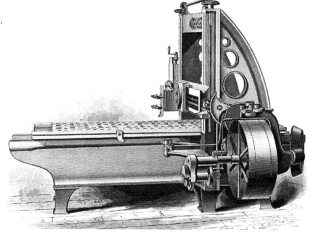

Figure 21 William Sellers & Co., planer, c 1876. Joseph Wilson, *The Masterpieces of the Centennial International Exposition*, vol. 3 (Philadelphia: Gebbie & Barrie, 1876).

Figure 22 Furness, Evans & Co., University of Pennsylvania Library, 1888. Courtesy of the University of Pennsylvania Archives.

The Centennial Exposition:
Disseminating the Machine Culture

Though Frederick Jackson Turner would famously proclaim the end of the American frontier at the 1893 American Historical Association meeting in Chicago, by the nation's Centennial in 1876, the massive cultural shifts toward an urban culture of industry and invention were well under way. To the quarter of the nation who visited the Centennial Exhibition in Philadelphia, the magic of the industrial and scientific future was present in the giant industrial halls and great machines. The board of the Franklin Institute concluded that Philadelphia should be the site of the fair not just because Independence Hall and Carpenters' Hall still stood in the old city but because "no other city possessed such advantages as are afforded by the vast industrial works of Philadelphia."[73] It was hoped that such an exposition would be an important step toward bridging the still evident regional divides persisting from the Civil War but, as the focus on the city's industry suggested, its true purpose was to present to a wide audience the transformation of the eighteenth-century city of the American Revolution into the nation's great industrial metropolis. With an eye to the underlying purpose of the fair, the symbolic opening act did not take place at Independence Hall or in the columned and domed Memorial Hall that had been constructed to house the fine arts and that looked to European classicism for its design. Instead it occurred in the giant Machinery Hall, a vast, clean, bright, and well-ventilated factorylike building. There while military bands played, the president of the United States and the emperor of Brazil started the prime mover of the fair, the giant Corliss engine that drove the vast array of machines that were the focus of the exhibition (Figure 23).

Nothing so directly expressed the progressive character of Philadelphia after the Civil War as the journey to the fair. Thanks in large part to the efforts of the Pennsylvania Railroad, this was one of the first modern travel experiences that combined ease and comfort at reasonable cost. In anticipation of a rising volume of rail traffic, the railroad had consolidated routes and unified rail gauges. The railroad was simultaneously engaged in double-, triple-, and sometimes even quadruple-tracking the route across the nation, making it possible to separate lumbering freight traffic from the fleet express passenger lines. To further speed travel, the Pennsylvania Railroad devised a trackside, telegraph-based signal system that told the locomotive engineer the position of his train relative to others on the system, thereby ensuring operational safety and speed. With the railroad's electronic signal systems, its multitrack operations, the luxuries of Pull-

Figure 23 "President Grant and the Emperor of Brazil Starting the Great Corliss Engine." Frank Leslie, *Historical Register of the Centennial Exposition* (New York: Frank Leslie's Publishing House, 1876).

man dining and sleeper cars, and comfortably upholstered passenger seats, even so distant a place as Chicago was only a day and a half's ride from the Centennial grounds by train, and it would be a pleasant ride at that.[74] A 9:00 A.M. departure from Chicago would arrive in Philadelphia early in the afternoon of the following day, with sleeping cars providing a good night's sleep on the way.[75] At the time of the American Revolution the "Flying Machine," a horse-drawn carriage, covered the ninety-five miles between New York and Philadelphia in two days with much bumping and physical discomfort; in 1876 the Pennsylvania Railroad trains sped nearly eight hundred miles, crossing rivers and mountains from Chicago in Illinois through Indiana, Ohio, and Pennsylvania in less time, considerably more comfort, and at a cost that most could pay.

Trains to the fair stopped at a new red brick station on the west banks of the Schuylkill at Thirty-Second Street. Designed by Joseph M. Wilson, then the staff architect of the railroad, it was constructed with an eye to the projected Centennial crowds and was capable of handling more trains simultaneously than any other station in the nation.[76] The new industrial age was announced by a sheltering porch around the building of cast iron columns spanned by a lattice frame of light iron members. The fairgoer also could ride directly to the fairgrounds, disembarking at a temporary station also designed by Wilson. Decorated with corner towers and braced by external framing that gave the visual effect of decorative half-timbering, it opened through an array of doors into a vast and airy hall that was part concourse and part retail emporium.

Passengers to the fair probably did not fully comprehend the nature of their experience, but Wilson was treating them with the ruthless efficiency with which a railroad man would treat freight. By placing the Pennsylvania Railroad's Centennial station directly opposite the main entrance to the fairgrounds, the sequence from train to station to exhibition delivered the fair-goer either to the main point of entry or to the temporary hotels that sprang up almost overnight south of the fairgrounds. Indeed, the planning of the entire fair was organized as a rationalized logistics-based system with each entrance serving a different audience and transportation system. At the east end of the Main Exhibition Hall, nearest to the city and the new Girard Avenue Bridge, was the carriage trade entrance. At the far west end of the Machinery Hall was another entrance for streetcar riders. The rail traveler arrived at the main courtyard midway between the two principal buildings. That the Pennsylvania Railroad was an early and principal supporter of the fair was obvious from its advantaged position at the main entrance, while the Philadelphia and Reading Railroad's station was placed on the opposite side of the grounds and a considerable distance from the main buildings. Most tickets to the exhibition were sold as a package together with the railroad ticket, but tickets also could be purchased at each gate. These gates opened onto the main courtyard and provided direct access to a monorail train, anticipating the Tomorrowland monorail at Disneyland by nearly eighty years. This novelty train, pulled by a steam locomotive on a single elevated monorail, provided a leisurely ride around the grounds, passing the Main Exhibition and Machinery Halls before circling the Agriculture Hall and returning to its point of departure.[77] Miniature trains would become a staple of future fairs moving the public around the fairgrounds in much the same way as the original construction materials had arrived. Once again it was clear that the future had arrived early in Philadelphia.

After several rounds of competitions for ever grander buildings to house the fair, the national financial crash of 1873 forced economical solutions. The main exhibition buildings were designed by a team that could only have been assembled in Philadelphia. They were led by two men delegated from the Pennsylvania Railroad engineering staff, Joseph Wilson and his chief assistant, architect Henry Pettit (1848–1921). They proposed to build what they knew best—an engineered iron frame for the Main Exhibition Hall and a heavy timber mill for the Machinery Hall. Both were clad with little more than industrial sash on the vertical planes and roofed using the industrial system of hot tar and roofing felt.[78] By coordinating and bringing together the products of regional manufacturers such as William Sellers & Co., by utilizing the delivery systems of the Pennsylvania Railroad, and by shaping the buildings to the goals and values of the engineers, Wilson and Pettit were able to design and construct vast structures that could be erected almost overnight using off-the-shelf parts and materials that served the already highly rationalized and organized mill construction business. A description of the Main Exhibition Hall in the *Journal of the Franklin Institute* noted: "This building being a temporary construction, the columns and trusses are so designed that they may be easily taken down and erected again at another site."[79] The fair would essentially rent the materials. Because they adapted preexisting systems from regional factory construction, they could build the required thirty-five acres of exhibition space for a cost of just over $2 million, less than $65,000 per acre. The anticipated costs were approximately two-thirds of the minimum lowest estimate of the earlier schemes and had the further advantage of meeting the deadline to receive the first exhibits in January of the Centennial year. The downturn in the economy further benefited the designers and contractors by reducing demand for materials and making construction crews available. William Sellers's Edge Moor Plant on the Delaware River outside Chester had recently increased its capacity and was able to produce the iron fittings that connected columns and trusses at a reasonable cost. Sellers negotiated a lease for the power shafting and couplings that would run the machinery with the intention of reselling those materials afterward. Despite the down economy of the period, Sellers was able to keep his plants operating while reducing the costs to the Centennial Board of Finance.[80]

As Wilson understood, in the midst of a massive recession, the Philadelphia fair could afford neither the baroque grandeur of the recent French exhibition or the fairy gossamer of Paxton's iron and glass Crystal Palace of twenty-five years earlier, which he readily acknowledged from his perspective as an engineer was the model for an exhibition. Accordingly, "the amounts of material used had to be kept strictly to the requirements for proper strength and no more." Nevertheless, Wilson was proud of the buildings, writing: "It is generally believed that the general effect of the building is quite satisfactory."[81] Indeed, the industrial character of the buildings became their strength, reinforcing the Franklin Institute's intended lessons by constructing a realistic setting that described the untraditional culture centered in Philadelphia.[82] Because of the efficiency of the construction, the fair buildings came in so far under budget that the planners could add the Horticultural Hall, a giant Victorian greenhouse, again largely made of predesigned, cast iron elements and industrial trusses, to further delight the fairgoer.

As could be expected from his role as the Pennsylvania Railroad's engineer, Wilson's account of the Centennial emphasized the Pennsylvania Railroad's mastery of logistics in the planning of the fair, ensuring its successful and timely completion (Figure 24). Rail lines were constructed parallel to the main halls so that the construction materials, and later the exhibits themselves, could be offloaded directly "alongside the buildings for which they were destined and . . . [trains'] contents unloaded almost at the spot at which they were to be exhibited."[83] Through the

Figure 24 "The Transportation of Foreign Goods to the Main Building." Frank Leslie, *Historical Register of the Centennial Exposition* (New York, 1876).

numbering of the columns of the interior, exhibit materials could be delivered to exact locations in the vast complex, a system that remained the basis for mail delivery during the fair. This was part of a larger system of subdividing and organizing of the exhibits that was masterminded by Melvil Dewey which he later applied to library collections in the familiar Dewey Decimal System.[84]

Despite the limitations imposed by the budget, the Centennial Exhibition's buildings afforded a new sort of grandeur that has characterized the modern world ever since.[85] This was not the conventional majesty of giant blocks of stone on stone in the manner of Boston's Trinity Church or Philadelphia's City Hall, then rising at Center Square, but, rather, the power of atmospheric vastness that had been imagined by Étienne Boullée's fanciful designs a century before and which was reappearing in the airy retail gallerias and department stores that were the new cathedrals of commerce. The Main Exhibition Hall provided one of the best examples of what would become a typical modern American experience—vast numbers of fellow citizens engulfed in a gargantuan, often temporary, space. Dining in one of the palatial hotel dining rooms that seated a thousand at a time in nearby seashore resorts, attending a band concert at an amusement park's outdoor amphitheater or a sporting event in the new stadia which began to appear in major cities, strolling in the mobs of the Easter Parade on the Boardwalk in Atlantic City, or, in our time, venturing into the crowds on Black Friday in modern shopping malls—these mass experiences were all anticipated by the buildings that Pettit and Wilson created.

The scale of the complex was also modern. The Main Exhibition Hall and Machinery Hall framed a central court measuring five hundred feet on a side, the size of a typical city block, while the entire ensemble from one end of the great halls to the other was nearly three-quarters of a mile in length—some six or seven city blocks, or roughly the distance between the new City Hall at Center Square and Independence Hall at Sixth and Chestnut Streets. In *American Building Art: The Nineteenth Century*, engineering historian Carl Condit gave Joseph Wilson his highest praise for his great train sheds of the 1890s, asserting that he "anticipated three cardinal doctrines of modern architectural theory—simplicity, volume rather than mass, and free-flowing space."[86] The same appraisal can be applied to Wilson's and Pettit's Centennial buildings that introduced the world to its industrial, mass future. Condit might have also pointed out that in his refusal to "allow precedent to fetter his reason or prevent him from properly adapting his work to local conditions and special wants," Wilson showed a modern understanding of the role of design as a catalyst for a new experience rather than resorting to old precedents clad in old styles.[87] In Victorian America, it was a strategy that only a Philadelphia engineer could have conceived.

Wilson's account of the design process of the Machinery Hall made it clear that engineering concerns, not aesthetics, governed the dimensions of the 1,500-foot-long building. Interior heights and construction systems were determined solely by the standardized requirements for hanging the industrial shafting that would power the exhibits; the central aisles were higher for light and ventilation, again following industrial models. Where the length, 1,876 feet, and height, 100 feet, of the Main Exhibition Hall referenced respectively the centennial year and the height of the first dome of the U.S. Capitol building, the Machinery Hall's length was determined by the engineers' assessment of the effective limits of piping runs for steam-powered machinery while the interior spans were determined by the timber framing common to the city mills.[88] In essence, the Machinery Hall was a giant mill, but rather than the usual masonry skin, it was covered with pre-manufactured industrial sash, tinted with whitewash on the glazing in the standard factory manner to reduce solar load. It was larger than most industrial buildings and it was open to the public, but it was a mill nonetheless.

While the Memorial Hall was intended to remain as the permanent art museum for the city, it was immediately apparent from the reaction of the crowds and from published reports that the actual star of the fair was the Machinery Hall, where the giant Corliss engine powered the miles of drive shafts and leather belting that turned the wheels of locomotives and ran the machines—the printing presses, carpet looms, and powered pumps, the man-made cataracts of the industrial world.[89] Many years later, Ashcan School artist John Sloan remembered that he had to be dragged away from the famous Corliss engine.[90] Sloan was five years old at the time but he was not alone. It was the machines that brought people to the fair and became its focal point. The fair had the requisite art, the manufactured historical symbols and memorabilia, the new foods, from Hire's root beer to ice cream cones, and the symbols of the nation's liberty—even the arm and torch of the yet-to-be-completed Statue of Liberty—but what people remembered was their introduction to the speed, energy, and excitement of the industrial world through the great machines and the buildings that housed them.

Ironically, the simple industrial framing and lack of ornamentation of Philadelphia's Centennial buildings had a more powerful impact on future European exhibitions and their architecture than on subsequent American fairs, including the Columbian, Louisiana Purchase, and Sesquicentennial Exhibitions. The main exhibition hall of the Palace of Industry of the Paris Universal Exhibition of 1878 and the Gallery of Machines of the 1889 Paris Universal Exhibition reflected Philadelphia's industrial mode. The great halls were spanned in modern materials, while the tower of steel by Gustave Eiffel achieved what the Phoenix Iron Company had proposed for the Centennial Exhibition but, for budgetary reasons, had been unable to build—a thousand-foot tower of cast and wrought iron, with a spiral perimeter stair and an internal elevator in the iron core that reached a viewing platform at the top.[91]

In his cultural history of America, John Kouwenhoven used the Philadelphia exhibition and the starring machines to differentiate the innovative American culture from the traditional forms of old Europe, noting, in particular, the foreign admiration for the American industrial achievement and their later regret when America shifted to conventional taste and historic forms in the buildings of the Chicago Columbian Exposition.[92] But he too missed a critical point. The fair and the great machines exhibited within it were not broadly American; instead they were deeply and specifically representations of Philadelphia's engineering culture, the new industrial client, the new design theories that would be used as the basis for design, and the resulting new architecture that the new theories would support.

Every corner of the Centennial city held more evidence of its new industrial agency and power. In the old downtown, a block to the east of the State House (Independence Hall), the visitor would have seen the banking district, which already boasted five banking houses designed by Frank Furness, each more flamboyant than the last, with the most recent, the Guarantee Trust & Safe Deposit Company building, framing a view down Carpenter's Court to the Revolutionary icon Carpenters' Hall. Furness's banks glowed with the light of day introduced through their skylighted and iron-framed roofs, while their machine-produced tile surfaces decorating the interiors added glitter and delight to the act of banking. To the west at Tenth Street were the foundations of Furness's factorylike hospital for Jefferson Medical College that contrasted with the medical school's earlier column-fronted lecture hall and marked the direct transfer of industrial characteristics into medical architecture. To the north at Broad and Cherry Streets was Furness's factorylike Pennsylvania Academy of the Fine Arts, displaying its giant exposed steel truss along its north façade and with wrought iron girders and iron columns and steel beams accenting its galleries below great skylights made possible by wrought iron trusses carrying glass shingles and industrial ventilators on the roof.

Furness and Wilson were not the only Philadelphia architects to design in the new manner. At Logan Square, James Windrim's design for the new build-

ing for the Academy of Natural Sciences presented visitors with a schizophrenic experience, an academic Gothic façade in green serpentinite and yellow sandstone (copying the University of Pennsylvania's new buildings) screening an unadorned industrial interior of free-standing riveted steel columns and spanning steel girders (Figure 25). On the west side of the city, in the Rittenhouse Square neighborhood at Twenty-Second and Spruce Streets, Henry Sims's chapel of ease for Holy Trinity Church contrasted conventional detailed Gothic walls of brownstone with exposed, riveted-steel flying buttresses (Figure 26). Across the city other buildings displayed steel beams and girders spanning entrances and interior spaces. No one who visited the fair and looked at the city's architecture could miss the new potency of its buildings. It was this city, led by engineers and designed with an eye to the mechanical culture,that became the setting and the impetus for Furness's imaginative architecture over the next two generations. There was other evidence as well of changing ideas and techniques that would continue to transform architecture. From the front steps of the Fine Arts Academy, the visitor could see the giant traveling cranes, operating from a self-sustaining scaffold invented by Joseph Wilson, easily lifting massive blocks of stone onto the rising walls of City Hall (Figure 27). In every

Figure 25 Academy of Natural Sciences, Philadelphia. Main Hall, 1876. ANSP Archives Collection 049.

Figure 26 Henry A. Sims and
James P. Sims, Holy Trinity Chapel,
1873. Photograph by George E.
Thomas, 2012.

direction of the city, from the Exhibition halls to the Academy, from the railroad stations to the banks, Centennial-era Philadelphia and its architecture were pregnant with the future.

In this setting, Frank Furness, more than any of his contemporaries, found the means to express its possibilities. Given the scattering of Furness-influenced buildings from Belfast, Maine, to Kansas City and beyond, the Philadelphia method did not need a name nor did it require a manifesto. The fruits were obvious. But history needs slogans and narratives. Over the next generation, the narrative of modernism would be hijacked to the later arena of Chicago. Furness's relative muteness—perhaps caused by unwillingness to compete with the towering verbal skills of his father and his brother—left only Sullivan's compel-

Figure 27 Wilson Brothers, stone hoisting machinery, Philadelphia City Hall. Wilson Brothers & Co., *Catalogue of Work Executed* (Philadelphia: Lippincott, 1885).

ling narrative, which would be written after World War I, long after Furness's heyday. Just as victors get to write the histories, so too, the unspoken creator disappears when other systems rise to the fore and are uncontested in the historical record. But the Centennial city, the industrial culture, and the design theory of Philadelphia machine designers are evidence of a new American architecture and culture that was developing on the banks of the Delaware.

Future scholars might also look to the influence of the Philadelphia Centennial. Clearly the 1878 and 1889 French International Exhibitions adopted the industrial character but a more direct line of connection is to be seen in the 1888 Universal Exposition in Barcelona, organized by Eugenio Serrano de Casanova (1841–1920) who had represented the Spanish government at the Philadelphia Exposition. He suggested Barcelona as the site for an international exposition to celebrate its industries. With the radiating industrial halls of the Palace of Industry recalling a railroad roundhouse as the centerpiece, it was a worthy successor to Wilson and Pettit's vision while the strident coloring, expressive use of iron, and original ornamental character of the Catalan Renaissance raises the possibility that Frank Furness's brilliant Centennial-era colorism affected the Old World.[93]

TWO COMPETITIONS

BOSTON'S TRINITY CHURCH AND
PHILADELPHIA'S PENNSYLVANIA
ACADEMY OF THE FINE ARTS

The opening of the new Pennsylvania Academy of the Fine Arts building in the spring of 1876 links the building to the nation's Centennial celebration. The nearly simultaneous competition for the new Trinity Church in Boston's Back Bay offers a way to compare the civic and the resulting architectural cultures of the two cities, demonstrating the growing divide between industrial Philadelphia and cultivated Boston. In the decade after the Civil War, as Philadelphians moved to control the related turfs of industry and transportation, their northern rivals were shifting in relation to each other, gradually taking on roles that are now familiar to us.

The efforts of Philadelphia and Boston notwithstanding, New York continued on its own course. It had become the nation's marketplace thanks to its nearly instant connections to Europe via the transatlantic cable, its matchless year-round harbor, and its growing control and centralization of American financial and capital markets. The Castle Garden Immigration Depot and later Ellis Island made Manhattan the immigration gateway and gave the city its polyglot late nineteenth-century character. In the last third of the century, New York took on Philadelphia's eighteenth-century role as the nation's global city and reveled in its domination over its eastern rivals.[1] In the next generation, its island site and the egos of its financiers would drive the development of ever-taller buildings that would transform office buildings into aspirational spires and in turn would force the development of high-speed ground transportation systems to solve the city's traffic congestion brought on by its density. Many of those developments required the Philadelphia engineers and industrialists who shaped the Centennial Exhibition. In the late 1870s, Joseph Wilson's firm, Wilson Brothers, designed the structures and stations for New York's elevated railroads; in that same period, William Sellers's businesses provided the structural steel for the Brooklyn Bridge that, for the first time, connected Manhattan to Brooklyn; and at the beginning of the new century, Philadelphia engineer and financier Alexander J. Cassatt, by then the president of the Pennsylvania Railroad, led the construction of the great railroad tunnels under the Hudson and East Rivers that for a century have linked the city to the New Jersey mainland and to Brooklyn and the commuter towns of Long Island.

Figure 28 Sturgis and Brigham, Museum of Fine Arts, Boston, 1870. Building now demolished. Photograph c. 1901, Detroit Publishing Co. Courtesy of the Library of Congress.

Boston was changing as well. In the eighteenth century its Puritan monoculture had driven Benjamin Franklin to seek out the open society of Philadelphia. The nineteenth-century addition of the Irish immigrants with their immense Roman

Catholic churches brought diversity to the city. The Roman Catholic newcomers would spread throughout New England, grasping political power and rivaling but not supplanting the earlier Puritans and their subset, the Unitarians, who together continued to run the cultural institutions central to Boston's identity. Beginning in 1857, the old Back Bay, behind the neck on which Boston had been built, was filled in, forming a new district for elite downtown living that was larger, richer, and more architecturally varied than Philadelphia's Rittenhouse Square and more permanent than New York's northward-moving residential districts that were constantly overrun by commerce. The new architecture of Back Bay's mansions revealed Boston's culture, looking to Paris and London for sources with mansarded rows flanking grand avenues that attested to the city's identity as the hub of New England.

Boston held firm to its historic role as the center of the nation's intellectual and academic culture.[2] Its Museum of Fine Arts was incorporated in 1870 and its new building was opened on the Fourth of July 1876 in a prime site in the Back Bay. Designed by the local firm of Sturgis & Brigham, it was part of a new generation of American museums, a deliciously ambitious structure whose brilliantly polychromed exterior was highlighted by a colorful blend of brick, stone, and terra cotta shaped into Gothic arcades reminiscent of Venice's Doge's Palace (Figure 28). Great sculpted panels gave legibility to the building's purpose. New York's Metropolitan Museum also was organized in 1870 but its building would only get under way in 1872 when its directors commissioned a brick and stone design from Calvert Vaux and Jacob Wrey Mould.

After the Civil War, Boston, New York, and Philadelphia continued their competition in multiple realms. Boston's Massachusetts Institute of Technology was founded by a Philadelphian, William Barton Rogers (1804–1882), whose father had taught at the University of Pennsylvania. MIT immediately established the first college-based architecture program, organized by William Ware in 1865. Penn's program would follow three years later.[3] Boston founded its famous symphony in 1881, following only New York in that endeavor. Boston's journals and magazines, including the *American Architect and Building News* (founded in 1876), gave a patrician Yankee tone to the architectural discussion of the Centennial decade and maintained Boston's position as a center for architectural comment and criticism even after the design professions had departed for New York.[4]

Despite the forces of new immigrant populations and the rising tide of scientific inquiry, Boston, at the end of the nineteenth century, remained the city of Henry Adams (1838–1918). The great-grandson of one American president and the grandson of another, Harvard educated, and exposed to the Western civilized world at a young age, Henry Adams found himself, as the twentieth century dawned, profoundly aware of the limitations of his education, which had focused on the past and ignored the present and the future. Where educated and cultivated Philadelphians formed institutions that exposed the new industrial culture to everyone, Adams, in *The Education of Henry Adams*, recognized the gulf between the world that he studied and understood—the traditional forms of the church, the Virgin as emblem of that church, old culture vested in academic robes—versus the New World, whose engines and dynamos rendered irrelevant most of his knowledge.[5] Aspects of Adams's Boston continue to characterize the New England city to the present, signifying the ongoing power of the ideas and values of New England's constituent and unifying culture. In 2014, when Harvard University's Fogg Museum reopened after its transformation by the Renzo Piano Building Workshop into a great machine for viewing and conserving art, a curator's address discussed the building as a successor to the Mouseion at Alexandria as described by the geographer Strabo shortly after the end of the rule of Augustus.[6]

Trinity Church

In March 1870, Boston's elite Trinity Protestant Episcopal congregation embarked on a process that would lead to the creation of its ecclesiastical landmark.[7] In the previous year, it had called to its pulpit one of the most remarkable preachers of the day, Phillips Brooks (1835–1893). After graduating from Harvard College, he had been the rector of Philadelphia's Holy Trinity Church on Rittenhouse Square, where he had commissioned Fraser, Furness & Hewitt to complete the tower for the late John Notman's brownstone church.[8] The decision by the Boston vestry to build a new church in the Back Bay was driven by the encroachment of Boston's expanding commercial district around the Summer Street location. The move of many of its congregation to the Back Bay reinforced the desire to move away from the noise and commerce of the downtown.[9] Raising the funds and coordinating a building committee for a new church would be part of Brooks's mission. With hopes fueled by peace and the rising economy, the Trinity trustees purchased a property facing the small triangle of open space optimistically called "Art Square."[10] At the moment however, the "square" was neither a square nor a center of art, being, instead, little more than a left-over wedge where the diagonal of Huntington Avenue and St. James Street crossed at the front of the future site of the Museum of Fine Arts.

The Pennsylvania Academy of the Fine Arts: Site, Exhibition, Teaching, and White Fungus

In 1864, six years before the Bostonians began to discuss a new site for Trinity Episcopal Church, the board of the Pennsylvania Academy of the Fine Arts had been forced to evaluate its building. The modest temple-fronted museum and school, originally set back on a lawn, by then was screened by rental shops that continued the line of retail along the 1000 block of Chestnut Street in the expanding downtown. In a message to his fellow trustees, John Sartain explained that the building was no longer suited for hosting the annual exhibits that were central to their fund-raising and did not support the proposed addition of life classes to the earlier teaching method of drawing from classical plaster casts. Further, the collection was being damaged by a white fungus when paintings were stored in the basement during the annual exhibits.[11] He concluded that the existing building might, at great expense, be made to suffice but it was clearly better to consider a new building. The war stopped the discussion for the moment, but in August 1867, in another board meeting, Sartain laid out requirements that could only be met in a new building at another site:

> The space required for the proper accommodation of the Academy is an area of about 100 feet, by 225 feet or its equivalent comprised in other proportions. This, when subdivided into galleries, can be made to yield a wall 2000 feet in length. Nearly 1200 feet of this is wanted for the effective display of the present permanent collection, even without further augmentation, and the remaining 800 feet are calculated for the Annual and other occasional exhibitions. This space is required because these galleries must all receive their light through the roof. The other various wants of the Institution would have to be provided for in a story constructed below the main suite of galleries.[12]

Before a design could be commissioned, the search for a site produced a comedy of errors that nearly sank the Academy. Board members first looked for free sites with their focus on Broad Street, which was becoming the city's center of clubs and mansions. One idea was to adapt Center Square at Broad and Market Streets as sites for the Academy and its peer cultural institutions, the American Philosophical Society, the Academy of Natural Sciences, and the Philadelphia Library Company, through whose combined effort "a grand result might be obtained in the adornment of the city."[13] As a fallback to the Center Square site, the Academy board purchased several properties across the street from the southwest side of the square. Unfortunately, these purchases were separated by three house lots. When the owners of those lots realized that the Academy board was trying to create a single property, their prices became exorbitant. The popular vote to build City Hall on Center Square instead of the previously selected site surrounding Independence Hall ended the dream of free land and raised the price of the holdout properties that the board needed to complete its parcel.

With no site meeting all of the board's criteria, board member, mechanical engineer, and Franklin Institute member Joseph Harrison proposed to combine the missions of two of the boards on which he served—the Academy and Fairmount Park. With engineer's logic, he suggested that the Academy find a site in the new Fairmount Park that could initially serve as the permanent art building for the coming Centennial Exposition. The site would be free while the Academy could take advantage of any public funds that would come from the fair.[14] Unfortunately the location on the west side of the Schuylkill was deemed inconvenient for both students and faculty who typically lived within walking distances of the Academy. The board was finally forced to make a decision when it sold the existing building in the postwar boom for commercial real estate prices along Chestnut Street. The Academy board settled on the best available site at the north end of the new civic zone, the lot at Broad and Cherry Streets. That site was purchased over Harrison's strenuous objections because he feared that the construction of City Hall would produce years of dirt and noise. Other board members were concerned about locating in the déclassé area north of Market Street.[15] The ensuing battle of words in the minutes and in the boardroom eventually led Harrison, the board's wealthiest member, to resign, leaving a board position that was filled by Fairman Rogers.[16]

Selecting Architects: Boston

The selection process and the final choice of architects for Boston's Trinity Church and Philadelphia's Academy of the Fine Arts tell us much about the cultural identities and the psychological boundaries of their cities. Trinity's potential architects included three hometown favorites: Sturgis & Brigham had recently won the commission for the new Fine Arts museum. The socially connected firm of Peabody & Stearns had opened its office a few months earlier after Robert Swain Peabody's return from study at the École des Beaux Arts. Ware & Van Brunt, whose partners were both Harvard graduates and veterans of Hunt's New York atelier, had recently opened a Boston office; their flamboyant take on Ruskinian

Gothic had been accepted for Harvard's Memorial Hall, and Ware was teaching the new architecture course at the Massachusetts Institute of Technology.[17]

The Trinity building committee also looked outside Boston to New York. As could be expected, Richard Morris Hunt, arguably the nation's best-known architect, was invited. Another New Yorker, William A. Potter (1842–1909), was invited because of family connections to the hierarchy of the Episcopal Church. The son of the Episcopal bishop of Pennsylvania and nephew of the Episcopal bishop of New York, Potter had won the commission for a significant Congregational church in Springfield, Massachusetts, the previous year. The outlier of the invitees was Henry Hobson Richardson, who was working in New York after six years in Paris. He had formed a partnership with fellow Harvard graduate Charles Gambrill, another veteran of Hunt's atelier. Though he was raised in New Orleans, Richardson's Harvard degree and membership in the Porcellian Club connected him to both the chair of the building committee, Robert Treat Paine, and its most active member, Charles Parker.[18] The Trinity vestry would have been familiar with Gambrill & Richardson's winning design for the Brattle Square Congregational Church (1870) that was rising two blocks from the Trinity site.

Taken together, the architects selected by Boston's Episcopalians represented the rising Eurocentric strain of elite American architecture. Notably, of the Boston project invitees, only Hunt had any significant professional experience before the Civil War. Clearly, the Trinity building committee intended to choose a contemporary direction rather than select from the previous generation of monochromic classicists, such as Gridley J. F. Bryant (1816–1899) or Edward Cabot Clarke (1818–1901), who had dominated Boston architecture in the previous generation.[19] An original design seemed readily attainable because the congregation's church on Summer Street remained adequate, giving it the luxury of an open-ended schedule. The Trinity Church building committee was named in March 1872 and, in a week, produced a conventional program for a church seating 1,000 on the main floor with another 350 in the balcony together with the parish house located at the rear of the site.[20] Plans, elevations, and sections were to be submitted by May 1 to meet an estimated budget of $200,000.

The Trinity Church Competition

The Trinity competition allowed little more than a month for the production of plans, sections, and elevations, suggesting that church design required less research and study than the Academy, which allocated more than four months for its competitors.[21] In addition to the winning Gambrill & Richardson elevation, two of the Trinity competitors' projects can be gauged from perspectives that were published in the *New York Sketch Book of Architecture* (1874) and the *Boston Architectural Sketch Book* (1874). The New York publication shows Hunt's scheme, a first-generation Romanesque design with round-headed arches and corbel tables along the eaves, not unlike Richard Upjohn's Bowdoin College Chapel of a generation earlier. The plan's chief feature was a crossing tower that would have been an architectural focus for the small plaza in front of the church. Sturgis & Brigham's scheme, as depicted in the Boston publication, offered a more conventional English rural Gothic scheme with a corner tower and a compact plan with short transepts and apse. Both architects accepted the limitations of the narrow lot that the congregation had purchased. Gambrill & Richardson's winning plan, like Hunt's, offered a Romanesque building with corbel tables lining the apse gable. In the firm's presentation drawing, however, the slender crossing tower broke through the border of the drawing to emphasize its height (Figure 29).

Shortly after the May deadline, the competition was decided in favor of Gambrill & Richardson. A leisurely postselection process ensued, resulting in multiple schemes and studies that attempted to reconcile the congregation's desire for grandeur with the filled Back Bay site's inability to carry the load of the great central tower proposed by the architects. At the recommendation of the architects, a side lot was acquired that permitted a more interesting composition, even as it raised the cost of the project. The schedule changed on November 9, 1872, when the great Boston fire destroyed much of the downtown and, with it, the existing church. Planning for the new church was accelerated. Its construction became a part of the much larger reconstruction of downtown Boston.

With the larger site in hand, the architects revised their plans, resulting in the familiar monumental Greek-cross-planned building surmounted by a two-stage crossing tower and flanked by the Sunday school that controls the remainder of the site. This design was enlivened by a roughness of texture in the stonework and bulkiness of proportion that hinted at the future expression of the final design. The broad and short plan offered advantages to Brooks because it brought members of the congregation within easy vocal range of the minister. It also compressed the nave and the giant apse, making the service more immediate and emotional than the usual elongated Episcopal church plan. While Richardson's scheme suggested the directions of the eponymous mode that came to be identified with him, in the end, the design was like those of his peers, looking to history.

Figure 29 Gambrill & Richardson, "Competition Design for Trinity Church, Boston, Mass." Courtesy of the Houghton Library, Harvard University.

FRONT ELEVATION

The Pennsylvania Academy and the New Philadelphia

The new building for the Academy was part of a vast change in Philadelphia's downtown. By the 1830s, it was obvious that the quarters of city government in the antique buildings of the Revolution centered on Independence Hall were too small to serve the lusty industrial city. The old downtown along East Market, Chestnut, and Walnut Streets had few spaces for the new commercial buildings that represented the quickening pace and national spread of the city's businesses, and there was no obvious space for a new city hall. To preserve the proximity between government and business, the selected architect for City Hall, John McArthur, Jr., devised a plan that literally wrapped the new City Hall building around Independence Hall. It would occupy the east, south, and west sides of Independence Square but required the demolition of the eighteenth-century city hall (later the U.S. Supreme Court) and the city court that served both houses of Congress. This plan was initially approved but later rejected because of the rising awareness of the importance of the icons of the American Revolution. In 1870, after much debate, Center Square, William Penn's original site for government, at the intersection of Broad Street and Market Street, was selected as the site of the mammoth building. Where Boston and New York built new city halls in the immediate vicinity of their previous buildings, preserving the relationship between government and downtown offices and commerce at the expense of their oldest buildings, Philadelphia engineers saw the value of reconceiving the downtown in a new center removed from the old port along the Delaware River.[22] Over the next generation much of the business district gradually moved to the neighborhood adjacent to the new City Hall, filling Broad Street south to Locust Street and north to Cherry Street as well as several blocks on Market Street to the east and west.

The initial concentration of the city near the port on the Delaware River meant that Broad Street, the largest street in Thomas Holme's plan for the city, was largely unoccupied through the period when the city was the nation's capital. Only in the 1820s did Broad Street gradually become the site of the city's cultural institutions, beginning with the Philadelphia Asylum for the Deaf and Dumb (now the University of the Arts). It was followed at midcentury by the construction of the pretentiously named American Academy of Music, together with the Pennsylvania Horticultural Society, clubs such as the Union League, several fashionable churches, and numerous mansions. In the ten blocks between South Street and Cherry Street stood a mixture of houses, clubs, and churches that formed the city's equivalent of New York's Fifth Avenue. Immediately after the Civil War, but before the decision to move the site of the new City Hall to Center Square, the area just to the north of the square became the site for the nation's most ambitious Masonic temple along with two important churches that faced each other across the intersection of Broad and Arch Streets.

In 1870, when the Academy board decided on the new site, Broad Street was still becoming a civic zone. That process would be disrupted by the construction of the City Hall, which quickly transformed Broad Street into a commercial and office district. The Academy, however, was also changing. Instead of its being controlled by the artist members and principally aimed at an annual exhibit of recent paintings as an economic engine for the artists, John Sartain proposed that the Academy add instruction to its purposes by retaining Christian Schussele (1824–1879) as the instructor in painting. An Alsatian-born, École-trained artist under Paul Delaroche, Schussele moved to Philadelphia in 1848, opened a studio, and produced works of art focused on historical topics, many of which were engraved by Sartain. His career was threatened by an increasing tremor in his hands, leading Sartain to find a means to support his friend. This new purpose for the Academy required new teaching rooms and demanded a new building.[23]

Selecting Architects: Philadelphia

Considering that the new building would shape the future of the institution, the Academy's board meeting minutes are surprisingly terse about its architectural competition. A preliminary meeting in February 1871 recommended purchase of the property at Broad and Cherry Streets. John Sartain was asked to "draw up a plan for the arrangement of rooms and galleries adapted to the wants of the institution."[24] A building committee was appointed on June 12, 1871, and a week later issued an "Invitation for Proposals to Erect a Building for the Pennsylvania Academy of the Fine Arts."[25] The program that was the core of the invitation was largely written by Sartain, who relied on his earlier thoughts and poured into it his deep knowledge of the needs of the institution. The board minutes list the architects who were to be invited to compete together with their advocate on the board: Fraser, Furness & Hewitt [Fairman Rogers], James Windrim [Sartain], Thomas Richards [Sartain], Addison Hutton [Caleb Cope], John McArthur [Sartain], Collins & Autenrieth [Sartain], and Henry Sims [Henry Gibson].[26] After the invitation, there was no further mention of the competition entrants until the minutes of the November 13 meeting.[27]

Much can be learned about the board's goals for the Academy by looking at the firms that were invited to compete for the new building, those that were left out, and those that chose not to compete. Given that this would be one of the city's most important new buildings, it is not surprising that most of the principal architectural offices received invitations. Unlike Boston, however, the Philadelphians invited only local architects, though whether this was the result of provincialism or the already independent course being set by the new client group is unclear. In any event it freed Philadelphians to choose without the implied criticism of designs by architects from other regions who might have taken more conventional directions. Several local architects chose not to take part. The most notable refusal was from John McArthur, Jr. (1823–1890), the architect of the new City Hall. Whether because he was aware of the vastness of the task facing him or realistic about his lack of connections to the Academy board, McArthur sent his regrets. The German-trained masters of the utilitarian brick *rundbogenstil* style, Collins & Autenrieth (active 1852–1904), who had no obvious connections to the funding members of the board, also declined. James Windrim (1840–1919), who was then supervising the construction of his design for the Masonic Temple across Broad Street, communicated with the Academy about the competition and was invited to enter but in the end did not to compete.[28] Henry A. Sims (1832–1875), who had recently returned to Philadelphia from Canada, was advocated by Henry Gibson but Gibson had recently commissioned Fraser, Furness & Hewitt for his home on Walnut Street and was perhaps a less than reliable advocate—as would prove to be the case in the final tally of votes.

Of those who entered the competition, Addison Hutton (1834–1916) was already a veteran of Philadelphia design battles. In the same year that Furness had left his home for New York to study with Hunt, Hutton, after training as a carpenter, had entered Samuel Sloan's office.[29] Two years later, Sloan thought enough of Hutton to delegate him to supervise projects in North Carolina. In 1868, Hutton's stylistically conservative, forbidding, monochromatic gray granite design, for the Philadelphia Savings Fund Society offices at Seventh and Walnut was selected over submissions from Windrim, Fraser, Furness & Hewitt, and Stephen Button, enabling him to open his own firm.[30] When the Academy announced its competition, Hutton's white, Pennsylvania marble design for the Arch Street Methodist Church had just been finished across Broad Street. It showed the influence of A. W. N. Pugin's Gothic revival that had revolutionized English ecclesiastical architecture before midcentury, but in its monochromatic treatment and early English style it was more past than present. Hutton's bid for the Academy's design was strengthened by his connections to the regional Quaker community, then reengaging with the civic life of the city after a century of disengagement, and his membership in the Franklin Institute tied him to the regional industrial culture from which many of his clients came.[31] His board advocate Caleb Cope was, for the moment, president of the Academy.

Thomas Webb Richards (1836–1911) was also a veteran of Sloan's office. He opened an architectural office in 1856, sharing space in the 816 Walnut Street studio of his brother, the noted seascape artist William Trost Richards.[32] The crash of 1857 caused him to leave Philadelphia for Baltimore, where he formed a short-lived practice with Lind & Murdock, who were then designing the Peabody Institute. The cast iron structure of the Baltimore landmark reflected Richards's Franklin Institute–based knowledge. A talented renderer, Richards was elected an associate of the Pennsylvania Academy in 1860, where he evidently formed a strong friendship with Sartain.[33] Richards had recently won the competition for the University of Pennsylvania.

Henry A. Sims had trained in Canada as a civil engineer and later worked in an architectural office there. He remained in Ottawa during the Civil War, thereby missing the pivotal experience of his generation. (His brother's term as a prisoner of war perhaps influenced his decision.)[34] When he returned to his native city in the late 1860s, he did not fully comprehend the new forces engulfing its architecture. His brag that he alone had "the only pure knowledge of the Gothic" in Philadelphia denoted his previous training and his own aesthetic interests but missed the new directions of the industrial culture. Sims was active in founding the Philadelphia chapter of the American Institute of Architects and was connected to the Pennsylvania Railroad by his brother, John Clark Sims, who became the secretary of the corporation in 1868.

The other invited firm was that of Fraser, Furness & Hewitt, who were the most politically and culturally connected of the competitors. There was a twist to the Fraser, Furness & Hewitt story. In the spring of 1871, Fraser was in Washington, D.C., looking for government work for his firm when the invitation came. His young partners entered the competition without him. Fraser, enraged, attempted to reopen the competition, to no avail.[35] The Academy chose to stay with the invited firms and their original schedule and refused Fraser's entreaty to be permitted to compete on his own.

The selection process for the new Academy building exemplified the changing identity of Philadelphia. Most of the Trinity Church competition invitees had some degree of advanced professional training and many had links to Harvard College and to old Boston families. Of the Academy competitors, none were graduates of Philadelphia's University of Pennsylvania nor were any descendants of the Philadelphia gentlemen who had shaped the city before the Civil War and claimed ancestry from the early Penn settlers or the revolutionaries of 1776. Hutton and Richards came out of the working class of the city. Both had studied at the Franklin Institute and represented the old line of the builder-trained architect but with hard-won professional expertise in building practices. Furness and Sims, on the other hand, were from elite families and marked the beginning of the academically schooled generation.

As evidenced by their later careers, the Boston competitors represented the most up-to-date architectural fashions, forming the backbone of published projects in the national architectural publications over the next generation. The Philadelphia group represented a considerably broader range of practice and manner. Hutton showed his pre–Civil War stripes as well as his strength in blending new technical information with old design practices in his victory in the competition for the Ridgway Library on South Broad Street. Its three classical porticoes across the façade were the last gasp of Philadelphia's identity as "the Athens of America" but the cool gray granite walls masked an iron and glass framed skylighted interior and its innovative iron book stacks suggested that Hutton knew of Labrouste's French libraries as well as evolving library theory that separated storage and circulation. Richards's most important project, the brilliantly hued and multipurposed College Hall that housed the arts, the sciences, and the administration of the University of Pennsylvania's new campus, was already under construction. Henry Sims had recently been awarded the commission for the most ambitious of the post–Civil War downtown churches, the Second Presbyterian Church (now First Presbyterian Church) on Walnut Street just west of Rittenhouse Square. Its rich synthesis of color and Gothic detail would be a feature of his Academy design.

Building Committees: Boston and Philadelphia

The building committee for Trinity Church was led by Robert Treat Paine, a Harvard classmate of Phillips Brooks. Paine was New England royalty, connected to governors and presidents of Harvard, and namesake of a signer of the Declaration of Independence. Harvard graduates constituted the majority of the nine-member committee, which included Martin Brimmer (Harvard, 1849), the nephew of the architect of the 1828 church building and a legislator and cofounder of Boston's Museum of Fine Arts; Charles Codman, an attorney and classmate of Brimmer; as well as the previously mentioned Charles Parker (1816–1908), a banker and attorney and the senior member of the committee by age.[36]

Most of the members of the Academy's building committee were trained in civil and mechanical engineering and other scientific professions. London-born John Sartain (1808–1897) was a longtime board member and on the Academy's school committee.[37] A second-tier artist who made a business engraving copies of portraits, he was a member of the Franklin Institute and was deeply imbued with the values of the city's industrial culture, which he applied in his business. James Claghorn (1817–1884), financier and, after 1872, president of the Academy, was a holdover from the pre–Civil War financial elites who represented the old order of collectors and supporters of the arts. Henry Gibson (1830–1891), a distiller and real estate developer, but also an art collector, represented flashy new money, with a mansion on Walnut Street under construction. The most famous member of the building committee, added in 1872 to replace Claghorn, was Matthew Baird (1817–1877) who had worked in the Baldwin Locomotive Works since its inception and at the time was the sole proprietor of the city's greatest factory, which stood just to the north of the new Academy site. Henry G. Morris (1839–1915), a civil engineer and son of an industrialist and partner in one of the city's great ironworks, Morris, Tasker & Co., likely was chosen for his knowledge of the new materials of the industrial age.[38] The chair of the committee was Fairman Rogers (1833–1900), who trained at the University of Pennsylvania as a civil engineer and had applied his engineering knowledge to the Academy of Music's building when the institution was choosing its architects. He was a member of the Unitarian church, whose minister was Frank's father, and he was part of Furness's extended family—Frank's brother Horace had married Rogers's sister.

Furness's connection to Rogers was one of the inherent conflicts in the competition, but he was not alone. Richards, for example, had a special connection with the head of the school of the Academy, Sartain. Hutton had designed houses for Henry Morris in Philadelphia (while in the Sloan firm) and Newport, Rhode Island, in the previous decade, but as he reported in his daybook he was invited to enter the competition by Academy president Caleb Cope, a fellow Quaker who had hired Hutton for his new bank building.[39] Henry Gibson, who recommended Sims, was beginning a lengthy relationship with George Hewitt, starting with renovations to his own house on Walnut Street just before the Academy project and continuing into the 1880s with his Scottish castle, Maybrooke, in Lower Merion.[40]

Fairman Rogers and the New Philadelphia Client

With Harrison's resignation and the appointment of Rogers to the Academy building committee, the competition for the new building was aligned with the forces that would shape Philadelphia's architectural future. Rogers's father had made his fortune in hardware, while his grandfather, Gideon Fairman, was a well-known inventor whose engraving machines were used to produce bank-notes as well as Sartain's engravings. Their resources aimed young Fairman Rogers at the modern profession of engineering. His bachelor's degree was followed by a master's degree in civil engineering, the first in that subject to be granted by the University of Pennsylvania. Upon graduation, he was appointed as the university's instructor in civil engineering and soon began to work on the creation of what is now the School of Engineering and Applied Sciences, which would eventually include the architecture school that employed Thomas Richards as instructor.

Rogers's interests were encyclopedic, spanning from the practical design of highways and bridges to the problem of capturing and stopping movement with a camera to broad aesthetic questions. During the Civil War, the federal government gave Rogers the task of figuring out how a compass could be made to ac-curately point to magnetic north when embedded in an iron-hulled ship. His work on this question enabled the U.S.S. *Monitor* and later the ironclad ships of the U.S. Navy's Mississippi River Squadron to be navigated. As the war contin-ued, he taught engineering courses at the university during the school year but used the university's summer vacation time to design bridges for the Union mil-itary.[41] As early as the 1860s he had devised a means to photographically record animals in motion, anticipating and improving on the work of Eadweard Muy-bridge. Afterward, when Muybridge's west coast funding evaporated, Rogers stepped in to help organize support for the famous animal locomotion series, many of which were shot at the University of Pennsylvania, where Rogers also was a trustee. His interest in the arts brought him to the Academy board and the chairmanship of the building committee.

After supervising the building of the new Academy of Fine Arts, Rogers took on the question of the new types of instruction that the new building might support. He collaborated with Thomas Eakins in creating the Academy's new curriculum, one that turned from old methods of cast drawing to using the live model.[42] Their shared focus on the way that reality could be verified and recorded joined the two men in a peculiarly Philadelphia collaboration.[43] The 1878 publication of the results of Muybridge's animal locomotion photographs led to extensive communications between Rogers and Eakins and in turn re-sulted in the commissioned work *A May Morning in the Park: The Fairman Rogers Four-in-Hand*. In it Eakins captured not only the gait of walking horses, based on Muybridge's animal locomotion photographs, but also the relative rotational speed of the larger and smaller wheels, the latter blurred in comparison to the former, the glint of sunlight at the angle of the specific morning and even criti-cal gestures in coachmanship that Rogers knew from his study of the art.[44] In short, Rogers was a scientist with a strong interest in the arts. One suspects that, even if Furness had not been related by his brother's marriage, Furness's design, with its strong links to the real world, would have appealed to Rogers and his peers on the board more than fictive worlds from the past.

Theory into Practice: Industrial Forms and Possibilities

The crossover between the rising Philadelphia industrial culture and Furness's work was quickly apparent. Even before Sellers's lecture on Philadelphia's ma-chine design theory in 1874, Furness & Hewitt had incorporated aspects of lo-gistically based factory planning and hints of the new machine aesthetic into their competition entry for the Pennsylvania Academy of the Fine Arts. While the members of the building committee were certainly predisposed by their own training and backgrounds to new design strategies, still the young archi-tects and their Academy clients made a remarkable leap, the distance of which can be traced in the sequence of drawings from their entry for the competition to the final building. Of the Furness & Hewitt competition drawings, the best evidence is a perspective based on the firm's initial design that was published in *Lippincott's Magazine*.[45] Fortunately Henry Sims prepared a record of his entry in the form of a printed booklet illustrated with black and white photographs of the six required drawings.[46] Sims's scheme was something of a cathedral crossed with Pisa's domed baptistery (Figure 30). The Italian Gothic references were certainly intended to recall Peter B. Wight's design for New York's Na-tional Academy of Design of the previous decade (1863–1865), which incorpo-rated the Gothic arcade, decorative diaper work, and cornice of the Doge's Pal-ace in Venice that English critic John Ruskin so admired. For the Academy, Sims proposed a Gothic arcade containing windows along the lower level of the Cherry Street wall, to light the ground-level teaching studios, while the second-story galleries were directly supported on the lower studio walls. As per the program, skylights on the roof illuminated the upper galleries but, even then,

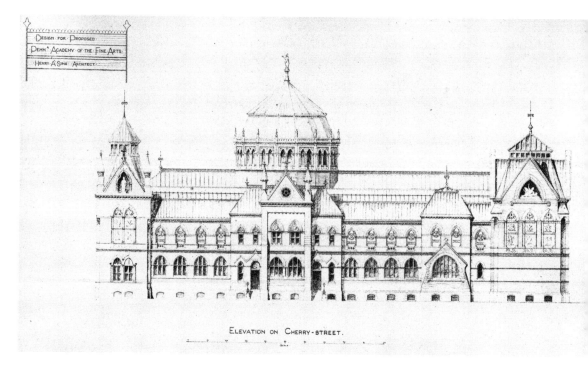

ELEVATION ON CHERRY-STREET.

Figure 30 Henry Sims, Photographic reproduction of the Cherry Street Elevation, Pennsylvania Academy of the Fine Arts Competition, 1871. Courtesy of the Pennsylvania Academy of the Fine Arts.

Sims needed additional windows in the side walls to light the transeptlike cross wings of the gallery.

The most innovative aspect of Sims's design was his plan to cast in terra cotta the vast array of sculptural ornaments that he proposed to enliven the façade. He estimated that casting from clay models instead of carving from stone would significantly lower the cost but acknowledged that "objection [is] always raised against cast ornaments for exteriors on artistic grounds."[47] Sims countered that this criticism need not "apply in all respects to terra cotta, as all the finer parts of the latter are moulded by hand." He was so sure that the various regional clays would produce a rich variety of colors that he did not produce the required second scheme finished in marble "because it would be incompatible with the style of his present design, especially if [it] were only carried along Cherry street for a short distance."[48] In the end, the judges of the competition must have seen the fundamental limitations of Sims's scheme: the masonry underpinning for the great dome forced all of the other elements out of alignment, limiting rather than freeing the plan. The gallery supported by the lower studio wall meant that the light into the studios would be unpleasantly glaring, and the plan did not manage the separation of the various traffic flows: the public, the students, and the giant works of art and the animal subjects that needed to be moved into the building. Still, for someone looking for the authority of history and finding security in ornament, Sims's project captured the eye and the vote of at least one board member, presumably his initial advocate, Gibson. Sims's scheme placed third.

While none of Hutton's competition drawings survive, his contemporary work at the Ridgway Library and various regional banks, especially the Philadelphia Savings Fund Society building at Seventh and Walnut Streets, suggests the likelihood of a monochromatic, classically proportioned design. A tiny sketch in his daybook for October 6, 1871, depicts his basic plan, which may have been rooted in Washington's Corcoran Gallery by James Renwick a decade earlier (Figure 31). The principal gallery was placed the full width of the Broad Street front, pushing the stairwell back toward the center of the building. The stair was certainly skylighted and was framed by additional skylighted galleries on the sides and rear that presumably denote in their general configuration the lecture rooms and studios below.[49] The date in Hutton's daybook, less than a month before the competition entries were due, suggests that he was delayed in getting to the competition and had yet to begin a serious study of the complicated issues of the building. In any event his scheme attracted no votes and placed out of the money in the competition.

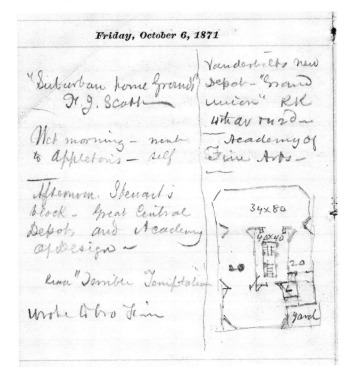

Figure 31 Addison Hutton, sketch floor plan, Pennsylvania Academy of the Fine Arts Competition, 1871. Hutton Daybook, October 6, 1871. Courtesy of the Haverford College Library.

We know nothing about the scheme offered by Thomas Richards other than that it was thought good enough to tie with the Furness & Hewitt project for the first prize. It is reasonable to assume that he offered a polychromed Victorian Gothic scheme in line with his winning entry for the University of Pennsylvania's campus. Because of his close association with Sartain, he probably would have followed quite literally the director's spatial assessment of the pedagogical needs of the school. The battle within the board may well have been as fierce as that between the competitors, raging over the two weeks from the submission of the drawings until the board meeting on November 13. A letter from Sartain to his protégé Richards, prior to the actual vote, offers a hint of the discussion: "[It] remains to be seen ... whether you or Furness erect the building. I am bent on having you if I can do it (and conscientiously too). But alas! I give not a cent of money, while Fairman Rogers no doubt gives thousands—more or less, perhaps, according to circumstances."[50] When the first round of votes were counted, Richards and Furness & Hewitt were tied, presumably backed by two votes each, with Sims third, presumably with Gibson's vote, and no votes for Hutton's scheme. The building committee reported to the board:

> Your committee are unable to recommend to this Board the adoption of any one of the plans as a model to build from. Of the two that are certainly the best, neither, judged as a whole, interior and exterior combined, should be preferred, because each possesses peculiarities to itself, not found in the other. All are agreed, however, that the third best plan is that of Mr. Sims, and that it is therefore entitled to the premium thereto belonging.
>
> Having now obtained all that can be expected from a competition, and with the result stated, we deem the best way of further procedure would be to select an architect from among the competitors, and secure his services at such a rate of compensation as the two contracting parties may agree on.

With Sims's and Hutton's schemes dropped from the tally, Furness & Hewitt won the next vote, likely with the addition of their client Gibson's vote. By the slimmest of margins, the young firm had won its most important commission. Negotiations began with the winners, who signed a contract on November 13, 1871.[51] Rogers's summary of the negotiation with the architects was recorded in the minutes:

> In the endeavor to obtain by competition a suitable plan for a building intended for Academic uses, as was described in the minutes of the date

above referred to, the result was a failure, all the plans having been rejected; but it was agreed to appoint Messrs. Furness & Hewitt architects, and the Board of Directors confirmed this action of the Committee. The Committee then requested the Secretary, John Sartain, who was chairman of the committee of our plans, to draw up plans to submit to the Committee embodying his ideas of what he deemed necessary and appropriate arrangement for the uses of the Academy in its schools on the lower floor and the exhibition galleries in the upper. This was done, and the drawings submitted at a meeting of the Committee held at the residence of Mssr. Henry C. Gibson Jan. . . . 1872. After a critical study of the arrangements, their reasons and purposes, the designs for both floors was adopted, some trifling amendments having been previously agreed on. These were to make the risers of the steps in the grand stairway six inches instead of seven as proposed, also to open a third flight of steps (after passing the landing) directly westward into the sculpture gallery, instead of having only the two flights returning and ascending eastward to reach the floor level of the exhibition rooms. Later in the evening the architects arrived by previous invitation, and the adopted plans were handed over to them with directions to design their architecture in conformity therewith. This has been done, substantially, and the exterior design in one of the competing plans of Furness & Hewitt was also realized, substantially, in the building as it stands.[52]

The board's ideas significantly improved the entrance sequence, both in projecting the main stair forward, thereby energizing the hall, like a pressure vessel pushed by a piston, while the added run of stairs breaking through the back wall of the stair brought the light of the skylighted galleries to the entrance.

The Victorian Bias Toward Traditional Forms

Despite the dramatic changes that were flooding across western civilization, in both Europe and the Americas, tradition shaped aesthetic criticism and practice. The past remained the basis for authority such that biblical and classical standards remained guidelines for the future. These biases were especially hostile to innovation in architecture, and even more so for civic buildings that carried high cultural meaning. When the English critic John Ruskin was asked about the use of iron in the Crystal Palace, he rejected out of hand the architectural use of the new technologies and materials of the industrial age because unlike the culture-laden meanings of masonry, the new industrial materials were mute. Favoring preexisting social orders, craft methods, and old meanings over new materials and the possibility of new meanings, Ruskin reasoned that iron and glass would never be of much use to architects because such a use would undo the common biblical metaphors:

> I cannot now enter into any statement of the possible uses of iron or glass, but I can give you one reason why it is not likely that they will ever become important elements in architectural effect. Assuming then that the Bible is neither superannuated now, nor ever likely to be so . . . it will follow that the illustrations which the Bible employs are likely to be clear and intelligible illustrations to the end of time.
>
> Now I find that iron architecture is indeed spoken of in the Bible. But I do not find that iron building is ever alluded to as likely to become familiar to the minds of men; but on the contrary, that an architecture of carved stone is continuously employed as a source of the most important illustrations.[53]

Ruskin was not alone in interpreting new schemes and new materials through the lens of historical and cultural values. When the American engineer John Ericsson offered his revolutionary design for the U.S.S. *Monitor* to the U.S. Navy, Commander Charles Henry Davis, a graduate of Boston Latin School and in 1825 of Harvard College, was selected for the official review commission because of his theoretical training. Davis signed off on the design despite his misgivings, stating, "Mr. Ericsson, you can take that little thing [the model of the *Monitor*] home and worship it and it will be no sin, for it is not made in the likeness of anything under the heavens above or the earth beneath, or the waters under the earth."[54] In an age when precedent was valued over innovation, even so educated a professional as Commander Davis had no means to begin a review when a design departed from biologically and historically based schemes.

Before the Civil War, Horatio Greenough had praised the American functionally driven evolution of the clipper ship toward ever greater speed but he still presumed wings of canvas and refinements to age-old technology. Ericsson's U.S.S. *Monitor* marked the type of total reinvention that was possible when an engineer's knowledge reconceived a warship as a cannon platform, powered by steam, with its hull almost entirely below the waterline. In the next generation, the possibilities implicit in the new age would unleash a host of innovations leading to our own time, but the past reigned until the telephone, electric light,

X-rays, and radio transmission became common experiences and the general public made everyday use of automobiles, airplanes, and radio. By the 1870s, however, Philadelphia's elite board members were unique in that they were attuned to new types of industrial design that reduced and then eliminated references to classical ornament in machine design and in the great locomotives that were the city's best-known product. Furness benefited from this new clientele.

Over the next few years, Philadelphia's engineers and industrialists who funded projects asked that their workaday world be given its own aesthetic due. Fortunately, there is visual as well as written evidence of the alternate cultural frame of Philadelphia in projects by Furness's rivals James Windrim and Henry Sims. Windrim's exposed steel frame for the interior of the new Academy of Natural Sciences has already been mentioned in Chapter 2. Sims, who had lost the competition for the Academy by being too literally Gothic, quickly adapted Gothic design to the new materials of the industrial age. In 1873, he used exposed steel girders and struts, riveted together and expressive of their own materiality, in lieu of flying buttresses for the Holy Trinity Episcopal Chapel in the heart of Philadelphia's Rittenhouse neighborhood. The following year, he embraced the new strategies even more directly when he was given the commission to design the architectural aspects for the new Girard Avenue Bridge that was to bring visitors across the Schuylkill River to the Centennial Exhibition grounds. The bridge was engineered and fabricated beginning in 1874 by Clarke, Reeves & Co. and its parent company, the Phoenix Iron Company of nearby Phoenixville, the same group that had provided the steel and structural design for Furness & Hewitt's Pennsylvania Academy of the Fine Arts. The engineers' instructions to the Sims firm read like a manifesto on the new materials of the industrial age: "1st. That there should be no sham ornamentation, no concealment of parts and no effort to make one thing look like another. The ornament is merely an emphasizing or accentuating [*sic*] the prominent lines of construction. 2d. Each kind of material is allowed to suggest for itself its appropriate treatment so as to show what it is. For example *iron is made to look like iron and not like stone or wood*" (my emphasis).[55]

In the previous decade, the largest bridge across the Schuylkill at Chestnut Street had been designed by Strickland Kneass, who described it thus: "In general design, this bridge is of Ornate Gothic."[56] Fifteen years later in the industrial age, historic details were rejected and with no sense of irony; in Philadelphia, iron was subjected to the values that John Ruskin reserved for handcrafted material. In industrial Philadelphia iron was to have its own expression and not to be hidden behind the usual classical fripperies of egg and dart moldings or

Gothic arches and other extraneous features. Unfortunately, Sims's death in 1875, in the middle of the bridge's construction, prevented him from further exploring the new territory that he and Furness were discovering.[57]

The celebration of iron in Philadelphia architecture was widespread. In the late 1870s, Charles Marquedant Burns, a protégé of Sims, was commissioned to design Bryn Mawr's Episcopal Church of the Redeemer. It was funded by Charles Wheeler, a partner of Henry Morris in the Morris, Tasker & Co.'s Pascal Iron Works. As a condition of his donation, Wheeler required that the columns of the church interior be "of iron or steel."[58] Despite Wheeler's wishes, the nave arcade of the church was built of conventional stone. When Wheeler died in 1885, the church vestry commissioned a rood screen to Wheeler's memory and restated Wheeler's requirement that iron be celebrated. The *American Architect and Building News* illustrated the Burns rood screen accompanied by a lengthy text that noted: "This screen erected to the memory of Charles Wheeler of Philadelphia was constructed in the shop of Louis Koenig in the short space of three months. Above the arches run two heavy horizontal beams of wrought iron on which are to be seen the *bolts and rivets of the construction as forming a portion of the ornamentation*" (my emphasis).[59] From these accounts, as well as the pre–Civil War structures in which the new materials and the new engineering possibilities were incorporated into an array of buildings from banks to the Academy of Music, there can be no doubt that in Philadelphia, the engineers and industrialists were active participants in shaping the aesthetic of the city and bringing their materials and their values into the design discussion. Was such a condition included in the fund-raising for the Academy? Was the giant exposed truss suggested by one of the many iron makers or engineers who funded the building? Unfortunately, we have no information on this point—but it is clear that industrial Philadelphia provided the context for this design feature.

Building the Academy

Because Richards and Furness & Hewitt shared the top two prizes, the winning competitors were each given a premium of $400, with an additional fee of $5,600 (roughly 2.5 percent of the estimated construction budget) going to Furness & Hewitt. This fee was to pay for the working drawings and construction supervision over approximately three years, in the expectation that the building would be completed early in 1875, well in advance of the coming Centennial celebration. The new building was financed by subscription. Many of the city's leading industrialists and businessmen committed to regular payments that equaled the estimated cost of the project. Among the donors was Rogers, who agreed to pay $2,500, 1 percent of the anticipated cost of the project. William Sellers made a similar commitment, while board member and industrialist Henry Morris committed to $5,000. Locomotive builder Matthew Baird, who was added to the building committee in 1872 and lived a few blocks to the north of the proposed site, offered a similar sum. Leaders of the Pennsylvania Railroad, including Henry Houston, Thomas Scott, and J. Edgar Thomson (respectively, the general manager for freight, the president, and the future president), all gave significant gifts.[60] Thanks to the booming economy of the early 1870s the entire subscription was filled within a few weeks.[61]

The difference between the donors of the original 1807 building, largely drawn from the legal profession, and the contemporary supporters was not lost on banker and board member Caleb Cope, who in his 1872 address at the laying of the cornerstone pointed out the new economy that supported the building: "With few exceptions great fortunes are not made by those who practice the law at least in this city, but they are made by those who are called *business* men especially by that class who are directly or indirectly engaged in the conversion of the raw material into useful and consequently merchantable forms. It is chiefly the manufacturing interest (more particularly that connected with the manipulation of iron which has aggrandized so large a portion of our industrial people, and enabled them to become the patrons of art) upon which we must rely for a liberal support of our Institution in all its requirements."[62]

While funds were being solicited, Furness & Hewitt spent the first several months developing the plans and details. By late summer the basement was excavated and the foundations and shallow brick vaults supporting the first floor were built and the walls would have been rising to street level. At the time of the cornerstone laying ceremony on December 7, 1872, Rogers ended his talk on the future building with an important strategy: "Partly for commercial reasons, but mainly because it is desirable, in a building the construction of which must occupy a considerable period, to have the longest time for the study of those problems which present themselves, the system of working by separate contracts has been adopted, and we are therefore yet free to decide upon such plans for the roof, the sky lights, and the artificial lighting of the galleries as a careful consideration of these comparatively unsolved difficulties in the construction of art galleries may point out."[63]

Again an engineering-based perspective appears in Rogers's note. In traditional construction there were few issues that would have required additional study, but in Philadelphia, in the heart of the quickly evolving industrial culture, new materials and new possibilities were expected and would be incorporated as they were discovered and tested. Two weeks before the cornerstone ceremony, the Academy commissioned Steward & Stevens to provide the iron beams that would carry the shallow brick vaulting of the first story, providing evidence that the materials of the industrial age would receive their due in the new design.[64]

The sequence of board discussions at the time of Rogers's statement offers some hints about the specific issues for which contracts had yet to be drafted and signed. The most important question remained the means of carrying the gallery wall above the continuous band of glass roofing over the studios. The size of the skylighting was determined in February 1873 by selection of a standard "hammered" plate glass panel, ten feet in length, a size that was available from local suppliers.[65] This determined the offset of the gallery from the street wall of the studios along Cherry Street. A month later it was reported that steel trusses would be ordered from the Phoenix Iron Works to carry the north gallery wall. Did this idea come from bridge designers Clark and Reeves, the staff engineers for the steel supplier, who had offices around the corner from Furness & Hewitt's office? An alternate collaborator for the idea would be civil engineer Rogers, who surely saw the possibilities of spanning the brick walls between the studios as a bridge would span from one masonry pier to another.[66] In any event, the drawing entitled "Section Through Antique Galleries" (Figure 32) showed the paired trusses carrying the gallery wall and seated on the studio wall separating the gallery for drawing from the antique plaster casts (the "Antique Galleries"). The same solution of steel trusses spanning from pier to pier would be adopted to carry the roof trusses over the octagonal crossing of the long gallery in the center of the second floor.

Early in 1872, while the foundations were being excavated, Furness made a trip to Washington, D.C., to study the recently completed Corcoran Gallery. Construction of the Corcoran had started in 1859 from the designs of James Renwick, Jr. (1818–1895), and it was under roof in 1861 when it was commandeered as federal offices during the war. It was only returned to its owner and finished in 1871, making Furness one of the first to visit the completed gallery. There, he received a set of photographs of that building for the Academy board and promised to exchange a set of photographs of the new Academy for the Corcoran's files.[67] The gallery cannot have provided much in the way of inspiration, being more like a Victorian McMansion, featuring modest skylighting and much decorative plaster and faux marble but with none of the modern technologies that would shape the Academy.

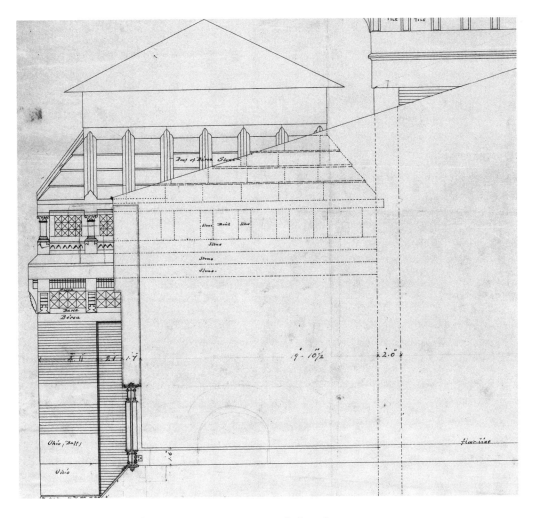

Figure 32 Furness & Hewitt, "Section Through Antique Galleries," detail, c. 1873. Courtesy of the Pennsylvania Academy of the Fine Arts.

From the outset of the project, it was agreed that the Academy would have a superintendent of construction. Jacob Myers (1842–c. 1915) was hired at $1,500 per year but the architects were to be in charge of the specifications and prices and thus, it was hoped, would be able to obtain the lowest possible price while maintaining the standards of their design. Myers was a conventional builder, trained in the office of builder-architect John Crump, for whom he served as foreman on some of the major projects in the city.[68] After the successful completion of the Academy, he opened his own contracting office and built many of the city's principal buildings over the next thirty years. Myers was an expert at calculating costs but did not bring the level of engineering knowledge or knowledge of the vertical assemblage of industries from stone quarries to construction that Norcross Brothers, the builders of Trinity Church, brought to the Boston church.[69] Where James O'Gorman points out that builder Orlando Norcross was nearly Richardson's equal as a partner in the production of the buildings of the Bostonian's career from Trinity Church to the Allegheny County Courthouse, Furness had no such colleague.

Beginning in the spring and summer of 1873 Furness & Hewitt managed the bidding for the various materials and systems. In doing so, the firm negotiated significantly reduced prices, although it is unclear whether the lowered costs were entirely due to its review and management or were a consequence of the suddenly contracting economy. In March 1873, the selected stone supplier for the decorative stonework, William Struthers (who had resigned from the board in an effort to avoid the appearance of a conflict of interest), quoted $60,000 for the interior sandstone of the monumental stair, the granite columns, the marble pedestals and newels of the stairwell, the sandstone door frame of the entrance, and various window dressings, together with the arches and piers of the façade. By the summer, even before the September panic precipitated by the fall of Jay Cooke's banking house, consultation with the architects resulted in Struthers reducing his bid by nearly a third, to $42,955.[70] The additional hours spent negotiating contracts were time consuming and, in 1874, with the job dragging because of unforeseen delays caused by the market crash of the previous autumn, the architects wrote to Rogers requesting additional payments to cover their mounting hours. They suggested an annual fee of $3,000, half of their original estimate for the entire job. In their communications with Rogers, they made it clear that the original agreement remained in effect and that they would be satisfied with any additional payment. In the context of the economic downturn, there was no budget for additional payment but the Academy committee offered $1,500, which was accepted.[71]

By May 1873 four spans of trusses for the Cherry Street wall had been ordered from the Phoenix Iron Works.[72] Despite a strike over wages by the city's masons the project moved rapidly forward through the summer of 1873. The basement was excavated and brick vaults were constructed, the brownstone walls of the ground level and the brick walls rose out of the ground, and the final decorative stonework specifications were written. In December the walls "were now nearly covered in to protect them from the weather during the approaching winter."[73] The autumn brought the national recession, which quickly turned into the depression that forced Furness to let Louis Sullivan go. By the following summer, the outlook was bleak. The direness of the situation became clear in April 1874 when the Academy board offered to pay the masons, Atkinson &

Myhlertz, with ground rents on their properties facing Penn Square. The builders' response to Sartain's inquiry was swift: "Dear Sir! Yours of yesterday just received. We are very sorry we cannot oblige you, but what we want is cash. Stone is cash, Wages is cash. . . . We took the Contract low, our margin is very small, but we looked upon it as a Cash job."[74]

As the depression deepened, the Academy board attempted to sell the institution's Penn Square properties while badgering subscribers to complete their donations. In April 1874 the roofing contract was discussed and it was determined to roof the building in slate rather than tin but by June with subscriptions lagging, Rogers reported to the board that while the exterior and interior walls were nearly finished, the building was not yet under roof because another contract, for the iron work and roof trusses to be provided by the Phoenix Iron and Steel Company, had yet to be signed.[75] Nonetheless, Rogers expected that construction could be completed by the summer of 1875.[76] The plumbing and heating systems were under contract in late spring of 1875; the sale of one of the Penn Square properties and the sale of the mortgage on the former building provided funds to finish the new building.[77] In February 1876, the building committee confirmed that the building would be sufficiently finished to open the Academy's annual exhibit in the new building in late April. In the same meeting it was reported that Furness had been authorized to speak to "Mr. Kemp, the Sculptor, and ascertain . . . at what Price he would carve the six slabs of stone in the Academy front to represent as many groups in the Delaroche's Hemicycle."[78] In two months, the carvings were finished and installed and the building was open for the annual exhibit. A few details including the carving of the name of the institution on the arch above the main doorway did not appear in the first photographs of the finished building, indicating that they must have been undertaken at a later date.

A Factory for Art

When the new Academy building opened in April 1876, it was a brilliant summa of the possibilities of its day in Centennial-era Philadelphia, colored by the rich array of materials that railroads brought to any building site in America (Plate 1). At first glance, the front façade was like many other public post–Civil War buildings influenced by the French Second Empire manner with a raised central pavilion and lower flanking wings. It differed, however, in the clash between the Ruskinian Gothic's pointed arched openings and the Neo-Grec classical frieze and in the violent contrasts of color of the materials (Figure 33). In both its stylistic complication and its color, it stood out against both the uniform red brick buildings of the industrial city and the monochrome whites and greys of the institutional city such as Hutton's recently completed Arch Street Methodist Church, Windrim's Masonic Temple, and McArthur's City Hall.[79]

A more careful look at the design revealed radically different sources and themes that hinted at Furness's direction in the next generation. The core of the scheme was a new type of logistical planning of the sort that organized contemporary Philadelphia factories. In their analysis of the Academy project, the architects anticipated three main movement streams into the building: the art-loving public; the students, faculty, and staff; and finally the paintings and sculptures that were to be raised to the galleries and the animals that were the subjects of the studio classes and were raised to the studio level. The public entered at the center of the principal façade facing Broad Street and followed a clearly directed route through a short vestibule and into the stair hall where the oversized great stair visually closes off all other directions and forces the visitor up to the main galleries. The studios (Figure 34) dominate the north façade; as at the far northwest corner of the building, the students received their own entrance from Cherry Street with a pair of doors secured by iron gates not unlike the main entrance, with a special bit of ornamental carving above. This division of entrances had the advantage of separating the bohemian art students from the paying public. On the rear alley, a giant industrial door, on the central axis of the building, opened into an immense cargo elevator that still lifts sculptures and paintings directly to the gallery level and is also used to raise animal models to the studio level. The logistical practices of the up-to-date industrial plant that differentiated the entrance for management from that of the workforce and, in turn, from the freight portals through which raw materials arrived had been applied to the planning of the Pennsylvania Academy of the Fine Arts and a couple of years later would also guide the principal Centennial buildings.

The ventilation system of the Academy again found Furness looking to contemporary sources. The architects proposed to utilize the heat buildup of the glazed attic to create the temperature differential necessary for a strong airflow that would pull cool air from ground level up and through the entire building. In the winter, a furnace simultaneously

Figure 33 Pennsylvania Academy of the Fine Arts, 1876. Photograph by Frederick Gutekunst. Courtesy of the Pennsylvania Academy of the Fine Arts.

Figure 34 View of the Pennsylvania Academy of the Fine Arts from Cherry Street. A visible steel truss runs along the side of the building among the decorative brickwork motifs. Photograph by Lewis Tanner, 2011.

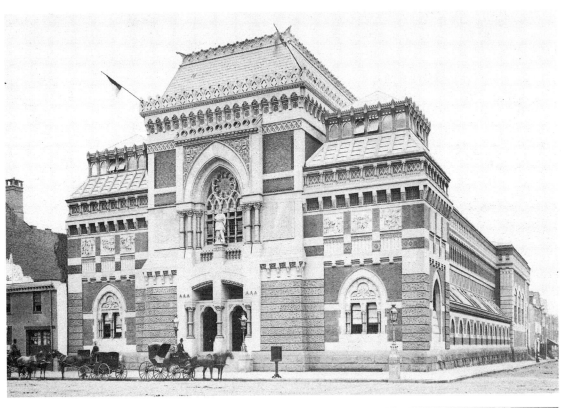

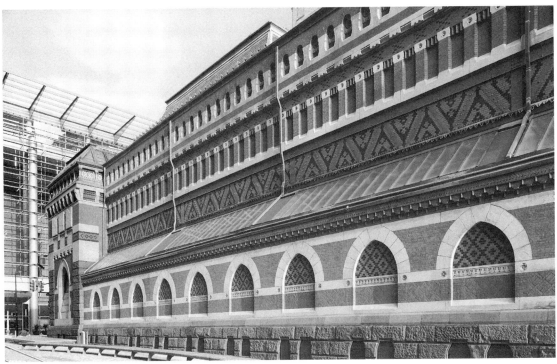

generated steam that radiated through a network of pipes while the by-product of heated air rose through ducts in walls. Excess heat was drawn off through the decorative vents in the cast iron frame of the skylights that exhausted through the roof monitor louvers. Mechanical arms attached to the louvers enabled them to be operated by a standard factory system of chains and pulleys, accessible in tiny chases at the gallery level. At night when solar heat gain did not provide the energy for the ventilation system, additional heat was provided by the gas chandeliers that lighted the building. Similar louvers were a prominent feature of the ventilators that crowned the galleries on either side of the central pavilion.[80] By starting from the problems and devising a plan that solved them, Furness established a method that must have been absorbed by Sullivan during his time in the office.

The connections between Furness's new method and the machine culture of Philadelphia are less obvious on the main façade, which was conceived as a billboard about art. Victorians demanded legibility that visually expressed the function of their buildings, as when architects used Gothic sources for churches and castellated schemes for prisons. In the case of Henri Labrouste's Bibliothèque Ste. Genevieve in Paris, this even extended to the outline of bookshelves chiseled into the limestone of the façade and inscribed with author's names. To make the point that the Academy was about all of the arts, the façade was a fusion of the principal historical styles, Gothic and classical, together with sculpted panels that made the purpose clear.[81] The Neo-Grec styling that Furness had learned from Hunt is evident in the giant grooved blocks in the upper levels of the façade, which are more or less in the position of the triglyphs of the frieze of the Doric order. However, instead of the usual band of metopes alternating with triglyphs, here the metopes were stacked above the triglyphs in a jazzy syncopation that disrupted the usual classical order, even as their vertical pairing produced a larger-scale compositional feature that was uniquely Furness's own.

In an obvious nod to the École des Beaux Arts, the figurative panels in the metopes were adapted from Paul DeLaroche's mid-nineteenth-century Awards Hall murals at the École. Entitled the "Hemicycle of the Beaux Arts," they depicted two conversational groups, the Venetian colorists, led by Titian and Veronese, and the Roman school, headed by Michelangelo and Raphael, that flanked the central figures. On the Academy, the figures were rather stiffly adapted with the Venetian school of colorists on the left and the more figural Roman school on the right, centered on Michelangelo, who is recognizable as an adaptation from Raphael's Vatican Stanze fresco. At the École, the center of the composition depicted Ictinus, architect of the Parthenon, and Apelles, the best-known classical painter, flanking the central figure of Phidias, the sculptor of the great Parthenon figures. The Furness & Hewitt 1872 perspective of the firm's design published in *Lippincott's Magazine* had depicted the large panels flanking the main portal embellished with busts and the inscribed names of Apelles and Phidias. As noted earlier, the budgetary crisis eliminated these last carvings but the core idea—that the arts go back to Greece, an idea that Furness carried forward from his training in Hunt's atelier—was affirmed when an antique, headless figure of Demeter, from the Academy's collection, was placed on the plinth above the main door.[82]

Countering those elements from the Neo-Grec and Parisian design sources are the pointed arches and the traceried window lighting the "Washington Gallery" that were derived from the Ruskinian Gothic revival. Most remarkable were the enameled tiles, backed by gold leaf to reflect light out through the colored surface, at the top of the building. This is one of the instances in which Furness, perhaps recalling Emerson's command, drew on natural sources. He later described the iridescence that resulted from the same technique of gold foil backing an enameled panel above the entrance of the Centennial Bank as "a good imitation of the green on a beetle's wing."[83]

Into this mix of conventional historically derived iconography and iconology, the architects made multiple references, some obvious, some subtle, to machines and industry. On the Broad Street front, the two side wings were originally capped with massive iron ventilators with operable glass panels that could be opened to move heated air out of the building. Topped by galvanized iron roof crestings, these elements were central to the original design composition of three adjacent masses, each with its own peaked roof. Instead of the standard Second Empire inflection toward the center, the effect with the raised monitors was rather like the clusters of furnaces that would have been familiar to anyone looking at the city's industrial buildings.

The industrial culture appears in a second and less obvious way. Every element of the walls and roofs above the obviously and heroically handcrafted foundation stones was produced by industrial process. The bricks were machine produced; the yellow sandstone bands and the decorative ornamental panels were uniformly smoothly sawn to a flat, essentially machined finish and decorated by steam-powered sandblasting in William Struthers's stone yard; the sawn roof slates and cast glass slates of the roof were also industrial products (Plate 2). Even the ornamental bits—the Ruskinian florets along the side elevation, the abstracted floral ornaments above the windows—were clearly the product of the drill and not the chisel and were probably crafted by Franklin Institute–trained workmen in the Struthers stone yard.[84] The pink marble columns flanking the entrance, repeated in miniature in the frieze below the sloping roofs, are machine turned and polished to a high finish that brings out the color. Their lack of entasis and detail made them look like pistons, the energizing agent of the engines of the industrializing city. These columns reappear in the stair hall and again in the brackets of the central gallery, tying the exterior entrance zone to the processional sequence for the public. From the short brackets below the frieze to the grooves of the triglyphs, and on to the pierced openwork at the very top, each element was machine sawn, planed, and drilled, with only Alexander Kemp's metope figures requiring any degree of handwork.

That Furness intended this industrial interpretation is evident in the splendid bronze lamps that frame the entrance and originally were duplicated in a second pair located on the sidewalk (Plate 3).[85] A sketch in ink in Furness's notebook attests to his authorship of this feature. Cast and signed at the base in an elegant script with the name of the manufacturer, the Robert D. Wood Company, they are accented at eye level by bronze knobs not unlike those that controlled the machines of the day. In a similar vein the shafts of the lamps are encircled by small beads that look like nothing so much as a ball bearing assembly, as if the head of the lamp could rotate.

Furness reiterated the industrial iconography in ornamental metal elements that continue into the great stair hall and then into the galleries themselves. The pistonlike granite columns of the main façade are echoed in the cylindrical welded wrought-iron columns of the galleries, fabricated by building committee member Henry Morris's business, the Pascal Ironworks, which had been making similar pipes since 1830, when it introduced the product to the United States.[86] The columns in turn carried steel beams of bolted together U channels, manufactured by the Phoenix Iron Works, whose name can be read in raised lettering on the vertical surfaces (Plate 4). In the exposed ceilings of the entrance vestibule, the auditorium, and the studios, all on the first floor, exposed steel beams span the masonry walls, carrying shallow brick vaults.[87] The gallery floor above the auditorium rests on iron beams carried on a pair of immense built-up riveted steel plate girders that span the auditorium and, again, represent a solution common to factories but unique in public assembly spaces. In a cost-saving mode, the floors of the galleries are concrete, darkened with cinder ash and ground to a smooth finish that is waxed to a high polish.[88] Once again, the stonework and stone ornaments of the interior are machine finished, with no hint of handcraft. Finally the cast plaster ornaments on the stairwell's upper walls were mass-produced castings.

Among the most remarkable examples of the transfer from industry to art in the Academy are the midlevel brass rods of the monumental stair railing. Instead of the usual decorative balustrade, derived from Renaissance forms, Furness adapted the drive shafts and universal coupling housings that transferred power from the great steam engines to the leather belts that drove the machinery in the neighborhood's giant factories (Plate 5). While these are not true transmission shafts, which would have been made of iron, nor true universal joints, whose internal elements would have rotated to transfer power in multiple directions, they were likenesses that would have been as universally understood as a punch card in the 1960s computer world.[89] An even more directly industrial quotation is seen in the general interior lighting in the galleries. Instead of chandeliers, the lighting system consisted of circles of iron pipes suspended below the skylight with gas jets lining the top of the pipe that could be lit like giant gas burners to provide illumination (Figure 35).[90] Recalling Ralph Waldo Emerson's call for an art made out of the constituent facts of modern life, Furness literally brought the factory and

Figure 35 Furness & Hewitt, gas lighting, main corridor, detail, 1876. Photograph by Frederick Gutekunst. Courtesy of the Pennsylvania Academy of the Fine Arts.

the Academy together, both in the collision of the front palace and the rear industrial loft, and in the details that would have been widely understood by the 1870s audience as adapted from industrial sources.

Some of these choices resulted from the financial crisis of 1873 that forced economies in the construction but, as would later be the case in the buildings for the Centennial Exhibition, the industrial solutions furthered the message intended by Philadelphia's industrialists. The initial competition drawings depicting the main stair hall for example show the upper walls above the arcade constructed of decorative brickwork. In high design and where money was no object, masonry had traditionally been the preferred material for the walls surrounding a monumental stair. Such is the case in the massive blocks of stone that form the great corner stair towers of McArthur's new City Hall and in Henry Hobson Richardson's later monumental stair hall in Pittsburgh's Allegheny County Courthouse. In the Academy project, as the economy worsened and with every penny being counted, costs forced the switch from perfectly laid patterns of decorative brick to rough construction brick clad with cast plaster lozenge-shaped tiles, with incised floral ornaments that now seem so appropriate. Something like the effect intended in the original scheme can be seen in the decorative brickwork of the interior of the Centennial Bank. The architects' section drawings originally depicted stone columns and diaphragm walls separating the side wings of the "transepts" from the long central gallery. With costs in mind these elements were simplified, beginning with the elimination of the central stone archway between the flanking columns of the passage between spaces. Later when this feature was actually constructed, rolled steel pipe columns replaced the stone columns and steel lintels replaced the stone arches. Similarly the switch from tile to concrete for the gallery floors, again as a cost-saving measure, significantly improved the galleries, because the concrete formed a better background for the art than Minton tile flooring with its distractingly bold patterns and strong colors.

Richardson's great church was not impeded by budgetary constraints but the difference between the interiors of the two buildings was not a consequence of costs. Richardson's interior evolved from a simple patterned masonry to a Byzantine dematerialization of hand-set mosaics and brilliant gilding, making an ethereal and airy space of intense Victorian color that countered the massive stonework of the exterior. Furness used matte surfaces to provide an appropriate setting that did not compete with the art, but his building was focused by light that guided visitors into and through the building. The darkness of the first lobby, with its wood entrance vestibule, led into the brilliantly lighted great stair, which was illuminated from above both by the skylight over the main stair and by the light from the gallery skylight that was visible through the opening in the wall at the head of the stairs. This light pulls the visitor up the stairs toward the exhibit spaces (Plates 6 and 7). Top-lighted galleries illuminated the art on the walls and the sculptures in the broad octagon at the crossing of the axes of the galleries. The school was lighted by the band of glazing that illuminated the studio spaces along the north side of the building, with light-hued walls bouncing light into the interior.

In the Academy, Furness & Hewitt achieved a fundamental reinvention of the museum and the art school along the lines of modern life. Its new construction systems were far removed from Richardson's great Boston church, which relied to the greatest extent possible on historical materials crafted by hand and in which the architect eschewed modern steel construction. Where Richardson was making a building that would capture the historical imaginations of the New England elite, Furness's factory for art anticipated the loft spaces that were adopted by post–World War II artists in New York's Soho area when the New York school artists discovered the cheap space and high ceilings of the loft district of lower Manhattan (Plate 8).

Historians have always been kind to Trinity Church. In the words of Professor O'Gorman, Boston's great church represented "American culture's coming of age."[91] It would be fairer though to accord that role to Furness's early masterpiece, which utilized the architectural and cultural forms of his own time, and to praise Richardson for extending lines of development that Eurocentric history would later reincorporate and claim as its own. Where Trinity connected American architecture to the European past in an unbroken skein of cultural references, the Academy marked the crossing of high architectural design with the potential of the future, a coupling whose genes would lead to Sullivan, to Wright, and on to Robert Venturi and Denise Scott Brown, Frank Gehry, and Renzo Piano. Heretofore, museums had been leftover palaces, repurposed civic buildings, or new buildings made to look like these hand-me-downs. Because they were planned for other criteria, the gallery windows of those adapted buildings usually produced glare at the same level as the art. Of all of the new galleries constructed after the Civil War, Philadelphia's Academy was the most progressive and the one that connected to the future.

Between 1873 and 1877 Richardson's great church rose from Boston's Back Bay on a parallel pace to that of the Academy. Each block of stone was carefully sized and hand cut and then was laboriously hoisted by muscle power; each bit of ornament reflected the mind of the architect and the handcraft of the mason, eventually creating an edifice that Bostonian aesthetes such as Henry Adams could appreciate.[92] Reiterating his commitment to tradition, Richardson even bragged that his building depended on no iron or steel for support or structure.[93] As late as the 1890s familiar features, such as the carving of the front porch and the small towers that animate the narthex massing, remained unfinished. Allowing for almost a year of delay in the depths of the economic crisis, Philadelphia's Academy was built in less than three years and marked the rise of a new design culture, one centered on the materials of the industrial city and the great engines that powered its factories. With its planning based on modern logistics, its materials expressive of the industrial age, and its broad forms representing the breakthrough to an expression of function, the seeds of the future lay within the walls of the Academy. These elements would be at the heart of Furness's designs for the next generation.

When the new Academy building opened in April 1876, the Reverend William Henry Furness gave the dedication address. He had been called into service at the last minute when the intended speaker, board member Theodore Cuyler, died a week before the opening. The Reverend Furness's remarks captured the possibilities of the new age, speaking of "the rejuvenescence of our venerable Academy" and a "new day that now dawns upon the Beautiful Arts, that help so powerfully to gladden and refine and elevate the life of man."[94] Two years earlier, Coleman Sellers had predicted a "new order of shapes, founded on the uses to which they are to be applied and the nature of the material of which they are made." Instead of old cultural values, Sellers's position on design fitting purpose was manifested in Furness's design for the Academy and would be expressed with ever greater force within a few years in the mature work of Furness and his Philadelphia peers.

4 BUILDINGS AS MACHINES

THE MATURE ARCHITECT

There comes a time in every man's education when
he arrives at the conviction that envy is ignorance;
that imitation is suicide; that he must take himself
for better, for worse, as his portion.

— Ralph Waldo Emerson, "Self-Reliance" (1841)

In the decade after finishing the Academy, Furness largely freed himself from
the stylistic mannerisms that had carried forward from his training under
Hunt, though he sometimes permitted them to reappear as comic touches
far into his career. His function-generated designs were like the casings and
housings of the great machines of the day, but because they were buildings and
not machines, they were enlivened by the wealth of ornament through which
Victorian architects expressed meaning. In these years, Furness found his own
independent stance, one that increasingly differed from the works of his peers
and the values of his ever-more academic and traditional profession.

As their profession evolved, architects were increasingly controlled by the organizations that they created. The most obvious control was whether an architect's work was published in the various American architectural magazines and
journals that flourished beginning in the Centennial year. The national architectural journals were controlled by historically minded Bostonians, and in the 1890s,
by the fashion-centered culture of New York. Philadelphia's architectural journal
of the 1860s had long since folded, victim in the case of *Sloan's Architect* with its
identification with a single architect, Samuel Sloan. While the locally published
Lippincott's Magazine touched on architectural topics, as when it provided an
overview of the history of the Pennsylvania Academy with the early photozincograph of the Furness design, or when it published Sullivan's essay on the skyscraper,

"The Tall Building Aesthetically Considered," it was at heart a literary magazine with the usual poems, short stories, and travelogues.[1]

Without a regional press to support his work, Furness relied upon his friends in other centers for publication. In 1876, as a vestige of his New York student-days friendship with A. J. Bloor, the *American Architect and Building News* reported extensively on Furness's work in Philadelphia as a part of its coverage of the Centennial, praising his designs as the most interesting in the city and noting several of his buildings for discussion. At the same time the Jefferson Medical College Hospital was given a full-page illustration showing plans and sections (Figure 36). But the first year of the *American Architect and Building News* was the last time that a Furness building would be given the national attention of a full-page image in that magazine.[2] Philadelphia's industrial cultural links to the Midwest are evident in the numerous illustrations of Furness buildings that were published in Chicago's *Inland Architect* into the twentieth century. The machine-influenced buildings of Philadelphia were not alone in being excluded from the journals. Other

Figure 36 Furness & Hewitt, Jefferson Medical College Hospital. *American Architect and Building News* 2 (September 9, 1876): 292.

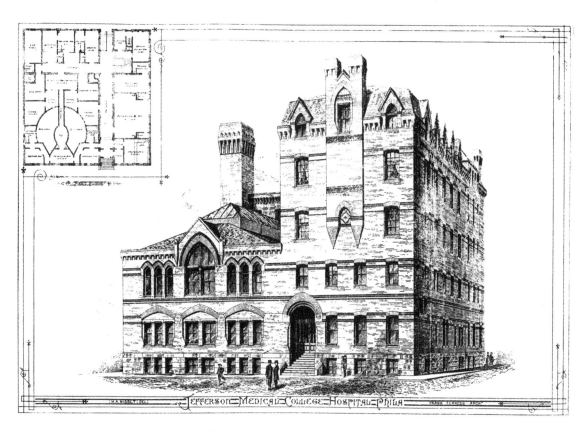

regional design strategies, particularly the Bavarian- and Austrian-influenced, hyperornamented, and encrusted Victorian schmaltz of St. Louis and Milwaukee, which served their German communities, were largely ignored as well.

From "Unfailing Originality" to "Furnessque"

As is evident from the number of commissions that Furness received, Philadelphians continued to welcome his innovations. By the late 1870s his buildings sufficiently stretched regional imaginations that leading reporters linked them not to a historical style but to their author. In 1877 a medical writer reporting on the nearly complete Jefferson Medical College Hospital for the *Boston Medical and Surgical Journal* commented: "The style of architecture may be termed eclectic, not being modeled after any one school. Mr. Furness has evidently depended upon his unfailing originality, and as usual has given universal satisfaction."[3] The next year a critic for the *Philadelphia Evening Telegraph* made a similar remark in assessing the appearance of the Provident Life and Trust, which was finally complete after a long construction delay (Figure 37). Unlike most routine designs on Bankers Row, the Provident had "put a constant strain on the public mind" because Furness's ornament was "larger and more out of proportion than ever," implying that it was common knowledge that the architect supersized details for effect. The author continued, comparing the building to a cartoon in the British humor magazine *Punch*, in which a short homely chap accompanying a tall handsome fellow called attention to himself by walking with his cane raised to his nose.[4] Seven years later, after the completion of the even more astonishing façade for the National Bank of the Republic, a writer in the *Philadelphia Press* gave the style a name, terming it "Furnessque," suggesting that Furness had arrived at an eponymous manner comparable to the "Richardsonian" style of his contemporary Henry Hobson Richardson.[5] When the First Unitarian Church was completed in 1886 a perceptive newspaper writer again placed the building in the context of its designer's life and career: "The design will be readily recognized as the work of Frank Furness, the youngest son of the former pastor, whose contributions to Philadelphia architecture have been so original and important."[6]

The notion that Furness was exaggerating detail to attract attention for his clients and for himself captures one of the aspects for which his architecture is celebrated. Architects of the day worked from a kit of parts using historical details whose forms and proportions were increasingly known from published representations in engravings and later photographs. New Yorker Montgomery

Figure 37 Roof trusses of the Provident Life and Trust Company Bank exposed during 1959 demolition. Photograph by Theodore F. Dillon, 1959. Courtesy of the Library of Congress, Prints and Photographs Division, HABS, HABS PA,51-PHILA,256–6.

Schuyler's critique of the Hale Building, by Furness's contemporary and frequent imitator Willis Hale, was rooted in the presumption that historic models were absolute; therefore the Philadelphia approach was a corruption of truths received from the past. In his biting analysis of Hale's design, Schuyler placed it in the immediate context of Chestnut Street, the center of Philadelphia's commercial buildings, many of which were by Frank Furness.

> One is driven back upon Philadelphia when one is in quest of architectural aberrations that are bad enough to be good enough. The commercial architecture of the town is, in the mass, abnormal because the authors of it do not perceive, or willfully disregard the fact that there is an architectural norma. We are speaking of the designers who have given Chestnut street its distinctive character, and not of the minority of trained architects who are pursuing the thankless task of educating Philadelphia to an appreciation of architecture; and, speaking of this majority, it is fair to say that historical architecture is to them a field not for

study, but for pillage, as it was to the barbarians who incorporated in their own rude buildings such columns and capitals and other fragments of classic architecture as they found.[7]

Schuyler, like most out-of-town critics, missed Furness's intent. Furness never intended to re-create specific buildings or particular historical details, forms, or plans with any degree of specificity or accuracy. Instead Furness's bank buildings along Chestnut Street were manifestations of their commercial environment, out-shouting their neighbors with tops that were too big, arches that were cut in half, ornamental passages that were personalized and distorted to visually express the loads that were being carried, and more often than not used elements scaled as if for much larger buildings. Like the sketches in his notebooks that were part of a family tradition reaching back to his father, the devices of the caricaturist are clearly part of his art that enabled him to extract motifs without descending to historical imitation. Whimsical touches continue to the end of his career, suggesting that Furness liked being the class clown so long as it brought attention to him and his clients. Crossed eyes focus on tiny noses on lintels; sad-eyed mustachioed faces peer out from keystones; brackets are undercut to the point of irrelevance and entirely disappear on opposite halves of a span; fig leaves hide the groin of steel beams and brick piers. All were part of the Furness comic mode whose humor is still apparent even in an age when historic norms are scarcely remembered.

So long as Philadelphia engineers and industrialists chose their own identities over the national architectural norms, Furness received commission after commission from their institutions and their industries. When Boston's Henry Hobson Richardson complained that he had yet to receive a commission for a factory or other industrial building, Furness was designing buildings across the entire range of architecture of the day—factories, ferryboats, and railroad cars, hospitals, libraries, and residences from small row houses to urban and country mansions. Notably, however, the ferment within the profession that Furness had unleashed remained restricted to the broad westward routes of the Pennsylvania Railroad. In those cities where industrialists took a leadership role, beginning first in Philadelphia and continuing later in Chicago and, in the first generation of the twentieth century, Indianapolis, various strands of American modern design played out.[8] Two years after the Pennsylvania Railroad commissioned Furness to design what the railroad in its advertising called "The Greatest Railroad Terminal in the World," the opening of the Columbian Exposition in Chicago marked the triumph of New York's French-oriented Beaux Arts classicism under the architectural leadership of Furness's old teacher Richard Morris Hunt and his future rival Daniel Burnham. The collective vision of the fair was an apt parallel to the rising American empire, looking back to classical Rome, with each building related to the other in a transforming ensemble like a Roman forum, but with little to do with industrial America.[9] The chief exception to the endless rows of Roman columns was Louis Sullivan's Transportation Building, which was differentiated by brilliant swathes of color in the great arches that framed its entrances and decorated its elaborately ornamented façades; its interior was the simple industrial architecture that hearkened back to the 1876 exhibition halls. Of all the Chicago exhibition buildings, only Sullivan's reflected the energy of the new industrial power that embodied the nation to the rest of the world.

The gale off Lake Michigan was not a fair wind for Sullivan or Furness. As the sanction of taste was brought to bear on fin-de-siècle Philadelphia, Furness began to lose commissions to clients who for the first time looked to other cities for what the rest of the nation regarded as proper design. By the end of the century, Bostonians Peabody & Stearns were receiving important residential commissions on Philadelphia's Rittenhouse Square, and the Chicago impresario of the White City, Daniel Burnham, had designed an office building on Philadelphia's Broad Street for the Land Title Company and soon would be commissioned by the Pennsylvania Railroad to design its new terminal in Pittsburgh, followed by commissions for the Washington, D.C., Union Station and Chicago's terminal as well. But the White City of Chicago gets ahead of the story. From the Centennial well into the 1890s, Philadelphians continued to hire Furness to explore the possibilities of the machine age and to celebrate their independent identity.

Furness in the 1870s

The Centennial opened American and European eyes to the power of the new industrial culture that quickly spread its progeny across the United States. The Centennial Bank, which stood directly across Market Street from the main railroad station, attracted the eye of numerous architects (Plate 9).[10] Designed with an eye to purpose rather than history, Furness's scheme for the bank was both synthetic and expressive with a strongly focused massing that piled up eye-catching detail in the vicinity of the entrance. Oversized windows bathed the pale-hued brick of the interior in light (Figure 38), while the composition assembled disparate elements whose bastard fusion of forms raised the torch of the new industrial culture that was also evident in the great locomotives across the street at the

Figure 38 Banking room of the Centennial Bank. Photograph by Lewis Tanner, 2011.

Pennsylvania Railroad's West Philadelphia terminal. Applying the same type of strategic thinking by which he might have arrayed troops in a Civil War battle, Furness commanded the six-way intersection by placing the main entrance on the beveled front so that it simultaneously faced north toward the Centennial train station on Market Street as well as southwest toward the diagonal of Woodland

Figure 39 George M. Harding,
Belfast National Bank, Belfast,
Maine, 1878. Photograph by
George E. Thomas, 2012.

Avenue, even as it directly faced northwest toward Lancaster Avenue, the main route to the fair. The main banking room occupied the larger volume at the corner of Thirty-Second and Market Streets, while banking offices, lighted by an industrial skylight monitor, were located in a subsidiary rear wing. Accessed under a massive, exposed steel beam carried on cast iron columns, the transition to the office space is another example of Furness's celebration of the systems and materials of the industrial city (Plate 10).[11] Over the next decade the offspring of the Centennial Bank appeared from Maine (Figure 39) to the American Midwest. Insofar as Philadelphia architecture increasingly deviated from other metropolitan centers it might be concluded that it was provincial, but in the larger sense its designers were connecting to the global industrial and engineering culture, making it the vital center of the American movement away from tradition. Indeed for a moment in the mid-1880s, it might have looked as if Furness and the industrial culture were winning the debate, as architects across the Midwest, untainted by northeastern traditional design cultures, copied Furness's Chestnut Street bank buildings in Pittsburgh, St. Louis, and Kansas City, even reaching west as far as Salem, Oregon.[12]

The 1880s: Function and Form

Between the late 1870s and early 1890s Furness advanced beyond the harlequins of his first decade to design his most original work, the Philadelphia and Reading Railroad's suburban stations, the Undine Barge Club, the National Bank of the Republic, the Baltimore and Ohio stations including the main terminal in Philadelphia, important institutional buildings including the University of Pennsylvania's School of Veterinary Medicine and its library, and many of his best houses. In this period his formal innovation was characterized by finding the "new forms" and devising dynamic expandable systems that met newly arising needs. These designs expressed their functions while creating good workplaces in which effective light was provided for the increasingly close work of modern life in banks, libraries, and residences. All carried forward the use of industrial materials and systems that embodied the Philadelphia culture.

As the 1880s began, Furness turned toward an adaptable strategy of functional particularism that could be applied to city and country houses, small suburban railroad stations, and highly individualized designs such as the Undine Barge Club. Three hallmarks identify Furness's mature works. First, these designs almost uniformly reject symmetry for asymmetry to better represent the tasks at hand. Second, the violently contrasting colors of the Academy and the early banks and city houses gave way to more uniform hues that focused attention on form in the manner of the unifying coat of gray paint that clad the great Philadelphia machines. With his color palette limited, he instead relied on volume, texture, and pattern to carry the architectural narrative. Finally, Furness relied on oversized windows and skylights to connect the exterior to the tasks of the interior and, in the process, made light the salient element of his designs. Unmoored from history, Furness was free to solve modern tasks in a modern way, becoming contemporary in purpose and reaching toward new forms.

The Evolving Office

For the Pennsylvania Academy of the Fine Arts, Furness had relied on Clark & Reeves, the engineers employed by the steel suppliers, the Phoenix Iron Works, to design the steel framing of that building. Presumably Furness relied on other engineers supplied by the contractor or the steel manufacturer for the overhead steel trusses in the various banks. After the Centennial year, Henry Pettit joined the Furness workforce, bringing engineering knowledge that could be applied to new projects.[13] Because Pettit was Joseph Wilson's brother-in-law, he presumably had access to inside information gained in casual conversation with Wilson, bringing to the Furness office the most up-to-date insights about the new industrial materials and their use. In any event, after 1876 the Furness practice had the in-house capacity to conceive the trusses of the Undine Barge Club, the steel armature that supported the Baltimore and Ohio Terminal, the immense beams spanning the reading room of the University of Pennsylvania Library, and the transfer beams that made it possible to open most of the first floor into a single room for the new Provident Bank office tower at Fourth and Chestnut Streets. While Furness would continue to design from his internalized memory of stone construction with its arched openings, the enlarged office had the engineering talent to create the large spaces of the modern world.

Building a Brand: The Philadelphia and Reading Railroad

Much of Furness's growth as an architect occurred while he grappled with one of the most remarkable commissions to come to any architect of the period, the 125 structures for Philadelphia and Reading Railroad. In 1869 the railroad had been taken over by the dynamic attorney Franklin Gowen (1836–1885), who in the 1870s brutally put down the Molly Maguires, the secret organization of Irish coal miners in the anthracite region of eastern Pennsylvania. As president, Gowen aimed to transform the Reading Railroad from a minor coal-transporting business centered in Reading to a major force in the Philadelphia region. He did this by circumventing the prohibition against railroads owning coal fields, thereby increasing the railroad's balance sheet by capitalizing the coal in its anthracite fields. This enabled Gowen to parlay his railroad and its vast coal reserves into a regional powerhouse that for a moment could be portrayed as one of the most valuable corporations in the country.

In 1878 the Reading Railroad placed Furness on retainer to make visible Gowen's ambitions in a territory spanning from the Atlantic coast to the middle of Pennsylvania, with Philadelphia as its center of operations. Furness approached his task on two fronts, the first of which would now be called color branding. The Reading, like any railroad, had hundreds of buildings, some new, some old, some midcentury Downing cottages, others brick industrial buildings, and after 1878, buildings built in Furness's new manner. The task of linking the old and new buildings to their corporate purpose could be accomplished economically by creating a focused palette of colors and materials. For the Reading, Furness chose red brick, the basic building material of industrial Philadelphia, accented with structural steel and wood elements that were painted a rich rust-brown hue, while clapboarded panels were distinguished in a cream-yellow tone. At the cost of a coat of paint this color scheme simultaneously pulled the entire array of Reading's buildings together while differentiating them from the coloristically varied buildings of the rival Pennsylvania Railroad, whose building stock had also evolved over decades of growth.[14]

In the 1870s, the Pennsylvania Railroad began to apply its corporate policy of standardization to buildings within its system.[15] While saving on design and construction costs, this strategy had limitations because it was often hard for the passenger, lost in a newspaper, to be certain which station was which. For the Reading, Furness devised a more exacting strategy, one in which each new building, despite a general unity of color and size, was given a specific identity such that it functioned as a sign, enabling passengers to tell at a glance where they were on their routes. While not Robert Venturi's iconic Long Island duckling poultry shop, where the building is literally a giant concrete duck that is itself the sign, each station gained a striking degree of individualization. This second aspect of Furness's design strategy was accompanied by a shift toward greater formal freedom that differentiated Furness's stations from earlier railroad buildings including his 1876 proposed but unexecuted Shamokin Station.

There, Furness drew a symmetrical façade with a central door and waiting rooms on either side that belied the interior reality of the building. Henry Hobson Richardson's smaller train stations along the Boston and Albany Railroad are examples of this type as are a number of the smaller stations on the Pennsylvania Railroad's Main Line.[16]

For the later Reading stations, Furness clarified the path of the passenger from driveway to waiting room, to ticket window, to covered shelter, to train, while also reflecting the station's secondary function as the home of the station master, who received an on-site residence as a part of his salary. This secondary role enforced job loyalty while providing eyes on the site at the minor cost of a small addition to the building. Gowen borrowed this strategy from the regional coal mine operators, who owned their workers' housing as a means of controlling the workforce. The station master's quarters included a kitchen and parlor on the first floor, much like the standard workman's hall and parlor cottage. In the Reading stations, the parlor connected to the office in a bay that projected forward from the track-side façade to permit the station master to see the arriving trains on either track. The office also contained the ticket window, which opened into the waiting room so the station master could simultaneously sell tickets and verbally alert passengers to the arriving trains. Family bedrooms were on the second story, connected by a dogleg stair from the parlor. The station master's bedroom was in the bay above his office, again permitting him to keep an eye on the station and its surroundings. The architectural expression of these various activities permitted a wide array of boldly asymmetrical forms that made each station identifiable, even as they shared common plan features. These buildings and the pace at which he produced them, 125 in five years, while also continuing his general practice, made Furness a master of both the bold gesture and the purpose-driven, rational plan.

There was one other critical aspect that underlay this project—the fees. Furness was paid $250 per month as the architect of the railroad, meaning that the average design fee was little more than $100 per building.[17] Aspects of many of the stations were repetitive so that Levi Focht of Birdsboro, the builder for many of the structures, could work within nearly open design specifications like: "For the beam ends, give me your best detail." Still, there was little time for introspection.[18] Design development occurred over successive iterations of the same building type with each sketch leading almost directly to a building so that the gestural and forceful qualities of the designs were not refined away. Furness's ability to "caricature a plan," as Hunt had put it twenty years before, had become a working method with results that, at times, must even have surprised the architect himself.[19]

In the case of the Reading Railroad, the largest and most elaborate stations designed by Furness were on the Norristown Branch, which led from downtown Philadelphia past Gowen's home in Mount Airy. Heading out of the city, the train first reached Wyndmoor with its exterior wood skeleton, recalling the Pennsylvania Railroad's Centennial station by Joseph Wilson. Wyndmoor was followed by the Sedgwick Station, identified by a shingled, cylindrical tower, like a railroad water tank, with an attic dormer placed off center on the conical roof as if it were a head turned and looking down the tracks. Queen Lane was an amusing fragment of a building, little more than a warm waiting room with a large overhanging shelter, supported by an iron column that Furness later enhanced with an iron seat that was bolted to and encircled the column. Next was Gowen's home station at Mount Airy, recalling the concatenated forms of the coal breakers that were the focus of the railroad, with a miniature adjunct shelter reiterating the themes of the main station and cascading down from street to track level (Figure 40).

Mount Airy was followed by the Gravers Lane Station (Plate 11), which was designed at the end of Furness's work for the railroad and marked the maturing of his design method.[20] As might be expected from the modest monthly salary that Furness received from the railroad, the Gravers Lane Station appears to have been constructed from little more than the two ink-on-linen drawings that survive; one depicts the plan and the siting and the other, the side elevation that paid particular attention to the porch extensions at

Figure 40 Frank Furness, Mount Airy Station, Reading Railroad, Philadelphia, 1881. Collection of Theodore Xaras.

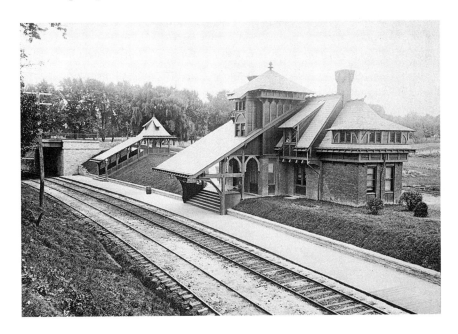

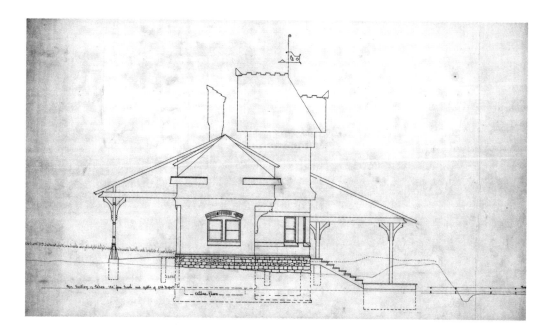

Figure 41 Frank Furness, Gravers Lane Station, elevation, ink on linen, c. 1881. Courtesy of the Architectural Archives, University of Pennsylvania.

the front and rear (Figure 41). Brief lines of shingle and brick denote the materials and there is remarkably little in the way of the architectural flourishes of leafy and foliate ornament or decorative materials that had characterized Furness's work in the previous decade. Instead, as befitted a building in the service of a great industry, the volumes directly express the particular functions within, and the composition of volumes has a matter-of-fact character that gives the building its energy—more like a giant machine or a deconstructed locomotive with headlamp, cylindrical steam chamber, and a whistlelike chimney than a conventional architectural composition. Each of these buildings had its own specific personality, recalling Sullivan's descriptive remark about Furness's designs as being "as though someone were talking."

Undine Barge Club

In the generation after the Civil War, men who had served in the military returned to passive office jobs, but many yearned for the strenuous life and camaraderie of their military service. In these years exercise became an attribute of urban elites, anticipating the fitness centers of our time and forming an obvious class signifier in cities between those who labored and those who exercised. Clubs were formed around fencing, racquets, and other sports and gymnasia were built in the downtown of Philadelphia, while preexisting rowing clubs were enlarged and new boathouses were constructed along both the Schuylkill and Delaware Rivers. Thomas Eakins's paintings, particularly scenes of rowing on the Schuylkill, but also those of baseball, boxing, and other sports, and Winslow Homer's watercolors of fly-fishing in Maine, celebrate the outdoor life that connects Furness's time to our own.

The Undine Barge Club had been organized before the war "in a meeting of several gentlemen" with a membership limited to twelve and with monthly dues of fifty cents. The members acquired a site on the Schuylkill "on the city side, having a cove with a good depth of water." The first question that presented itself was a name for the club. The name finally agreed upon was "the Undine Barge Association, based on the 'Story of Undine,' the spirit of the babbling brooks, so charmingly told by Friedrich Baron de la Motte Fouque."[21] In 1875 while still relying on its primitive boathouse near the waterworks dam, the club was the first to build an upriver boathouse that provided a "point to row to and a place where the dinners and other social functions of the Club could be held." Named Castle Ringstetten for the fabled castle under which the river nymph Undine lived, it was designed by Furness as a modest frame structure not unlike a seashore cottage (Figure 42), surrounded by a porch that accented the view of the river,

Figure 42 The Undine Barge Club's cottage-style Castle Ringstetten, the upriver boathouse and social club. Photograph by Lewis Tanner, 2011.

while the interior was warmed by a dining room fireplace not much smaller than the building itself.[22]

The main boathouse was built six years later (Plate 12). Initially Philadelphia's boathouses along the Schuylkill were little more than one-story sheds with large doors that opened toward the river. As Fairmount Park evolved, city regulations required ornamental boathouses. Most of the new boathouses were domestic in character, with boats jammed into what would have been the basement, while members, following the norm of Victorian houses, entered from the River Drive side, through a central doorway. Furness's mastery of logistical design for the railroad stations solved the problem of storing and moving increasingly fragile boats. The principal volume of the building was designed as a stone-walled, double-ended boat loft with oversized doors at both ends to permit the easy entry of boats from either the river or the road. The barnlike interior was spanned by timbers made into inverted trusses by an economical system of tie rods bolted through the stone walls that passed under cast iron queen posts, centered below the timbers, and then continued across the upper chords of the roof trusses (Plate 13). This system was taken directly from industrial spans of the small mills of the period and was simultaneously used by Furness for the covered porch at Gravers Lane Station. While stone walls and timber formed the bones of the building, the iron tie rods, presumably devised by in-house engineer Pettit, functioned like the tendons, making the clubhouse into a representation of the type of physical effort celebrated by the club motto, "Labor ipse voluptas" (Effort is itself pleasurable). At the street front, a bay, carried on massive corbels, juts out toward the entrance walk and is emblazoned with the club shield and its motto and an arm holding an oar and a boat hook. In a building dedicated to the pleasures of physical effort, the effort of spanning, load bearing, and carrying were given the lead architectural roles.

A projecting side volume houses the principal entrance vestibule and stair curving at the top, which is lit with a staccato sequence of small windows that offer fragmentary and rotating views of the water, even as they aim the visitor up to the club level. The newel at the base of the stair, like the Academy railings of six years before, was a representation, albeit in wood, of an industrial form, in this instance a drill bit with removable and replaceable cutting blades (Figure 43). The stairs terminate at a landing that provides access along the side to the visitors' porch for women, and continues directly into the club room. The club room is signaled on the exterior by a giant brick industrial chimney with flaring cap that marks the fireplace, whose hearth was the center for convivial male bonding over cigars and brandy (Plate 14). The room opens through large glazed doors onto a

deck toward the river, providing views of boats returning from races. In the opposite direction, doors lead to the locker room, which occupies the majority of the space above the boat barn within the trusses of the roof. Both the club room and the locker room were lighted by a continuous band of leaded glass in a crazy-quilt pattern that mirrors the stonework of the façade.

The exterior of the Undine Barge Club marked an important transition in Furness's color palette. Where the Reading Railroad buildings differentiated between the red brick and the yellow panels interrupted by brown-painted frames and ironwork, here Furness used a unifying cocoa-hued brownstone, accented with orange pointing, that relates to the hot-orange-painted window sash, the iron roof cresting above the slate roof, and the brilliant red-orange brick of the chimneys.[23] The wood elements, the turned posts of the ladies' porch, the wood paneling of the boat and entrance doors together with the door frames were originally painted a brown in the color range of the brownstone, pulling the entire façade together. The boat club, despite its tiny size marks the maturation of the Furness method. Over the next generation, Furness would receive commissions that covered entire city blocks and housed the great institutions of the city but in Undine he had learned to shape a building to purpose such that each function was clearly expressed and represented on the exterior. The boathouse had become a machine that supported rowing, as half a century later Le Corbusier would proclaim the house a "machine for living."

Domestic Architecture: The Suburbs

The new methods that Furness employed for the Reading Railroad buildings and the Undine Barge Club were also applicable to domestic architecture. In the late 1870s Furness's country houses such as the William Rhawn residence (Figure 44) in suburban Fox Chase and resort "cottages" like the Physick house in Cape May were still derived from the compact center-hall plans that he had learned from Hunt's Newport, Rhode Island, houses. These were typically cubic in volume with their mass emphasized by enfolding jerkinhead-style gables with their clipped peaks. In the 1880s some of Hunt's rural houses such as Idlehour, the Long Island summer home for W. K. Vanderbilt (1880), and Ellerslie, the country estate of Levi P. Morton at Rhinecliff-on-Hudson (1887), shifted toward a more elongated plan with an overlay of wood framing, based on the Norman seashore houses that Hunt had

Figure 44 Banker William Rhawn's country house in Fox Chase continued the square plan and cubic massing of early Furness houses. Wells & Hope, c. 1888. Photograph from private collection.

seen as a student in Paris. These were followed by Hunt's palatial structures at New-port. Furness's houses, by contrast, generally avoided historic motifs, and were de-vised as a tour de force of sheltering roofs settling uneasily on their stone bases.

William Henszey's house, Red Leaf (1881), on a prime Main Line site in Ard-more was a domestic version of the Undine design (Figure 45). For Henszey, the head of locomotive design and a partner in the Baldwin Locomotive Works, Fur-ness designed a multivolume stone structure, capped by dramatically shaped roofs and punctuated by industrial chimneys. Instead of a central hall flanked by pairs of rooms, Furness designed parallel ranks of rooms that shifted in relation to each other creating diagonal axes from one room to the next, adding the dynamic of the oblique to the plan. The best surviving example of this type is Furness's 1886 house for the actress Lotta Crabtree at the New Jersey resort of Lake Hopatcong, where diagonal room sequences focus on the views to the lake.[24] Furness's own summer house, Idlewild, near Media, explored similar spatial and compositional themes, but in miniature, and with the added jest of adapting the highly specific volumes of the university library to the purposes of his house.[25]

These strategies appeared at a larger scale in Clement Gris-com's suburban house, Dolobran, of 1881 (Plate 15). Griscom lived the standard bifurcated life of the city's industrial ti-tans, occupying a late Greek Revival townhouse at 1732 Pine Street two blocks south of Rittenhouse Square, with a sec-

Figure 45 Frank Furness, William Henszey house, Red Leaf, Ardmore. Wells & Hope, c. 1885. Free Library of Philadelphia.

ond house a half hour from center city near Haverford Station on the Main Line of the Pennsylvania Railroad. There it was part of a cluster of Furness designs for the captains of Philadelphia industry including the home of Pennsylvania Railroad vice president and later president Alexander J. Cassatt (Henry A. Sims, 1872; significantly altered and enlarged by the Furness office, 1880; later demolished), a nearby house for boardman and lawyer Theodore Cuyler (also demolished), together with another Furness house for Griscom's father (demolished). These houses were soon joined by houses for the families of Furness's partner, Allen Evans (demolished). Many of these same people organized and then encouraged the enlargement of the Merion Cricket Club (Furness, Evans & Co., 1892) at a central location near Haverford Station, marking its transformation from a young men's athletic club to a social anchor of the Main Line.[26]

Where the brick façade, marble trim, and simple detail of Griscom's city house was about the shared group identity of the old Philadelphia elite, the country house was more of an impressionist portrait, capturing both interests and family structure in the particulars of plan and elevation. Again Furness composed a cluster of modestly scaled volumes arrayed in two rows, one containing the hall and a small receiving

Figure 46 Ironwork windows on the porch at Clement Griscom's Dolobran, which open into the landscaped lawns of the house. Photograph by Lewis Tanner, 2011.

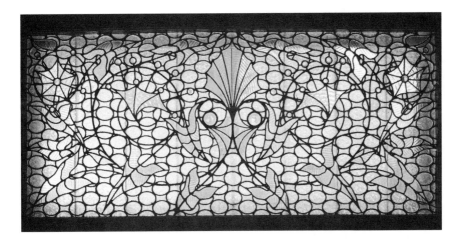

room facing the drive, and the other centered on the dining room and a parlor providing views toward the garden. Like most of Furness's domestic architecture of the period, the Griscom house was marked by muscular chimneys at each end with a wild array of volumes and roof shapes represent-

Figure 47 Leaded glass windows at Dolobran. Photograph by Lewis Tanner, 2011.

ing the various spaces within. The upper walls were shingled in the manner of the more informal so-called shingle style that spanned the East Coast from Florida to Maine.

The entrance of the Griscom house passed through a small outer vestibule into a stair hall focused on a freestanding, Japanese-influenced, walnut stair (Plate 16). The dining room in the second layer of rooms opened toward the landscape. It was originally wider than the hall and opened through sliding doors on one side, into an adjacent parlor. The parlor, in turn spanned the depth of the house, opening onto the porch on one side and into the hall on the other, again through sliding doors, creating a suite of spaces that look forward to the open planning of the end of the century (Figures 46 and 47). The Furness manner for these country houses belied the wealth of their owners and contrasted with the opulent Gilded Age palaces that would appear around New York and Boston in the contemporary works of Hunt and McKim, Mead & White. Where those New England and New York houses were increasingly about borrowed designs from other cultures, Philadelphia industrialists accepted Furness's strategy of reasonably sized and detailed spaces that were fitted to specific purposes (Figures 48 and 49). In the case of the Griscom house, the bays and windows were aimed at the remarkable landscape designed by Olmsted Associates that was the focus of the house.

Over the next generation, the office supervised multiple expansions that kept the house up-to-date, but it took nearly a generation before Furness solved

Figure 48 Fireplace in the downstairs office at Dolobran. Note the sculptural floral elements. Photograph by Lewis Tanner, 2011.

Figure 49 Bedroom fireplace with floral motifs, Dolobran. Photograph by Lewis Tanner, 2011.

the underlying problem of connecting the house to its site. The rear of the house looked out over a downward slope toward a ravine, which meant that the living and dining rooms were elevated above and separated from the setting. In 1897 Furness devised a ballroom extending from the basement of the main house so that the far end of the new room was at grade and opened directly into the gardens. The opposite end of the ballroom, within the original basement of the house, received a grand stair from the main hall that led to the lower level.[27] Where the ballroom extended beyond the original house footprint, its roof was spanned by Furness's patented reinforced concrete slab system carried on steel beams and protected from the elements by a hot tar roof that in turn was covered with stone tiles, making an outdoor terrace that extended from the dining room into the outdoors.[28]

As the 1890s advanced, Furness's clients were drawn to national tastes, forcing the office toward the fashionable Colonial Revival. Still, Furness battled against the normative designs as he enlarged eighteenth-century details, presumably with tongue in cheek, far beyond the original scale. In the case of a renovation of one house in the suburb of Gladwyne, the existing joists were sandwiched with bull-nosed step-stock planks, creating a supersized version of the beaded joists of eighteenth-century construction.[29] In spite of the more conservative turn, a few houses in the distant countryside continued the midcareer direct expression of function and construction essentially without detail, as in the case of the John C. Bullitt house near Paoli, but in general, after 1890 there were fewer and fewer of the head-turning designs of the first quarter century of practice. It is likely in these years that Furness's interests were focused on the banks, office buildings, and railroad terminals, where the new materials and values of modernity were still applicable, while most of the houses fell to Evans and the younger staff members.

City Houses

Philadelphia's pre–Civil War rows of uniform brick townhouses with their white marble lintels and steps were fixtures of the standard caricature of the dull Quaker City that drew the ire of critics from Charles Dickens to Frank Furness's own father. By the 1880s, due in large measure to Furness's efforts, the city's West Rittenhouse neighborhood was a riot of color with individual houses vying for attention in brownstones, green serpentinite, yellow Ohio sandstones, and blue Pennsylvania marbles and with the crisp sandblasted ornament, like that on the Academy, setting them apart. As the Rittenhouse neighborhood filled, it expanded to the west, gradually overrunning the stables, stone yards, and service facilities of the industrial waterfront along the Schuylkill. In 1886, Robert M. Lewis purchased a property on the 100 block of South Twenty-Second Street directly across from the "splendid and costly" St. James Protestant Episcopal Church, designed and built in 1870 from designs of Furness's former housemate New Yorker Emlen Littell (1836–1891). Within a couple of blocks were nearly two dozen Furness residential commissions (Figures 50 and 52), the armory that he had designed in the early 1870s for the socially prominent First City Troop, and the parish house and church that were under construction for his father's Unitarian congregation on Chestnut Street.

The chronological and architectural unity of the Twenty-Second Street block resulted from the 1880 sale of the property of the House of the Good Shepherd, a Roman Catholic "retreat for the reformation of unfortunates."[30] Its removal provided sites for a row of mansions, beginning with the astonishing pile that New Orleans cotton merchant George B. Preston commissioned of Furness in 1881 (Figure 51). Two years earlier, in 1879, Hunt had begun planning William Vanderbilt's

Figure 50 Exterior of the
Thomas Hockley house, built
1875, Philadelphia. Photograph
by George E. Thomas, 2012.

Figure 51 Furness & Evans, George Preston house, Twenty-Second and Walnut Streets, Philadelphia. Photograph from *Inland Architect*. Ryerson and Burnham Archives, Ryerson and Burnham Libraries, Art Institute of Chicago.

Figure 52 Exterior of the Dr. Horace Jayne house, built 1895, Philadelphia. Photograph by George E. Thomas, 1990.

limestone-clad French chateau on New York's Fifth Avenue while Furness's former studio mate George Post was designing another Fifth Avenue chateau for William's brother Cornelius. Both would have been well along as Furness began his drawings for the Preston house, but Furness did not follow their turn toward history. Instead Furness continued his own method, creating strikingly different façades on the two principal fronts rather than arriving at a fictive history-based unity in the manner of the New York buildings. A pair of overlapping gables capped the Walnut Street façade while the entrance opened from Twenty-Second Street, under a gargantuan bay shingled with California redwood and carried on immense brackets. Bands of brick and brownstone, highlighted with carved flowers and giant gouges, enlivened the street corner, while a favorite Furness motif, a window in the center of the chimney on the second story, placed a void above the fireplace of the front sitting room. Where Hunt and Post were mining details from European antiquities, Furness continued to rely on his own invention.

The lot to the north of the Preston house was sold to Dr. James Hutchinson, who in 1882 commissioned Boston-born and Harvard-educated Theophilus Parsons Chandler, Furness's chief rival for high-society clients, to plan his house. Chandler designed a French Gothic–styled double townhouse, of light red brick and brownstone, with a centered entrance flanked by large rooms. A year later banker Thomas Cochran commissioned Furness's former partner, George Wattson Hewitt, to build a double house in the "streaky bacon" coloration of the British Queen Anne style, but with details and color that were clearly derived from two recent Furness houses, the mansion for William West Frazier on Rittenhouse Square and the nearby Preston house.[31] The Cochran house was followed by another remarkable Hewitt-designed townhouse in a caramel tan brownstone, overlaid with hints of art nouveau in its delicate ironwork and stone carving, for John Christian Bullitt, the attorney for both the Pennsylvania and the Philadelphia and Reading railroads.

The block terminated at the north end with Furness's design for the Robert M. Lewis house (Plate 17). Lewis (1822–1899) was a member of the vestry of St. Peter's Episcopal Church in the old part of the city, which Furness had "restored" prior to the Centennial. He also was a nephew of Margaretta Lewis, the donor for Furness & Hewitt's Church of the Holy Comforter, an Episcopal mission chapel in the working class district of south Philadelphia.[32] Furness's scheme for Lewis's house made it something of a pendant to the Preston house at the opposite end of the block. Like the Preston house, the Lewis house was a strongly massed, gable-fronted building with the long side, along Sansom Street, dominated by an immense bay and accompanying monumental chimney that served the fireplaces of the main rooms of the house. But unlike the larger house, the entrance was on the gable end, facing the more important Twenty-Second Street. Where the Preston bay above its entrance was symmetrically supported by massive brackets, for the Lewis house, Furness slipped into comic mode, with a pair of brackets visually supporting one end of the bay, while the opposite end was left unsupported, confirming by their absence that the deeply undercut brackets adorned with a floral bouquet were entirely fictive as structure. Compact, brawling with its more refined neighbors, and with its giant bay over Sansom Street extended like the elbow of a pulling guard clearing the route for a running back, Furness's Lewis house transferred the visual battles for identity of Bankers Row to Philadelphia's premier residential neighborhood. Above the massive, rough- textured purplish brownstone first story, the upper brick walls were little more than a masonry frame, infilled with windows, that brought light into every nook of the interior. The varied windows, some squeezed be-

Figure 53 Wooden staircase in the Robert Lewis house. Photograph by Lewis Tanner, 1990.

tween brackets, some wider than they are high, were each sized to their interior purpose. Within, the plan follows the typical side-hall townhouse pattern with the entrance opening through a vestibule to a corridor and main stair along the party wall. Again there is a surprise. Instead of the usual dark core, the stair is bathed in light that filters down through the stairwell from a roof-mounted skylight (Figure 53).

Other contemporary city houses show Furness's talents as a colorist, using paint colors selected to complement and bring out the hues of the interior woodwork. The 1883 house for Alexander Cassatt's brother, J. Gardiner Cassatt (1849–1911), at 1320 Locust Street was part of a row of Furness houses midway between the old city and the new Rittenhouse neighborhood. While most of these houses are long gone or significantly altered, the Cassatt house has survived. The iron railing of the front steps is again ornamented with another industrial motif, giant, locomotive-scale spring clips (Figure 54). In the core of the house is a massive oak Victorian stair that was doubled into a monumental feature by a mirror (Plate 18).While most of the interiors were altered by Furness's former draftsman,

Figure 54 Ironwork railing ornamented with an industrial motif of locomotive-scale spring clips. J. Gardiner Cassatt house, Philadelphia. Photograph by Lewis Tanner, 2011.

Joseph Huston, in a Colonial Revival renovation at the end of the century, restorers in 1999 discovered and preserved fragments of an original painted cornice set off by a dark brown band accented with abstract gold leaf spots that provided glitter to the junction of wall and ceiling. Deeply undercut brackets frame the original Furness mantel in the rear dining room (Plate 19).

Machine details and rich colors reappear in the Joshua Z. Gregg house (altered by Furness c. 1888) at 1920 Spruce Street.[33] There the original orange-yellow walls complemented the golden oak of the hallway and rear dining room while deep rosy hues in the front parlor reflect the hues of the Honduran mahogany woodwork.[34] The Gregg house was further enlivened by a remarkable fireplace mantel in the rear dining room that was accented by short columns apparently made of stacked gears in wood that carry a shingled rooflet, a motif borrowed from the British Queen Anne style, but adapted to the Philadelphia industrialesque (Plate 20). The machine-sawn beams of the mantel lacked the texture of standard hand-adzed medievalizing craftsmanship that typified this type of design. Furness did not simply call for adze marks; rather his scheme called for abstract but regularized gouges chiseled or burned into the wood to give texture on modern terms. A decade earlier, the iron railings of the stairs and landings for two West Philadelphia rows of houses built for banker and developer Clarence Clark were ornamented with forms that recall the counterweights of locomotive wheels in the manner of his contemporary design for the Pennsylvania Academy of the Fine Arts gates. Crankshafts and whirligigs infill the iron railings of the

Evans row just to the south on Twenty-First Street while steel lintels span the recessed entrances as they also do on the Caroline Rogers Row. Well into the 1890s, locomotives and engineered designs remained Furness's urban muse.

The National Bank of the Republic: Architecture in the Furnessque Manner

By the early 1880s the conventional downtown bank façade with its grandiose central entrance and insistent references to classical design had become a cliché. Identity had always been a prime goal for Furness's commercial buildings, which demanded attention not unlike a 1970s urban teenager with a boom box at full volume on his shoulder or the tail-finned cars of the 1950s. Initially Furness had used violent color and pattern to enliven symmetrical elevations, whether for the voracious maw of the Guarantee Trust's entrance (see Figure 9) flanked by towers fronting Chestnut Street (1873–1875) or the gravity-defying tower that grew larger as it rose above the entrance of the Provident Bank (1876–1878). Beginning with the Penn National Bank (see Figure 80) at Seventh and Market Streets of 1882, as commercial buildings in brick and brownstone grew darker in hue, Furness found new strategies that would enable his bank designs to once again stand out from their peers. The Penn National Bank was made imageable by a light-hued but richly textured white marble façade that contrasted with its brick neighbors, while a plaque, apparently also designed by Furness, proclaimed the fact that this was the site of the house where Thomas Jefferson had written the Declaration of Independence. Entered through a pair of massive doors at the corner, its banking room was lighted by elongated Palladian windows and a skylighted ceiling.

The midblock red brick, red sandstone, red terra cotta, and red slate façade for the National Bank of the Republic (1883) was an even more rousing counterblast to the normative buildings of Banker's Row (Figure 55). Its aggressive scheme focused attention on the central axis not with the usual portal, pediments, and other elements lined up in the center of the façade but rather by dividing the façade in half and making each half wildly different from the other as if fractured by a funhouse mirror.[35] On the left, Furness placed a projecting entrance volume whose main doorway was spanned with the discordant element of a half arch. It was surmounted by a towerlike volume capped by a conical "candle-snuffer" roof that broke through the skyline to mark the point of public access. On the right, the façade was lighted by a large arch-headed window above an equally large rectangular opening that was a prelude to the sky-

Figure 55 Furness & Evans,
National Bank of the Republic,
1883. Courtesy of the Historical
Society of Pennsylvania.

lighted bank interior. A cascade of roof tiles added to the unsettling but engaging appearance.

Inside Furness repeated the device of the queen-post trusses of the Undine Barge Club to span the banking room, here supported at their ends by whimsically undercut brackets that again denied any structural role for these purely decorative elements. Where most urban banks with shared party walls were dark caverns with light at the ends, in the National Bank of the Republic the exposed trusses were open to skylights in the roof in the manner of the Academy, the Kensington National Bank, and the Provident Trust Company. The result was a light-filled workspace that anticipated Frank Lloyd Wright's Larkin Building by a generation. The discord of the front façade was repeated again at the rear of the banking hall, where a central fireplace, a favorite Furness accent that served the ventilation system, was flanked by half arches whose imposts braced against the fireplace and whose apex leaned against the outer walls.

In the 1890s, as banking became more corporate, the bludgeon-thy-neighbor style was supplanted by more conventional designs. The possibilities of radically taller buildings, carried on a steel frame and soaring above the old three- and four-story city, once again fueled Furness's competitive instincts. Height maximized an urban site's value and was an obvious device for identity as the continuing notoriety of the tallest building demonstrates to this day. In 1887 he joined his former partner, George Hewitt, in destroying the old order of the downtown around Independence Hall with office buildings that marked the new economic energy of the 1880s boom. Hewitt framed the eight-story Bullitt Building with an array of towers atop the office and bank entrances to call attention to the building from its midblock site between Chestnut and Walnut Streets. Where Hewitt's slab, capped by small towers, had the air of a Victorian exposition building, Furness's eleven-story tower for the growing Provident Life and Trust Company at the prominent site of Fourth and Chestnut Streets was a muscular jab at convention. His new tower incorporated features and textures of the original building's design but above all aimed at a progressive identity in the old business district, rising in contrasting layers of brick and stone to a massive chateau roof, which became the site for his architectural offices.

When the center of gravity of the city moved west following the gradually opening City Hall, Furness again was the banker's architect of choice. Instead of containing medium-height buildings elbowing each other for attention, South Broad Street was remade as a street of towers. In 1898, the Furness office designed the West End Trust at a prominent site directly across from City Hall, on the south side of South Penn Square and Broad Street.[36] Where the Provident

Plate 1 Front façade of the Pennsylvania Academy of the Fine Arts. Photograph by Lewis Tanner.

Plate 2 Roof of the Pennsylvania Academy of the Fine Arts. Photograph by George E. Thomas.

Plate 3 Detail of ornamental bronze lamp, one of two framing the Pennsylvania Academy of the Fine Arts entryway. The manufacturer's signature is visible at the base of the lamp. Photograph by George E. Thomas.

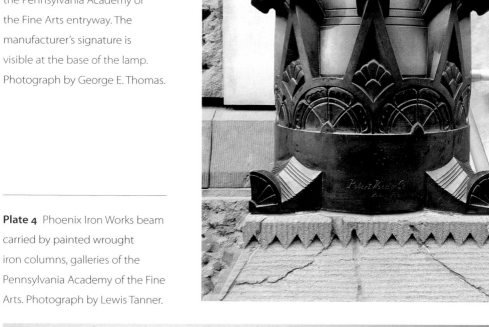

Plate 4 Phoenix Iron Works beam carried by painted wrought iron columns, galleries of the Pennsylvania Academy of the Fine Arts. Photograph by Lewis Tanner.

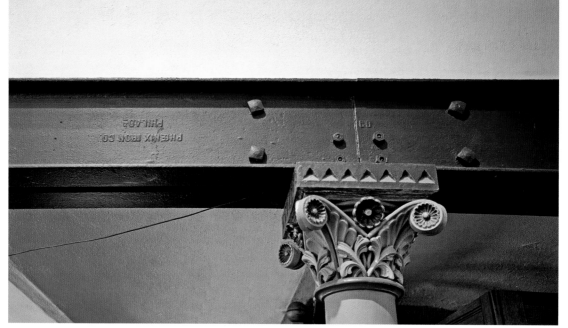

Plate 5 Detail of the Pennsylvania Academy of the Fine Arts stair railing, mimicking industrial machinery. Photograph by Lewis Tanner.

Plate 6 Main stair of the Pennsylvania Academy of the Fine Arts leading up to the gallery. Photograph by Lewis Tanner.

Plate 7 Upstairs galleries of the Pennsylvania Academy of the Fine Arts, looking across main stair. Photograph by Lewis Tanner.

Plate 8 Pennsylvania Academy of the Fine Arts attic. Photograph by Lewis Tanner.

Plate 9 Front façade view of the Centennial Bank's main entrance. Photograph by Lewis Tanner.

Plate 10 Detail of the painted iron columns, steel beams, and decorative brickwork in the Centennial Bank's interior. Photograph by Lewis Tanner.

Plate 11 Gravers Lane Station.
Photograph by Lewis Tanner.

Plate 12 Undine Barge Club exterior.
Photograph by George E. Thomas.

Plate 13 Interior of Undine
Barge Club's boat loft,
with visible timber beams.
Photograph by Lewis Tanner.

Plate 14 The Undine club
room, with monumental hearth
and leaded glass windows
in a crazy-quilt pattern.
Photograph by Lewis Tanner.

Plate 15 Exterior of Dolobran, Clement Griscom's house on the Main Line. Photograph by Lewis Tanner.

Plate 16 Entry hall of Dolobran, with Japanese-influenced walnut stair. Photograph by Lewis Tanner.

Plate 17 Exterior of the Robert M. Lewis house. Photograph by Lewis Tanner.

Clockwise from the top left:

Plate 18 J. Gardiner Cassatt house main stair. Photograph by Lewis Tanner.

Plate 19 Cassatt house fireplace. Photograph by Lewis Tanner.

Plate 20 Joshua Z. Gregg house fireplace. The unique design elements could be described as British Queen Anne style meets Philadelphia industrialesque. Photograph by Lewis Tanner.

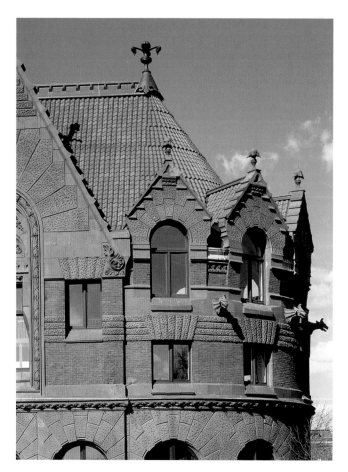

Plate 21 North end of the University of Pennsylvania Library exterior. Note the decorative gargoyles and the textured terra cotta blocks. Photograph by Matt Wargo, courtesy Venturi, Scott Brown & Associates.

Plate 22 Base of the grand staircase in the University of Pennsylvania Library. Photograph by Matt Wargo, courtesy Venturi, Scott Brown & Associates.

Plate 23 Main landing of the University of Pennsylvania Library's wrought iron staircase. Photograph by Matt Wargo, courtesy Venturi, Scott Brown & Associates.

Plate 24 Reading room of the University of Pennsylvania Library with visible skylight. Photograph by Matt Wargo, courtesy Venturi, Scott Brown & Associates.

Plate 25 Rotunda reading room of the University of Pennsylvania Library. Note the massive steel beams in the room's ceiling. Photograph by Matt Wargo, courtesy Venturi, Scott Brown & Associates.

Plate 26 Exterior view of the University of Pennsylvania Library's skylighted bookstacks. Photograph by Matt Wargo, courtesy Venturi, Scott Brown & Associates.

Plate 27 University of Pennsylvania Library steel-frame bookstacks. Note the tiers of copper ventilation panels and the skylight above. Photograph by Lewis Tanner.

Plate 28 Leaded glass window above the University of Pennsylvania Library's front doors. Photograph by Lewis Tanner.

Plate 29 Façade of the University of Pennsylvania Library with tower. Photograph by Lewis Tanner.

Opposite top left:
Plate 30 Exterior of the New Castle Library, Delaware. Photograph by Lewis Tanner.

Opposite top right:
Plate 31 Interior of the New Castle Library, with top lighting from skylights. Photograph by Lewis Tanner.

Opposite bottom:
Plate 32 Exterior view of Wilmington Railway Station. Photograph by Don Pearse for Bernardon Haber Holloway Architects PC.

Plate 33 Main stair of the
Wilmington Railway Station.
Photograph by Lewis Tanner.

Plate 34 Platform-level view of
the Wilmington Railway Station.
Photograph by Don Pearse for
Bernardon Haber Holloway
Architects PC.

tower had been a layer cake of brick and stone bands, Furness heeded his student Sullivan's essay "The Tall Building Artistically Considered" on the tall building as a "proud and soaring thing" for the trust, rising 204 feet in a classic Furness clash of colors.[37] Above the pink granite base, a fluted shaft of copper-clad bays and yellow brick walls rose without interruption to a crowning feature of immense gables in red tile and copper. For a moment it was the tallest building in the city, a title later taken by another Furness tower (1913) that was part of the Commercial Trust block west of City Hall. From the early 1870s until the beginning of the twentieth century, it would be Furness who led the way in the city's commercial architecture, taking his cues from the contemporary industrial world with but few nods to other cities and other sources.

The Baltimore and Ohio Terminal

While the suburban stations, the houses, the boathouse, and the old-city banks were relatively small and simple in program, in 1886 Furness was given a vastly more complicated problem for the new downtown Philadelphia station for the Baltimore and Ohio Railroad. Railroads fiercely guarded their turf and, in the case of Philadelphia, the prime downtown real estate was controlled by the Pennsylvania Railroad and to a lesser extent the Philadelphia and Reading Railroad. Together they used every stratagem including city council legislation to block competing railroads from entering the city.[38] In 1881, the Baltimore and Ohio (B&O) lost its access to the lucrative New York and Philadelphia markets over the Philadelphia, Wilmington, and Baltimore's tracks in a midnight purchase by the Pennsylvania Railroad. After several years of searching, the Baltimore and Ohio Railroad found an obscure route into the center of the city, via a charter that permitted a bridge across the Schuylkill River and provided for tracks on the east river bank where a terminal could be located near Chestnut Street. While negotiations were under way in city council, the railroad asked Furness to look into the possibilities of the site. Cornelius Weygandt (1832–1907), the vice president of the Western Savings Bank, was Frank Furness's banker and a diarist. In his diary for Tuesday, April 27, 1886, he reported: "Frank Furness came in today, to renew his note; and, upon inquiry as to whether he is busy now, I learned from him that he is likely to have the work of the Balt. & Ohio R.R. Co., for the stations upon its line between Balt. and Phila.; including the large main station and offices, at Chestnut Street near the Schuylkill river, which Furness says is a difficult and perplexing job, architecturally."[39]

The "difficult and perplexing" aspect of the project resulted from elevated bridges at each end of the site, carrying Walnut Street and Chestnut Street across the Schuylkill River. Furness would have to find a way to connect the usual street-level functions, waiting rooms, and the entrance to the office building for B&O's regional operations on the upper levels with the tracks and main concourse two stories below along the river bank. The site was further complicated because it was filled land and therefore of poor load-bearing capacity and it was known to flood fairly regularly. These circumstances led Furness to conceive an armature of steel columns carrying massive built-up girders on which the masonry of the station could be constructed at the elevated grade of the bridge. The scheme of a massive masonry building carried on stilt-like columns, seeming to float above grade, was unique in American railroading while the lower level, screened by a giant window sash between steel columns, was equally unconventional, looking like the Machinery Hall of the Centennial Exhibition of a decade before (Figure 56).

As the Philadelphia terminus of the Royal Blue Line of the Baltimore and Ohio Railroad's high-speed New York route, the new station was intended to give the railroad a presence in the city while making waiting pleasurable. Three decades earlier John Ruskin had argued that since no one

Figure 56 Furness & Evans, Baltimore and Ohio Terminal, looking southeast, 1887. Courtesy of the Library of Congress, Prints & Photographs Division, HABS.

actually wanted to travel by train there was no need to make train stations pleasant: "Now, if there be any place in the world in which people are deprived of that portion of temper and discretion which is necessary to the contemplation of beauty, it is there [in a railroad station]. It is the very temple of discomfort, and the only charity that the builder can extend to us is to show us, plainly as may be, how soonest to escape from it. The whole system of railroad traveling is addressed to people who, being in a hurry, are therefore, for the time being, miserable." Ruskin concluded, "There never was more flagrant nor impertinent folly than the smallest portion of ornament in anything concerned with railroads or near them."[40]

Once again Ruskin had it wrong about modern life. By the mid-1880s, railroad travelers expected comforts and services. Because the new station was located in a residential neighborhood separated from the business district, travelers had none of the facilities that surrounded the usual downtown station. Furness had to re-create the downtown. Furness placed the lunchroom and restaurant along the southern side of the station; the main waiting room paralleled Chestnut Street and the more private ladies' waiting room was located in the southwest quadrant (Figures 57 and 58). Despite the giant fireplace in the men's waiting room, the focus of the space was the grid of massive, riveted, built-up steel girders similar to those Furness had used to span the auditorium of the Academy of the Fine Arts. In gendered Victorian fashion, the ladies' waiting room had a plaster ceiling and a more domestically scaled fireplace, with rocking chairs for the more delicate traveler.

While the celebration of steel lay at the heart of the design, as in Furness's other masterpieces, the art of the terminal was about light. The principal entrances were located at each end of the building, one under the porte cochère entrance, marked by a clock tower, and the other at the west or river end. Both were brightly lighted by walls of clear leaded glass panels in sunburst patterns that illuminated vestibules leading into the main waiting room. By contrast with the brilliantly lighted stairs, the main waiting room was relatively dark, a place of calm. Once below in the domain of the trains, the ticket office in the center of the Chestnut Street side drew customers to the cashiers' windows by light from a skylight overhead at the sidewalk level.

The lower-level concourse was among the most original spaces of Furness's career, not for the delight of its ornament, though it was certainly remarkable, but rather as the boldest expression of the possibilities of the age of iron (Figures 59 and 60). In this space decorative elements were limited to the pattern of the clear leaded glass windows on the perimeter, the ornamental wrought iron rail-

Figure 57 Furness & Evans, Baltimore and Ohio Terminal, main waiting room, 1887. Courtesy of the Library of Congress, Prints & Photographs Division, HABS.

Figure 58 Furness & Evans, Baltimore and Ohio Terminal, ladies' waiting room, 1887. Courtesy of the Library of Congress, Prints & Photographs Division, HABS.

Figure 59 Furness & Evans, Baltimore and Ohio Terminal, stair to lower concourse, 1887. Courtesy of the Library of Congress, Prints & Photographs Division, HABS.

Figure 60 Furness & Evans,
Baltimore and Ohio Terminal,
detail of iron in main stair, 1887.
Photograph by Cervin Robinson,
1959. Courtesy of the Library of
Congress, Prints & Photographs
Division, HABS.

ings on the stairs, and the bold wrought iron lamp stands adorned with lanterns that lit the stairs. The principal feature of the concourse was the grid of massive riveted steel columns and girders that unabashedly carried the main station above. Here was a room entirely of iron, steel, glass, and concrete, the materials that bespoke industrial Philadelphia and the modern world. Its closest contemporary counterpart would be Daniel Burnham's great interior stair court in the Rookery in Chicago, which was also a showcase of glass and iron. But where Burnham's room was lacy, decorative, almost feminine, Furness's design was muscular, an architecture of power and structural force, an apt parallel to the machine age culture in Philadelphia that produced it.

The University of Pennsylvania Library: A Machine for Learning

While the Baltimore and Ohio Terminal was under construction, the University of Pennsylvania, under its new provost, William Pepper, was laying the groundwork for a university library.[41] Into the mid-1880s, the library occupied two rooms in College Hall that were sufficient to hold what were regarded as the "classics" of Western civilization. Teaching at Penn, like most universities, was based on the lecture and recitation method rather than original research so the library was rarely used and was only open on an as-needed basis. In 1884, Provost Pepper, himself a medical doctor and a proponent of laboratory research as the basis for scientific medical training and practice at Penn's medical school, hired Penn's first librarian to encourage students to use the university's collection. In this, he was attempting to keep up with Harvard and European universities, which had begun the transition from the dissemination of old knowledge to the creation of new knowledge that was the goal of up-to-date research faculties.

With the city's focus on engineering and the sciences, it is no surprise that the University of Pennsylvania library holdings were significantly weaker than those of its northern rivals where books were high-cultural signifiers and libraries were the central feature of their campuses. A decade earlier, Harvard's book collections had so outgrown the capacity of the shelves encircling Gore Hall's Gothic reading hall that they required a separate "bookstack" for storage (Figure 61). This self-sustaining iron and steel structure was designed by Furness's former atelier mates Ware & Van Brunt and an account of it was immediately published in the *American Architect and Building News*.[42] The resulting separa-

Figure 61 Gore Hall bookstack, Harvard University. From *Library Planning, Bookstacks and Shelving, with Contributions from the Architects' and Librarians' Points of View* (Jersey City, NJ: Snead & Co. Iron Works, 1915). Courtesy of the Library of Congress.

tion of reading room and book storage gave Harvard's library more desk and work space while isolating the book storage function.

Having hired a librarian, Pepper then put out a call for Philadelphians to contribute to the library "a record of the busy work of the world to-day" so that Penn's students could "use it and learn the methods of original investigations and research."[43] This request connected the university's teaching methods to the new goals of original research and the creation of new knowledge that are at the core of the modern university. The limited spaces of the university's library were promptly overwhelmed by an avalanche of materials that promoted Pepper's real purpose, making a new library building essential. The following year, the provost's report pointed to the crisis he had precipitated, which "renders more conspicuous the lamentable want of suitable accommodation for books and for readers. The time has now come when a separate fire-proof library building is imperatively demanded. It is a necessity for the instructors, over 148, and for the students, over 1048, who now have not good opportunity of using the library for reference still less for systematic study and investigations."[44] With a generous start of $50,000 from industrialist Joseph Wharton, for whom the university's business school would be renamed, and donations from other industrialists, many of whom had also contributed to the Pennsylvania Academy of the Fine Arts nearly twenty years earlier, Provost Pepper proceeded to raise funds for the new building.

The Design Team

Working from his professional culture as a medical doctor in the age of burgeoning numbers of medical consultants, Pepper devised a planning process that was unlike that for any other library of its day.[45] Instead of suggesting the adaptation of a model from some other institution, or employing an architect with a known predilection for a particular historical mode of design, Pepper assembled a consulting team to manage the project. Pepper charged the committee to develop plans for what would be the "best appointed library building in this Western World."[46] The committee was headed by university trustee and preeminent public scholar and lecturer Horace Howard Furness, who was charged with "securing competitive plans for a Library Building" and to "secure all available information and to entrust the data so obtained to an architect to be appointed by the board for putting the same into form. Second that the chairman of the Library Committee be requested to collect all desirable information including plans, cost and reports on the actual efficiency of existing libraries and that these be placed at the disposal of this Joint Committee for consideration before the architect employed is asked to do any designing."[47] Under the impetus of his charge from the board, Horace Furness selected two library experts to join him in planning the new building: Justin Winsor (1831–1897), Harvard's librarian and manager of the largest college library of the day, and Melvil Dewey (1851–1931), the leading theoretician of contemporary libraries and professor in the School of Library Economy at Columbia College. Finally, it was reported, "the Joint Committee recommends to the board that Mr. Frank Furness be appointed architect for the Library Building under the above plan of action."

Penn's library committee members were each at different points in their careers. Justin Winsor was a Boston Brahmin, a Harvard graduate, and the quintessential historian-librarian of his time. After working at the Boston Athenaeum, he had helped form the Boston Public Library and then was given the post as director of the Harvard library. Nearing sixty years of age, he was at the last stage of a distinguished career. He would focus on the critical issues of collection growth and management which had preoccupied him at Harvard.[48] Melvil Dewey, by contrast, was still early in his career but already had a significant reputation. As noted in Chapter 2, in 1873, a year before he graduated from Amherst College, he had devised the decimalized classification system that was first utilized to organize the exhibits of the Centennial Exhibition and was later used to organize human knowledge in library catalogs and on the shelves. Even though it has been generally replaced by the Library of Congress system, his system still has a presence in many libraries. He was also instrumental in the professionalization of the library workforce through his teaching at Columbia College. To that end, Dewey had founded a business, the Library Bureau, that, beginning in 1881, provided library supplies and equipment from card catalogs and card stock to book trolleys and other paraphernalia for library needs.[49] Though by all accounts a difficult personality, he was the premier expert on operations for the contemporary library and still had the fire of youth enlivening his imagination. He would push for a librarian-friendly scheme instead of the usual architectural monument.

Frank Furness was at the height of his profession. In the twenty years before the University library commission he had designed some four hundred buildings, including many for the leading institutions of the city, most of the important banks and financial buildings, many of its private houses in the city and suburbs, and an array of clubs and country houses from Maine to Maryland. There was no one in America better suited to understanding the core issues of a newly restated problem and designing a solution that fit its purpose.

The Victorian Library

As new methods of research and investigation produced new knowledge in the form of books and new journals, and as modern educational practices required original research based on primary sources, library designs evolved from the gentleman's book-lined study to the engine of learning at the research university. Like engineers in the pre–Civil War years, librarians asserted their professional status and demanded an active role in library planning. They too established journals and found professional causes. In the early 1880s, their immediate cause was focused on the plans for the Library of Congress. The result of an 1870s competition that was won by the Washington, D.C., firm of Smithmeyer & Pelz, the Library of Congress's bombastic spaces and rigid plan came in for particular censure by the nation's librarians. The attack was led by William Frederick Poole (1821–1894), the head librarian at Chicago's public library.[50] Poole's *Report on the Progress of Library Architecture* (1882) formed the theoretical frame for the new university library.[51] Summarized in the *American Architect and Building News*, Poole's *Report* focused on the conflict between the librarian seeking an effective scheme in which to work and the architect, whose goals for monumentality were often were at odds with sound library planning. Poole's incendiary introduction made it clear that battle lines had been drawn and the librarians were in no mood to take prisoners: "In the course of my remarks on that occasion [Washington, D.C., 1881 meeting of librarians] in which I made some suggestions as to the construction of this class of buildings, I said I know of no better rule to be observed in the library architecture of the future than this: avoid everything that pertains to the plan and construction of the conventional American library building."[52] Poole continued, "the conventional architecture of library architecture is very faulty and . . . we shall never have a general reform until better principles are applied to the largest buildings. The smaller libraries are constantly copying and perpetuating the confessed faults and worst features of the large libraries."[53]

Rather than grandiose schemes that boosted the egos of donors and municipal leaders, Poole instead called for designs that could solve the actual problems facing librarians, and he had little patience with the old orders of design that institutional boards often preferred but which librarians knew did not work. In the course of his articles he suggested that book storage capacities should be capable of being enlarged to meet collection growth. Poole closed with the thought that an informed public would shape the future: "Librarians are losing respect for antique absurdities and are not afraid to think for themselves. Committees ask not whether the plan is old and typical but whether it is convenient, useful, economical, and sensible. Architects are now seeking information from those to whom they formerly dictated conventional rules."[54]

The age when architects were gentlemen and librarians were servants had ended and conflict reigned over questions of tradition and style. Designers of university libraries too often began from the architectural style of the campus, which recalled the medieval foundations of colleges and universities. While Poole certainly remembered his first years in the Italianate, generally classical scheme of the Boston Athenaeum, by the time that he wrote "The Construction of Library Buildings" in 1882 he was particularly against libraries based on churches, though any form or style that was more important than the solution to the problem of efficient storage and access would have merited his ire as evidenced in his speech of the same title in early 1881 at the Washington Conference of Librarians:

> The seventh objection I will mention to this [ecclesiastical] style of architecture is the difficulty of enlarging it. How is this building to be enlarged when the growth of the library demands an extension? Shall it be extended heav-

enward and more galleries be piled on these with more wasted space in the nave, greater difficulty of access to the books and more extravagance in the heating? Shall transepts and a chancel be built so that the plan will represent the true ecclesiastical cross? Why library architecture should have been yoked to ecclesiastical architecture and the two have been made to walk down the ages *pari passu* is not obvious unless it be that librarians in the past needed this stimulus to their religious emotions. The present state of piety in the profession renders the union no longer necessary and it is time that a bill was filed for a divorce. The same secular common sense and the *same adaptation of means to ends which have built the modern grain elevator and reaper are needed for the reform of library construction.* (My emphasis)[55]

Four years after his lecture, Poole returned to the questions of library planning in a lecture on "Small Library Buildings" at the American Library Association's Lake George Conference of 1885. There he crossed the boundary from critic to designer, offering a scheme for a small library that would directly influence the University of Pennsylvania Library. Entrance and access to the spaces of the building were placed in a separate volume to exclude unnecessary traffic from the reading rooms; reading rooms, one connected to the circulation desk, the other more distant for quiet research, were separated from each other by a screen. Books were stored in their own wing and additional collections could be stored in added wings or by taking over reading room spaces, which in turn could move to unfinished spaces on a second floor. His conclusion was absolute: "Any plan which does not admit of enlargement, without disturbing the convenience and architectural symmetry of the building should be rejected."[56]

As Poole was writing his diatribe, several university libraries were being designed that were more to his liking. The most successful to date was the library at the University of Michigan, designed in 1883 by Furness's fellow student of a quarter of a century earlier, Henry van Brunt. In the context of Poole's pointed attacks on ecclesiastical schemes, Van Brunt's layered and rounded apselike end with its flanking towers recalling the apse end of the Abbeye aux Hommes in Caen would seem a flagrant example of this form of architectural abuse.[57] However, despite the visual similarity to the apse of Romanesque cathedrals, the library's roots lie in two entirely separate forms, both linked to ideas of efficiency. The functional source of the curved shape was the arrangement of the book shelves on the perimeter of the reading room in spokes radiating from a center, a scheme that shortened the distances of movement for the staff. A similar scheme had been used for the tents in Philadelphia's vast Mower Hospital during the Civil War and was common in other hospital designs of the day. Furness had explored the idea in the initial central stacks of the Mercantile Library (1873). The greatest problem with Van Brunt's plan was the inability to expand the core of the design. In the case of the Michigan Library, its collection had reached the limits of its shelving system within twelve years and quickly forced the construction of a separate bookstack.

A second and equally potent design source for the spoke system of shelving was the panopticon plan that was well known for prisons and other contexts demanding surveillance. The radiating wings provided visual oversight from a central position. This was the basis for the octagonal reading room with its elevated central platform for the librarian-warden for Princeton University's Chancellor Green Library (1871–1873) by William A. Potter and the similarly arranged reading room of the Library of Congress, both of which, in turn, looked back to Robert Smirke's gigantic domed reading room for the British Museum (1854–1857).[58] Despite these new models and the best efforts of leading architects across the nation, the university library, with its rapid expansion of collections and growing user groups, remained a problem whose solution had yet to be discovered.

As the University of Pennsylvania Library planning got under way, Henry Hobson Richardson's Billings Library at the University of Vermont was nearing completion (Figure 62). With its central tower, its rounded end (referred to

Figure 62 Henry Hobson Richardson, Billings Library, University of Vermont. *American Architect and Building News* 24, no. 679 (December 29, 1888) following 304.

as the "apse" in contemporary literature) that contained the special George Perkins Marsh collection, and its elongated reading room, lined with book alcoves, like a nave with side chapels, it has often been portrayed as an influence on the Furness scheme. In fact, the two buildings were profoundly different, as is evident in their planning and their conception. Library professionals saw through Richardson's scheme and reviewed it poorly. It was outgrown even before the building was finished, necessitating a separate rear wing within five years.[59] When Richardson's death was reported in the *Library Journal* it was with the comment that he had designed many "beautiful buildings, though not all perfect as libraries."[60]

Planning the Modern Library

The plan and form of the new university library resulted from discussions between Furness, Winsor, and Dewey in their April 1887 meetings.[61] Their scheme reflected the consensus of the library professionals who were already aware of the limitations of the Billings Library and other recent libraries that would outgrow their collection space within a decade of their construction. Penn's consultants would not start from an ecclesiastical form or from a classical basilica lined with books on the Labrouste model, which could not be enlarged, nor would they box themselves in with a collection storage system that could not be extended. The consulting team quickly arrived at a basic scheme for the site at Thirty-Sixth Street and Woodland Avenue whose core elements survived the relocation of the library across the campus to another triangle at Thirty-Fourth Street. This site had the advantage of offering more room for expansion to the south and, because it terminated the axis of Locust Street that intersected the main campus from the west, the library would be the visual focus of the campus. A year after their meetings on campus, Dewey wrote a letter to the provost outlining the significance of their scheme: "The plans I sketched with Mr. Furness late that evening, seem to me better than any college library has yet adopted. I should like to see your building by all odds the best model for similar institutions to follow and it will be a great pleasure if I can be of any service in that direction."[62] Shortly thereafter, Dewey made good on his promise when he saw to it that the new library plan was published in the *Library Journal*.[63] The published perspective showed the massing as it was eventually built on Thirty-Fourth Street, while the plan laid out the sequence of spaces— campus to entrance portico to stair tower to reading room—but because it was

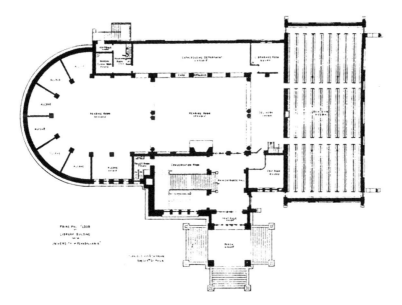

the old plan for the original site, it was a mirror-image reversal of the eventual building (Figure 63).

Figure 63 Furness, Evans & Co., University of Pennsylvania Library, plan at time of dedication. *Proceedings at the Opening of the Library of the University of Pennsylvania, 7th of February 1891* (Philadelphia: University of Pennsylvania Press, 1891).

Like the Academy nearly a generation earlier, the library began from a framework of logistical planning. The tower was placed on axis with Locust Street, which, into the middle of the twentieth century, formed a connection to the diagonal of Woodland Avenue in front of College Hall. The porch led directly into the great stair tower, which served multiple purposes, providing connections to every principal public space of the building while removing extraneous traffic from the reading rooms. Its secondary purpose was as a "conversation room," where students could talk without disrupting the work in the library. The axis from the portico doors led through another set of doors to the main reading room and continued directly to the card catalog, Dewey's search engine, which was given pride of place as the terminus to the entrance axis. The catalog cross-filed the entire collection so that it could be readily searched by subject, title, or author; its Dewey decimal numbering system made it possible to locate books, and after use, to return them to their proper shelf location. The librarian's desk to the side guarded the bookstacks and was where books were requested and delivered to the reader. To the north were two large reading rooms; the first, in which the catalog and the delivery desk stood, was for more casual readers but was made quiet by its vast, sound-absorbing height. The more distant reading room was conceived as a space for quiet study and was surrounded by alcoves, one for each of the major departments of the university, containing the books that a professor might want to have at hand to teach a seminar.

The cataloging department was placed in a distinct volume along Thirty-Fourth Street where it could be directly entered from the street. This zone contained a staff coat room and a delivery room where new books could be deposited before beginning their passage through the cataloguing process under a skylighted work space. The wood cases of the card catalog closed off the arcade between the reading room and the cataloguing department. The drawers could be pulled in either direction, by a reader in the library or by a librarian adding cards, saving the cost of a second catalog for the staff. The cataloguing department terminated with a direct passage to the bookstacks.[64]

The bookstack represented Winsor's special contribution to the problem. As he well knew, collections were growing at a ferocious rate and their growth was the central problem of the modern library. Following the model of Harvard's bookstack and working with the insights of Winsor, Furness designed parallel masonry walls accented by blind arcades on the east and west façades that represented the internal structural bays. The structure itself was a self-sustaining system of steel columns with the bookshelf supports forming a part of the structure. Its floor was made of thick slabs of rough-finished glass that permitted light from the roof's skylights to reach down to the basement. Natural lighting was preferred because it had been determined that gas lighting damaged the high-acid wood-pulp paper of recent books and journals. The shelving system was organized at heights that Dewey determined were ergonomically appropriate for moving and storing books.

The most ingenious feature of the book wing was its capacity for future expansion. Instead of imitating the symmetrical and rather cubic libraries of the classical revival designs of the imperial age after 1893, which resisted expansion from the very core of their design, Furness designed the stack wing so that it could be extended with additional bays. As evidenced by the original ink-on-linen perspective drawing, which shows nine projected bookstack bays extending to the south instead of the three actually constructed, Furness conceived a built-in expansion capacity that would allow the collection to grow at least 300 percent (Figure 64). No aspect of this remarkable building was more telling than the architect's willingness to forgo the satisfaction of a completed composition, governed by preset, final proportions. Instead, with its extendable bookstack, the building was intentionally unfinished, like the expandable factories created by Philadelphia engineers. It was, in Horace Furness's elegant phrase at

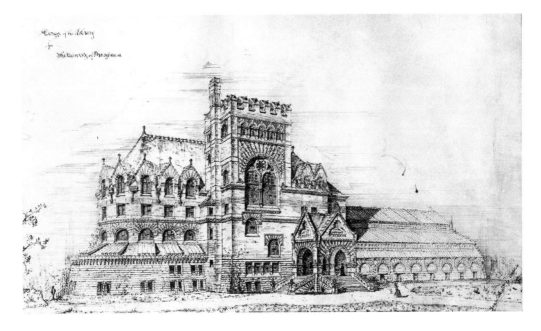

the cornerstone-laying ceremony, "a provision for the present and a prevision for the future."[65]

It is instructive to compare the speed at which the Philadelphia project was initiated, designed, and built with the state-supported libraries in Paris designed by Henri Labrouste half a century earlier. Labrouste's libraries were commissioned by the French nation and represented a vastly different process and method. The Bibliothèque Ste. Genevieve was designed over a decade and more, with a state salary providing the income for the architect over the bulk of his career. In such circumstances, every detail could be studied, restudied, and worked over and over again and every implication could be examined in multiple ways. In large measure, Labrouste's libraries were the product of a single remarkable intellect—but only a single intellect. By the time that Furness came to the university library project he had been designing two or three buildings a month for a generation, serving not one client but many and learning to work with modern clients and, in the case of the library, with a modern consulting team. Labrouste's designs show the effect of decades of analysis and revision; Furness's shows the impact of immediacy and the varied insights of his team. For all of the architectural interest in the French buildings, Labrouste's book-lined rooms were in many ways the old medieval library in which the books were the icon, light was distant, and the reading room was monumental. The Furness building was a new

Figure 64 Joseph Huston of Furness, Evans & Co., perspective "Design of Library for the University of Pennsylvania." Courtesy of the Architectural Archives, University of Pennsylvania.

and adaptable college research library, not an imperial commission. In Furness's conception, doubtless amplifying insights from the provost and the librarian, the purpose of a library was primarily as a work space that served a growing community and a growing book collection. In the end, Labrouste created a landmark in the continuing evolution of French classicism; Furness joined the library to the industrial culture, pointing the way toward the future.

Industrial Materials and Forms

The consulting team's plan established the relationship of spaces and functions but it was the massing and striking coloration that revealed the library's architectural character. The choice of brick as the principal façade material, rather than the heretofore customary green serpentine stone of the campus, tied the library to the great mills of the city. This unheroic material was given visual interest by Furness's decision to use cull bricks on the façade and in the great public rooms. Their misshapen forms are still visible in areas of the great stair hall that were protected from the sandblasting of the 1960s by bookcases that have since been removed. These bricks had the advantage of economy while also giving the resulting brickwork variations in texture and hue that contrasted with the monotonous red for which Philadelphia buildings had become infamous. The red of the brick was complemented by the deep orange-red glazing of the terra cotta blocks that were used for the more expressive elements. The crimson tonality was completed with red tile for the roofs, red sandstone from the Pictou quarries in Nova Scotia for the base and the curved end of the building, red paint for the wood window frames and sashes, and red copper for the metal cornices and the roof copings at the top of the building. To borrow a title from Arthur Conan Doyle, Penn's library was a "study in scarlet." The trustees joked that they might sign the name of the architect on a plaque at the end of the stacks by translating the sound of his name into Latin, as "fornax." Like the great industrial complexes of the city, Furness's library was indeed a furnace that powered an engine for learning.

The terra cotta blocks of the façade were cast as if they were rusticated stones, but, perhaps in a wink to Ruskin's call for each material to express its character, Furness textured the terra cotta blocks with an abstract pattern of gouges (Plate 21). These were similar to the giant chips of stone that the mason blasted out with a pick when finishing the rusticated surfaces of the Academy's foundation blocks, but here the gouges were transformed into a regular pattern that was both evidence of its industrial production and, at the same time, large enough and strong enough to catch light and break up the surface. Terra cotta could be cast as multiples and even large blocks were a manageable weight thanks to hollow interiors, significantly reducing the labor for masons on the job. By the 1880s, because of its economy and the growing number of terra cotta manufacturers in the Philadelphia region, Furness even used terra cotta ornamental panels on the façades of factories, such as the rope works of John T. Bailey & Co. on the waterfront in south Philadelphia.[66]

From the overscaled wedge-shaped voussoirs framing the giant arches of the library's entrance porch and surrounding the great window that lights the stair to the top of the tower, which was crowned with a floral version of battlements that catch light and dissolve the building into the sky, Furness shaped terra cotta to his expressive purpose. High above the entire building are the faceted planes of the giant terra cotta chimney cap, another reference to the city's great factories. The enrichment of the exterior made a critical point. A library was, after all, more than a warehouse. A Victorian building, no matter its architect, required more than just walls and roof; it must also provide delight, making it pleasurable and appropriate to its context. Industrial processes made it possible to manufacture richly textured blocks with strongly shaped detail at a minimal cost. With the exception of the hand-cut sandstone of the base, all of the materials of the exterior were manufactured.

Iron and steel were given special roles throughout Penn's library in carrying the narrative of scientific progress. Iron first takes stage center in the main stair that stands like a great sculpture in the entry tower. There each of the manufactured states of iron was shaped with its appropriate form and detail. The cast iron newels and columns were richly ornamented in the mold with crisp details and sharp edges; the wrought iron elements were bent and hammered into twists and spirals; and the rolled steel I-beams were articulated by patterns of the rivets where steel plates joined stringers and landings and the staccato of bolts denoted the location of the stair risers along the stringers (Plates 22 and 23). The differing attributes of the material are further represented in a dazzling array of forms and systems, sometimes supported from below, sometimes hung from above, sometimes cantilevered, sometimes carried on iron arches and cast columns. At the very top, and best seen from outside at night, the railings take on the pattern of triglyphs and metopes, as if remembered from the classical details learned in the Hunt atelier thirty years earlier, but transformed from solid stone into a web of iron and air by the values and forces of the industrial age.

Steel reappeared next at the top of the multistory reading room, where giant metal plates, themselves cusped on their interior curve as if left over from stamping circular-saw blades, were highlighted in dark blue at the top. These stiffen the trusses that span the reading room and carry the skylight that floods the room with light. The metal plates reappear in the same role, stiffening the trusses above the large auditorium at the north end of the building. The skylight, of course, was a carryover from the top-lighted factories and work spaces of the city, but also continued the themes of Furness's other notable public spaces—the Academy, the banking rooms, and the interior stairwells of his largest downtown houses (Plate 24). An intervening layer of clear, decorative leaded glass forms the laylight panels that are a highlight of the ceiling. Finally, in the quiet reading room at the end of the library, steel achieved heroic scale in gargantuan beams, riveted together like giant bridge girders and flaring at their imposts where they were carried by masonry piers (Plate 25). These beams were scaled to carry the dynamic load of the auditorium overhead, but Furness, with tongue in cheek, accented the juncture of beam and column with terra cotta fig leaves as if, with Victorian prudishness, to conceal the groin of a classical sculpture.

By contrast, the steel-framed bookstack was understated and minimal, both because of its role as service space and as a comment on the elegance of the apparatus itself. In later years, when Furness was commissioned to design shelving for the collection of Russian books donated by Charlemagne Tower, he added a bridge across the north reading room to house the collection. This brought the iron and glass of the bookstacks into the public spaces and adds the ghostly passage of people moving across the rough glass surfaces to the visual interest of the building.

As with all experiments, there were failures as well as successes. Librarians knew from experience that the top floors of skylighted bookstacks were problematic because of the heat build-up, which damaged both the paper and the spines. Dewey and Winsor were fully aware of this problem and it had been extensively discussed by Poole. Furness proposed to manage the heat gain of the glass roof as he had at the Pennsylvania Academy of the Fine Arts, with a secondary interior glass ceiling forming a plenum that could trap heated air, which would be vented by two tiers of operable, ganged copper ventilators running the entire length of each story of the bookstack. As imaginative as this solution was, it could not resolve the actual physics of the problem. Light energy entering through the two layers of glass was stored as heat in the books and turned the upper level of the bookstack into a furnace. Furness tried running a trickle of water across the glass from sprinkler pipes at the crest of the roof, but the light-heat energy transfer was occurring within the building and the water did nothing to improve the situation (Plates 26 and 27).

When the Furness office extended the bookstack in 1916, it continued the vocabulary of terra cotta and brick but in the new form of the Duhring Wing. Its punched openings and casement windows limited light into the building while the higher masonry walls, it was hoped, would shade the glazed roof of the original piece of the stack.[67] Despite these unforeseen problems, the core idea of the expandable bookstack worked and the collection was able to expand to many times the original projected size. While other libraries, like the one at the University of Michigan, were out of room within twelve years, the University of Pennsylvania library continued to serve its community until the construction of a new central university library in the 1960s.[68] By then, the original creativity of the scheme was long forgotten and university students had devised a legend that the building was a secondhand use for an abandoned Furness train station project that the frugal university had accepted to save money.

An Architecture of Light

As he had done in the Academy of Fine Arts and most recently in his center city banks and again at the Baltimore and Ohio Terminal, Furness used light to convey the architectural narrative of the university library. In the case of the library, light metaphorically represents access to knowledge even as it guides the path of the user (Plate 28). At the library, the visitor enters from a shaded porch into the darkest space of the building, the lower level of the stair tower. There the brightest object is the cream-hued iron stair, ornamented with decorative lamps like those of the Baltimore and Ohio Terminal, which directs the visitor to landings that accessed offices, the campus's largest auditorium, and the separate room originally devoted to house the collections of the university museum. The wall opposite the entrance is punctured by two pairs of doors that are lighted with leaded glass panels and above by a row of windows that glow with the light from the library. While the entrance zone was conceived as a space for student conversation, the path through it, from darkness to light, from ignorance to knowledge, leads to the library.

Furness had used a similar strategy in the sequence from dark to light in the design of the Academy and more recently for his new building for his father's First Unitarian Church. There the entrance was announced by a freestanding stone tower, capped by a pyramidal tile roof, carried on stumpy stone columns, and tied together by iron tie rods to resist the forces of the roof framing. The nave was lighted by the bold gesture of a ventilating skylight running along the central axis of the space that represented the Unitarian idea of the access of all to grace. For the library, Furness also drew on industrial light-management techniques that he would have known from the regional factories—diffused light from light monitors and skylights, even illumination via north-facing windows, and light-hued terra cotta in the reading room, like the industrial use of whitewashes on factory walls, to bounce light around the work space.

Industrial Sources

Furness didn't just refer to Philadelphia's industrial culture through the choice of materials and close attention to lighting work spaces. He also used architectural forms that were straight out of the city's factories. Hiding in plain sight is the great tower, which at first glance, might seem to be one of the picturesque features condemned by the librarians. However, one of Richardson's Billings Library towers, was a belfry and the other contained a minor stair; Furness's tower was far larger in volume, essentially a vertical room (Plate 29). Like the towers found in many of the city's great factories and in the public schools that looked to the same source, the library tower incorporated all of the vertical services, the public stairs, the toilets, their plumbing stacks, and the roof drains. A particularly close industrial example was the Compton and Knowles Loom Works, which stood until recently near the North Philadelphia train station (Figures 65 and 66). It was designed with a polygonal eastern end, like the library fitting into a triangular site, and an immense stair tower with a flanking chimney at the center of the long wall. It was designed by former Furness draftsman Joseph Huston, who, almost a generation earlier, had made the perspective drawing of the library. The ground level of the library tower was designated in the original plans as a "Lobby and Conversation Room," creating a gathering space where undergraduates could hang out outside the research and study zones.[69] But the library committee did not intend for students to simply hang out in the stair tower. Like the bells and whistles that commanded a workforce to its tasks in a factory, the message of the library's purpose was reinforced in the leaded glass window of the entrance doors, which proclaims, in a line of Falstaff's provided by Frank's brother, Horace, "Talkers are no Great Doers" (Figure 67). It was a not-so-subtle reminder to students to advance from the conversation space to the work that was their purpose at the university.[70]

The university library marked the maturation of Furness's method. Where the Academy had been informed by logistical planning and a mixture of high art

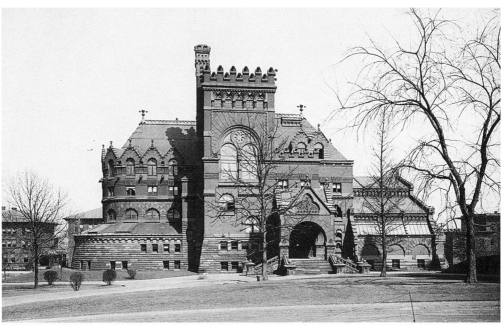

Figure 65 Joseph Huston, Crompton & Knowles Loom Works, 1902. Building now demolished. Photograph by George E. Thomas, 2002.

Figure 66 Furness, Evans & Co., University of Pennsylvania Library, 1887–1891. Detroit Publishing Co., c. 1900. Courtesy of the Library of Congress.

Figure 67 Interior library doors, with quote from Shakespeare. Photograph by Lewis Tanner, 2011.

and industrial iconography, its façade detail was still largely about the question of what style was appropriate and whether an amalgam of styles would become an American manner. Though Sullivan saw the power of Furness's new method of directly solving the problem at hand rather than finding parallel solutions in books and in history, in the early years Furness still relied on ideas learned in Hunt's atelier. A decade of building in the ecological niche of engineer-dominated Philadelphia had given Furness the means to rethink architecture in every dimension. Where most of his peers in other American cities were caught up in style as historical content and contemporary fashion, Furness was able to make the leap to an architecture that was based on planning to meet purpose, to design forms that encompassed and supported specific tasks, to use lighting to focus attention on tasks, and to devise ornament that connected the building to the larger context of meaning. Like the housings of the great machines of his time, the volumes of the library closely reflected the internal functions, but as a social and cultural product, architecture demanded expression in the spatial sequence of the plan, raised vertically into façades, and overlaid with ornament, which links the building to cultural purpose. In the end the library's purpose was like that of a machine—to effectively and efficiently serve a user in the contemporary world.

Ironically, or maybe simply out of perversity, the ornaments that Furness chose for the library, including the giant gargoyles of the north end of the building, have created confusion in that they seem to confirm that the building's source was the type of ecclesiastically derived forms that library professionals hated. On closer analysis however, the differences between ecclesiastical sources and the university library were obvious. Unlike ecclesiastical plans that focus on the altar at the end of a processional sequence, Furness's and Dewey's scheme for the library was based on assembling a sequence of functional zones that served specific tasks and work processes. The Penn library's apselike end can be explained as describing the horseshoe seating of the upper-level auditorium, and the tower obviously was not a belfry. In every way the planning and the interior spatial order of the Pennsylvania building were derived from the team's response to the particular problems of the modern library.

The Reception

When the library opened in 1891, it was viewed by professionals in the field as better meeting their goals than any other library of the day. *Harper's Weekly* gave it a front-page story with multiple illustrations above the fold.[71] At the opening, Horace Furness gave one of the dedicatory addresses and remarked on how the collaborative process begun by Provost Pepper's committee had started with Winsor's and Dewey's professional knowledge, which in turn had been incorporated into the architect's design: "Thus instructed in all a library's needs, and aided by the thoughtful suggestions of our own excellent librarian, Mr. KEEN, our architect, whom it does not beseem me to praise, and who needs no praise of mine, proceeded at once to give to these needs a form and habitation; and you have the result before you, wherein every door and window, gallery and alcove are placed and devised with sole reference to the one dominant idea of a LIBRARY—a library to be freely and commodiously used by the public, by the professors and by the students, and as indestructible withal as elemental clay and iron and glass can make any structure reared by mortal hands."[72]

Horace's choice of words reiterated the central theme that he had essayed in the cornerstone-laying speech three years before. The library that had been designed was not about a historical style or a current fashion, rather it was conceived in the way that the great machines of the city were conceived as "the employment of means to ends."[73] Here, with the results manifested, he could focus the audience on the purpose of "every door and window, gallery and alcove," all aimed at making nothing but a library and using the raw materials of the age—"clay and iron and glass."

In 1888, a year into the project, Talcott Williams, who had participated in the meetings between the consulting team and the architect, had described the building for the *Library Journal*. Then he had somewhat wistfully compared Furness's scheme with McKim, Mead & White's Boston Public Library (Figure 68): "I have no desire to be understood as criticizing one plan in the light of the other. This would be ridiculous. The Boston building is going to be a great architectural monument. The University Library proposes to be nothing more than a mere convenient library building."[74]

It was a backhanded compliment, but in his comparison Williams caught the essential difference between the two buildings. The Boston building was conceived as a "monument." The university's library was to be a "convenient library building." Librarians preferred the latter; the architectural press, imbued with the goals of historical precedent and monumentality, understood and praised the former. When the library was completed and turned over to the university in February

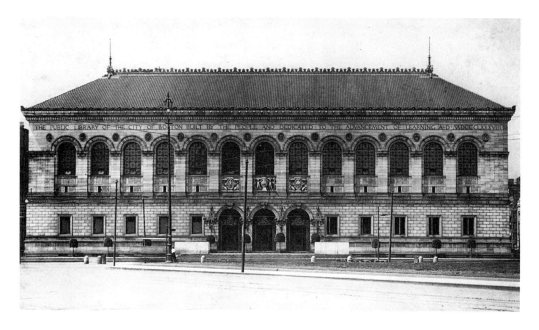

1891, Williams again gave an address that ranged across the history of libraries. On the one hand he proclaimed the library as the physical manifestation of human memory and history but he also proclaimed its purpose in supporting the new role of the university faculty, who had become more than simply teachers. They were now part of a group who "must produce and discover." The university's chief new tool for that purpose was "that laboratory of learning, its library."[75] In comparing the library to the laboratory, Williams caught its essential character as a part of the new wave of scientific knowledge that was reshaping life. At Penn as the sciences broke into their separate disciplines, the library was part of a wave of laboratories that transformed the campus.

A Library Whimsy

As the university library was being completed, the Library Association in New Castle, Delaware, commissioned the Furness office to design a new building for its collection.[76] What resulted is something of a fireplug of a building with an octagonal front, but chopped off flat at the rear, crowned by a peaked roof with a giant ventilator and an immense weathervane (Plate 30). At first glance the building appeared to have ignored all of the new information about library design that had been developed for the University of Pennsylvania Library. Instead of separating circulation, book storage, and other functions, every activity of the building takes place in one room and the collection was stored against the walls in the model of the old gentleman's library that Melvil Dewey abhorred. Moreover, unlike Furness's typical stylistically independent design stance, the New Castle Library is laden with obvious quotations from colonial architecture including the fanlight over the entrance, the panels of Flemish bond brickwork set into the center of the two angled planes on either side of the entrance, and the immense weather vane that caps the roof. These are paraphrases of features on the New Castle Academy building across the street, where the library had been formed, and where it had remained for the first four generations of its existence. However, as Furness had done in his design for the Philadelphia Library Company a decade before, his quotations demonstrated genealogy—but on his own terms.

The fanlight over the door is exemplary of Furness's approach. While an obvious reference to the town's Academy, it was quadrupled in size, making it nearly the full width of the façade and turning the fanlight into a Venturi-like sign. Similarly Furness "hung" bits of the Academy's Flemish bond brick walls on either side of the entrance, like a picture in his field of economically constructed common bond brickwork. To emphasize that they were quoted from the earlier building they were framed by an egg and dart molding and set off in the common bond brickwork of the main building. The old Academy's gilded weather vane is the quill, the instrument of literacy of the eighteenth century; Furness painted his weather vane industrial black and gave it the form of a giant industrial key or lever.

If the Colonial Revival details were signifiers of cultural connection, the library's core characteristics are Furnessic. The shape of the building—here an octagonal front that emphasized its plastic volume—makes a powerful street presence. The windowless walls, the pyramidal roof capped by plates of glass below the giant ventilator, the industrial chimney, and the vibrant colors recreated in a recent restoration, all mark the assuredness of an architect who was confident in his own voice. The library provides another example of Furness's rich color harmony even as it further differentiated his design from the cream and off-white trim of the Colonial Revival.[77] The Philadelphia hinterlands remained comfortable with their industrialesque choices even as the Chicago Fair was about to rise from the swamps of Chicago.

Despite Furness's adaptation of the colonial revival to convey the cultural context of the building, once again, the strongest forms of the building came from the industrial culture. Notable are the giant sheets of glass that crown the roof and ensured even top-lit illumination for the reading room while eliminating the need for windows on the side walls that would have introduced glare and reduced collection storage space (Plate 31). A square of glass slabs, carried in a steel frame in the center of the floor, conveys the light of the reading room into the basement. A decade later Furness used the same technique with a circle of glass in the floor of the Girard Trust, below the skylight of the dome, to light the safe deposit department in the bank's basement. Another industrial quotation is the oversized ventilator at the apex of the roof with its punched openings that forms the base for the giant weather vane. These elements represented Furness's rethinking of the heat buildup problem of the University of Pennsylvania Library by drawing heat off from the top of the building, while also reducing the amount of solar exposure. Unlike in the university library, with its reading room separate from the expandable bookstack, the miniature size of the New Castle Library collection meant it could be housed on the perimeter walls with balcony and basement storage providing access to less used collections. Still, the careful siting of the building provided a rear yard into which the library could have expanded had collection or user growth required it.

Influence

At the end of the century, in 1899, the *Library Journal* provided another comparison between the university library and the Boston Public Library. Philadelphia librarians were still showing off the university library as the best example of what a library should be while the Boston Public Library was undergoing a massive redesign as it attempted to make the building work for its various purposes.[78] In 1902, the *Architectural Review* published an issue devoted entirely to libraries. It opened with Charles Soule's article "Modern Library Buildings," which began with an illustration of Domenico Fontana's Vatican Library and then continued back through the history of monastic libraries before returning through college libraries in Oxford and Dublin. In his survey, Soule commented favorably on Ware & Van Brunt's bookstack for Harvard, which had yet to be replaced by Horace Trumbauer's Widener Library.[79] The remainder of the journal was devoted to recent libraries but with one or two exceptions, where bookstacks were given room for expansion, the lessons of Furness's library at the University of Pennsylvania were already forgotten. Instead, nearly every library showed the influence of McKim, Mead & White's Boston Public Library and by extension, the French libraries by Henri Labrouste. Poole's complaint of a generation before, that the big libraries affected the little libraries, remained true.

Nonetheless, a careful examination of the various plans shows that some of the university's library lessons had survived. In several instances bookstacks were placed at the rear of classical fronts in locations that would permit them to expand as needed. Examples included Stone, Carpenter & Wilson's Providence Public Library, which could expand into its rear yard, as could the stubby rear bookstack wings of Ferry & Class's Wisconsin Historical Society in Madison. For Newark, New Jersey's Free Public Library, Philadelphians Rankin & Kellogg devised a bookstack structure that was separated from the Renaissance main block and with the book catalog immediately accessible at the entrance. In the main, however, library architecture had been taken over by the classical box. The clear logic of Furness's, Winsor's, and Dewey's plan was lost until the free designs of the modern movement reappeared after World War II. Even Louis Kahn's library at Phillips Exeter Academy, designed while his teaching studio was in the upstairs auditorium of Furness's library, remembered his own Beaux Arts training at Penn by referring to Labrouste's Bibliothèque Ste. Geneviève scheme—a cubic volume incapable of expansion, with the tiny scholars' windows of the Paris building remembered in the tiny windows at each carrel in the upper levels. On the other hand the airy open core at Exeter, spanned by concrete beams, was certainly a reference to the vast volume of the reading room of the Penn library, which had yet to be subdivided when Kahn had studied there as an undergraduate. Most telling, when Penn's library was lovingly restored by Venturi, Scott Brown and Associates in the late 1980s, and the great reading room was reopened to its full height, the spaces that Furness had designed to serve the entire university remained well suited to serve as a modern library for the fine arts school, whose numbers were similar to those of the university of a century before.

Furness in the 1890s

Because the Civil War generation of engineers and industrialists remained in control of Philadelphia's institutions, directed its industries, and controlled the conversation of the city, the connection between industry and architecture remained strong. In 1889 Furness won the competition for the Bryn Mawr Hotel, on a site near the homes of many of his industrial clients, in the heart of the Main Line of the Pennsylvania Railroad. Instead of the conventional historical references that dominated hotel design in the national architectural journals, Furness tied the hotel to the railroad's industrial culture, combining an industrial palette from regional factory walls of rough stone with brick arched window heads, juxtaposed against the structural steel armature. Exposed massive riveted steel columns demand attention at all the entrances, the porte cochere, the front entrance hall, and the lobby (Figure 69). As in the library, the main stair rises from the lobby, carried on exposed steel stringers and steel girders (Figure 70). Once again it was a Philadelphia industrial version of a grand stair, not overlaid with plaster moldings, but with riveted steel frankly expressing the means of construction.[80] A year later, with the backing of A. J. Cassatt, who was soon to return to the Pennsylvania Railroad as its president, the Furness office added the new buildings of the Merion Cricket Club to the Montgomery Avenue row of civic institutions of the Main Line. While the hotel now functions as a school, the clubhouse still functions as the heart of its community, with its green lawn tennis courts setting off the red brick and terra cotta façade of the main building.

Figure 69 Historical photograph of the Bryn Mawr Hotel lobby (now the Baldwin School). Riveted steel columns can be seen on the left framing the stair. *Illustrated American* 8, no. 89 (October 31, 1891).

Figure 70 Stairs of the Bryn Mawr Hotel with exposed steel girders. Photograph by George E. Thomas, 2011.

The hotel was the first in a line of Furness-designed projects for the Pennsylvania Railroad leading three years later to the commission for the enlargement of the Pennsylvania Railroad's downtown terminal (Figure 71), across the street from the still rising City Hall. Furness's victory in a competition that included his Philadelphia rivals Wilson Brothers could still get the creative juices flowing. His brother Horace's account in the summer of 1892 to his daughter Caroline captured the moment:

> The next important item is the extreme content of your Uncle Frank over his appointment as architect of the Broad Street Station. 'Tis an enormous "job" estimated to cost about a million dollars and will closely occupy him for two years at least. The way in which he received the appointment, by a unanimous vote on the first ballot, was eminently soul-satisfying. He learned the good news last Monday at four o' clock. He came at once to Idlewild [his summer house near Media and close to Horace's Lindenshade] and he and Fanny drove instantly to tell us. We were at tea and I was summoned to the bow window where I found Fanny almost bursting with smiles and joyousness and your Uncle Frank wildly waving a handkerchief fastened to the whip.[81]

Like the library, the station was in two parts, an office tower toward City Hall, followed by a vast train shed, the largest in the world, designed in collaboration with his rivals, Wilson Brothers. Using a "wheeled timber traveler" designed by Wilson Brothers, the new train shed was a constructive tour de force that was built over the existing low-roofed sheds of the 1880 building, enabling the shelters to remain in service during the construction. The front terminal building and the architectural frame of the train shed were Furness's tasks. Furness accented the shed at each of the giant trusses with Gothic aedicules adorned with giant terra cotta panels by sculptor Karl Bitter that represented the great depots of the Pennsylvania empire, Philadelphia, Pittsburgh, St. Louis, and Chicago.

The headhouse of the terminal consolidated the offices of the railroad above the concourse and the passenger amenities. Here Furness wrapped the east end of the train shed with a monumental brick and terra-cotta-clad, L-shaped, structure that referenced the Gothic of the original Wilson Brothers wing, but in a free manner that was clearly Furnessic rather than historic. While the details might be termed a mannered Gothic, the core of the design was about introducing light into the eight stories of offices on either side of a double-loaded corridor, and, via skylights, into the passenger concourse on the elevated train level. Unlike the case of the contemporary downtown terminal for the Philadelphia and Reading Rail-

road, which was conceived by Wilson Brothers but was detailed by a New York architect whose presence represented the New York capital that had rescued that railroad from bankruptcy, the Pennsylvania Railroad was able to capitalize its building from its own vast resources. Furness's Broad Street Station continued to epitomize the values of the engineering culture in its choice of materials (red brick and red terra cotta), in the clarity of its planning, in its expression of function with large windows marking the waiting rooms and dining rooms on the second level, in its rational location of stairs and elevators connecting passengers to the street and railroad staff to their offices.

Figure 71 Furness, Evans & Co., Broad Street Station, Pennsylvania Railroad, 1892. "America's grandest railway terminal" (New York: Miller and Moore, 1893). Courtesy of the Library of Congress.

In 1900 Furness designed a pedestrian bridge across Market Street from the elevated train level of the terminal, to a giant stair in the new ten-story Arcade Building, also by the firm. The bridge made it possible to safely exit toward the offices of the downtown, while the office portion of the building served the growing railroad staff. The Arcade Building was a tour de force of speculative creativity and institutional power. Its site was created out of little more than two parcels of land at opposite ends of the block connected by the space above the sidewalk running along Fifteenth Street; the larger portion housed the banking offices of the Commercial Trust Company, a banking house formed by the railroad executives and trustees.[82] In the previous decade Furness had brought his hard-driving colorful style to the new downtown, designing the office buildings such as the West End Trust that soared nearly three hundred feet in the air. So long as the Philadelphia Civil War generation continued to commission and their favored architects continued to design, Furness's architecture was consistent with Philadelphia's industrial culture.

The Twentieth Century: Still the "Bravest of the Brave"

As the nineteenth century turned into the twentieth, the innovative and free Victorian Gothic that had fired architects' imaginations from Maine to Florida and west to California had faded to a few embers that stood out from the gray-white ash of the limestone and plaster civic architecture of the City Beautiful Movement. Only around Philadelphia did the fires of the industrial age still burn brightly, but nowhere so brightly as in the complex of station, office, and freight station of the Pennsylvania Railroad's Wilmington Division that the Furness office designed in the heart of downtown Wilmington, Delaware. This last major project of the firm in Furness's lifetime was part of a vast scheme directed by the Pennsylvania Railroad's new president, Alexander Cassatt (1839–1906). Trained as an engineer, Cassatt had risen through the ranks of the railroad, reaching the rank of first vice president in 1880. Two years later, when he might have been on the brink of presiding over the entire railroad, he resigned his position, turning to a career in finance that, over the next seventeen years, took him to Paris and New York. When he was persuaded to take the presidency of the Pennsylvania Railroad in 1899, he recognized that the company needed to not only transform its finances and its physical facilities but also its identity. Using the knowledge that he had gained in the financial markets, Cassatt proposed to create 2,966,000 new shares of railroad stock at the market rate of $50 per share, which would create nearly $150 million in capital—equivalent to billions of today's dollars. Instead of a windfall to stockholders, the new capital would be used to rebuild the Pennsylvania Railroad's by then aging infrastructure. The Pennsylvania Railroad's annual report for 1902 outlined Cassatt's vision. Tunnels under the Hudson River would connect the railroad directly to midtown Manhattan, where a new terminal would be constructed; tunnels under the East River would connect the railroad to Brooklyn and the vast suburbs of Long Island. Railroad consolidation in the corridor between Philadelphia and Washington, D.C., and along the western route to Chicago would result in new union terminals in Washington, Pittsburgh, and Chicago. Along its routes through urban centers, rail grade crossings would be eliminated by elevating or depressing rail lines to prevent collisions and to hasten rail traffic.[83]

In the previous generation Cassatt had commissioned Furness's firm for his in-town and country houses and had funded Furness designs at Haverford College and the Merion Cricket Club and therefore might have been expected to use Furness again for the great plums of the expansion, the railroad terminals.[84] He did not. With his cosmopolitan experiences in London, Paris, and New York, Cassatt had as his goal the transformation of the identity of his railroad away from the industrial culture of Philadelphia to the national corporate mode embodied in the modern Beaux Arts. New York's Penn Station was designed by McKim, Mead & White; Washington's Union Station, Pittsburgh's Union Station, and Chicago's Union Station were the work of the master corporate architect of the era, Daniel H. Burnham of Chicago.[85] Because Wilmington remained a part of Philadelphia's cultural turf, Cassatt appointed Furness, Evans & Co. as the architects for the Pennsylvania Railroad's new station, a related freight depot, and the district office building.[86]

The Wilmington project was announced in 1900 but got under way in earnest in 1902 with the creation of a new railroad, the Philadelphia, Baltimore and Washington Railroad Company. That it was entirely owned by the Pennsylvania Railroad was evident from its directors including Cassatt and longtime board member William Sellers, who was immediately elevated to the chairmanship of the board.[87] A year before, the Pennsylvania Railroad formed the Wilmington Terminal Corporation to manage the construction of the offices and new station as well as the elevated tracks through the city. The first phase of the project was the flaming red brick and terra cotta office building that was under way in 1904 and completed in 1905.[88] The new station in the same palette of materials presented significant difficulties. Most obvious was the new massive stone and steel railroad viaduct carrying the main passenger lines between Philadelphia and Washington, D.C., which sliced through the site, creating a situation not unlike that which confronted Rem Koolhaas in his recent design for the Illinois Institute of Technology College Center. While Koolhaas's building flows under the tracks to link two zones of the campus, its central purpose is not connections with the tracks above, which of course was the point of the new Wilmington station. For the B&O Station at Chestnut Street in Philadelphia Furness had designed the station above and alongside the grade-level tracks. At Wilmington Furness reversed the design with the concourse placed directly under the tracks and connecting by stairs up to the north and southbound platforms (Plate 32).

The results were brilliant. Instead of the usual dark, narrow, subterranean tunnel connecting the two sides of a through station, Furness created a vast well-lighted room whose ceiling was a dense lattice of massive steel beams that carried the railroad overhead (Figure 72). The riveted beams of the ceiling resonate with the power of the industrial age in a memorable synthesis of sound and form, as great locomotives hauling high-speed passenger trains and heavily loaded freight cars rumble above. Decorative stairs with cast iron risers and steel treads carried on steel stringers connect to extended passenger platforms (Plate 33). These are sheltered by canopies carried on exposed steel posts and with a cornice along the tracks made of small steel pieces like the lattice frame of Joseph Wilson's Centennial Station of three decades before (Figure 73). With the station's steel canopies and brilliant red brick and red terra cotta façades, and red tiled roofs,

Figure 72 Detail of Wilmington Station main terminal ceiling; the riveted metal beams support the train tracks above. Photograph by Lewis Tanner, 2011.

Figure 73 Detail of ironwork on the porte cochère at Wilmington Station. Photograph by Lewis Tanner, 2011.

there was no doubt that Wilmington was linked to industrial Philadelphia's identity (Plate 34). While architects across the rest of the nation had adopted the whited sepulchers of the Beaux Arts, into the twentieth century, Philadelphians—at least those who still hired Furness—were comfortable with industrial brick and exposed structural steel and iron as the material expression of the factual and progressive culture that they had created.

There is one other point. Despite the modernity of the Furness inflection toward the machine and to new sources and methods of design, the façade of the station is still Victorian in the physicality and expression of load-bearing weight. In the end, from his training in the Hunt studio, Furness was a product of the Stone Age. Even when his Philadelphia clients and builders led him toward the use of modern steel, the proportions and forms that were most natural to him were rooted in the lithic construction that he had learned from Hunt. This can be seen in the slight curve of the base of the steel beams spanning the north reading room of the university library and it can be seen in Furness's comfort with the dense mass of steel beams that form the ceiling of the waiting room of the Wilmington station. Unlike Wilson Brothers, who grasped the transformative potential of minimal steel structures to make the shift from mass to space, Furness's architecture was informed by masonry in the limited sizes of openings, the density of its walls, and his ongoing expression of the drama of weight. To fully read Furness, it is necessary to see both the Victorian weightiness and the artistry that Frank Lloyd Wright saw when he visited the university library in the 1950s. No architect can fully break free of his time and Furness was no different. He remained a Victorian to the end, but insofar as he brought the values of the engineering culture to planning and materials, and further, turned his aim toward a future unencumbered by overt historical references, he opened the course of the future.

Five years after completing the Wilmington project, Frank died. His brother Horace mourned him even as he welcomed the end to "a tedious, wearisome illness, so distressing that his release was a blessing. He left a noble record. He served in the Cavalry throughout our Civil War, and received the highest honour a soldier in this country can attain to:—a medal from the U.S. Congress at Washington for 'distinguished bravery.' Very, very few have ever received it. It stamped him as the bravest of the brave."[89] The "bravest of the brave" makes a good epitaph for Frank Furness. Beginning with the Pennsylvania Academy of the Fine Arts, the Jefferson Hospital, and the great banks of Chestnut Street and continuing through the university library to the Wilmington train station in the twentieth century, Furness's best designs embody a type of courage that a century later makes him stand out in his profession. Ever since Furness and his peer innovators broke with slow-to-evolve vernacular forms to incorporate new materials and to create new construction systems, architecture has been an experiment, one that requires architects and clients who are committed to solving contemporary problems in a contemporary way, using the materials of their industrial and modern times, finding forms and plans that best serve new purposes. By these means Furness served a culture of innovators who were secure in their values and beliefs. In a global age, interconnected by media, this becomes more difficult as architecture is increasingly judged against a conservative cultural frame that presumes the value of history over the possibilities of original design. It is the rare architect—Frank Furness, Louis Sullivan, William Price, George Howe, Robert Venturi and Denise Scott Brown, Rem Koolhaas, or Frank Gehry—who risks the ridicule of traditionalists to express the poetry of the present of the world in which they live and work. However, as long as there are clients who face the future, there will be those who will demand architecture reflective of their interests and values. In this sense, the architecture that Furness created for the engineering-centered ecology of Philadelphia was representative of the freedoms created in the regional industrial culture that arose from the Franklin Institute and then was transferred to the great railroads and industries of the post–Civil War generation. His best architecture riffed on the possibilities of its time, incorporating the new materials, new technologies, and new plans and forms in ways that have embodied the best of modern design ever since.

EPILOGUE

SULLIVAN, PRICE, AND HOWE

The birthplace of modern architecture, that is to say, of revolutionary ahistorical design, is usually placed in the Berlin office of Peter Behrens (1868–1940). There, beginning in 1907, Behrens employed several of the young men who, over the next generation, would do much to shape the familiar narrative of European modernism: Walter Gropius, who worked for Behrens between 1907 and 1910; Ludwig Mies van der Rohe, who arrived in 1908 and left with Gropius in 1910; and Charles-Édouard Jeanneret (Le Corbusier), who arrived as the others were leaving in 1910 and departed the following year. The students trained by Behrens—some for little more than a few months, others for a couple of years—followed strands of his interests in applying the discipline of industrial production to the problem of contemporary design. Behrens, however, was not the first to create such an extraordinary triumvirate of students. A third of a century before, beginning in the early 1870s, Frank Furness influenced a line of students, first Louis Sullivan, then William Price, and finally George Howe, who, together, laid the groundwork for much that has been credited to Behrens.

A comparison between Furness's seminal building, the Pennsylvania Academy of the Fine Arts, and the AEG Turbine Plant designed by Behrens is revealing (Figures 74 and 75). Both buildings reflect the underlying heritage of classical architecture that, after a century of close study of classical orders as the basis for architectural education, was buried deep in the subconscious of most architects. Furness linked the Academy to the iconography of high culture by incor-

Figure 74 Stamp honoring Frank Furness and the Pennsylvania Academy of the Fine Arts, issued 1980. Courtesy of the United States Postal Service.

Figure 75 Stamp depicting the AEG Turbine factory, designed by Peter Behrens, 1928, Berlin.

porating remnants of the classical frieze of Greek architecture across the upper level of the main façade and by drawing on the proportions and rhythms of Second Empire classicism that he had learned from Richard Morris Hunt. Behrens used the classical proportions and muscularity of Greek temples for the iconic façade of the AEG building. There was, however, a critical difference between the two buildings. Behrens was, after all, designing a factory while Furness was bringing the logic of industrial architecture and the machine to a museum and a school.

The connection between Furness's method and the American roots of modern design came into sharper focus in 1930, when George Howe, then deep into the project that would become his masterpiece, the bank and office tower for the Philadelphia Savings Fund Society, posed and answered the question "What Is This Modern Architecture Trying to Express?"[1]

In that year, Howe had reached a critical breakthrough in his own career. He had been a partner in the Furness office for nearly four years before departing for military service in World War I. Just before the United States entered the war, Howe had joined the firm of Mellor & Meigs which became Mellor, Meigs & Howe. There, for a decade, he designed Norman farmhouse–styled mansions in what he called "Wall Street Pastoral"; college buildings such as Bryn Mawr College's Goodhart Hall, which could have been a Hollywood stage set for a medieval romance, but was never very good as an auditorium; and commercial structures including the branch offices for the Philadelphia Savings Fund Society that harkened back to classical forms. Dissatisfied with the lack of a theoretical frame for his work, and, as William Price had done at the same point in his life when he reached the midlife point of forty years, Howe turned toward the future, leaving his partnership to form a new firm that would undertake work in a contemporary manner. In six years between 1929 and 1935, as the lead partner with Swiss architect William Lescaze in the firm of Howe & Lescaze, and then for a generation in association with other young Philadelphia architects including Louis Kahn, Howe returned to the core values of the industrial culture that he had absorbed in his first years of practice in the office of Frank Furness.

Howe & Lescaze's first scheme for the office building for the Philadelphia Savings Fund Society was a conventional modernistic shaft crowned by a great orb that was not far removed from the sleek New York skyscrapers of the era. "Iced" with details, it harkened back to Raymond Hood's winning design in the *Chicago Tribune* competition of eight years earlier and ultimately to William Price's presciently modern Traymore Hotel of 1914–1915. The final scheme eliminated all conventional ornament to simply give plastic and material expression to the tasks of the building. A new type of functional beauty would be derived from the proportional relations of the parts, the animating and energetic expression of purpose through the architectural devices of form and fenestration, and the beauty of materials sharpened by the rich hues of stone, polished to a mirror finish, that reflected the moving clouds and the city around it.

The building derived its value from the site's proximity to City Hall, both downtown train stations, and the subway along Market Street. At street level, the commercial first floor consisted of giant plate glass show windows, reaching almost to the ground, that were framed in glittering minimalist stainless steel bands. The spacious second-floor banking room was lighted by immense industrial steel windows and was easily accessible by an escalator from the Market Street entrance. Bank offices were located directly above the banking room, in a continuation of the dark stone-clad base. Above the banking spaces was a shaft of rental offices entered via a separate lobby on Twelfth Street. That zone was faced in cool gray brick panels separated by limestone-clad piers. The tower rose to a crowning conference room, for the bank officers, that provided dramatic views of the city; the roof level was topped by a giant radio antenna and the iconic angled blue sign emblazoned with the bank's initials, "PSFS." Outlined in neon against graphically modern lettering, these elements complemented the overall design and together expressed the contemporary commercial and technological worlds that Howe had embraced. The design for PSFS was Howe's answer to his question of 1930 and a powerful statement of principle for the American movement toward modern architecture.

In his essay on modern design, Howe differentiated between typical surface decoration, derived from the fashion of the moment, and his own goals for an art that had the capacity to reveal the essence of its time: "It follows that modern architecture has very little to do with what is generally understood as modern decoration, which is for the moment the product of individual fancy, untrammeled by basic restraints, and as variable and unimportant as the length of a woman's skirt. Fashion may change with the quarterly dividend, but the fundamental principles of architecture remain unalterable."

Howe continued with a thumbnail history of those Americans who had led the movement toward modern design. Instead of connecting to the familiar cluster of European post–World War I theorists, Howe made the startling assertion that its roots were to be found in the works of a group of American architects of the previous generation: "America has always been the land of lone prophets without much but posthumous honor in their own country, which has been too busily engaged in exploiting its vast resources to take much interest in the spiritual consequences of its art, and [Frank Lloyd] Wright, [Louis] Sullivan and [William L.] Price were among the first to grasp the architectural possibilities of the new life and the new means of construction. Their names were known in Europe while they remained comparatively obscure among their countrymen."[2] These Americans formed a genealogy that Howe clearly intended as his own. He, Sullivan, and Price shared a common experience—early training in the office of Frank Furness.

Louis Sullivan was an obvious choice for Howe's genealogy because Sullivan's recently completed *Autobiography of an Idea* (1924) made the connection between his experiences in Furness's office and his insights into architecture. Sullivan's narrative captured the transfer of allegiance from history to modernity, expressed as the idea of Furness making "buildings out of his head." Sullivan's aphorism "form ever follows function" was a direct expression of the values of the industrial culture that had found expression in the work of his teacher,

Frank Furness. William L. Price, also mentioned by Howe, had followed Sullivan into the Furness office five years later, entering in 1878 and working there for a year or so.[3] Like Sullivan's first projects, Price's early independent works paid the homage of direct imitation to Furness following the formal vocabulary of functional expression learned during his time there. In the 1890s Price turned to historical sources in the manner of most of his contemporaries. At midcareer, impelled by the opportunities of new construction materials and the aura of the twentieth century, he returned to the core values of Furness's methods. Price explored the possibilities of modernity in modest ahistorical houses that he built for his experiments in communal living in Rose Valley, Pennsylvania, and Arden, Delaware, and in massive reinforced concrete hotels and railroad buildings that reflected the impact of the growing mass culture and the new structural materials of his age that were part of the region's modern identity.[4] Price's practice like Furness's spanned the territory of the Pennsylvania Railroad from the Atlantic Coast to the Midwest and carried the lamp of ahistorical design forward to the beginnings of World War I. His Traymore Hotel in Atlantic City with its tapering forms and setback upper stories was chosen to represent American modern design in an exhibit sponsored by the American Institute of Architects that was shown across Europe after World War I.[5] It continued to be cited as an example of the best of American modern design into the 1930s.[6]

Howe would have also been well aware of Price's importance in developing the forms and vocabulary of American modernism because his successor firm, under the leadership of the former head draftsman, Ralph Bencker, remained a major force in Philadelphia design, continuing to work in an overtly modern manner long after Price's death in 1916. In the mid-1920s, Bencker was awarded the commission for the modernist Pennsylvania State Building for the Sesquicentennial and, as Howe was writing his essay, Bencker had just finished designing the skyscraper for the offices of N. W. Ayer & Co., the nation's premier advertising agency, on Washington Square near Independence Hall. Moreover, Bencker was simultaneously designing the iconic hypermodernist Automat buildings that established the regional identity of the nation's first fast food empire, the Horn and Hardart Company, from New York to Washington, D.C.

Frank Lloyd Wright (1867–1959) was the outlier of Howe's lineage of American modernism in that he had not directly studied with Furness, but he was connected to the genealogy as Sullivan's pupil and recognized his debt to Furness as well. Wright certainly met Furness during the latter's extensive visit to Chicago in 1892, when Furness was commissioned by the U.S. government to evaluate the buildings of the Columbian Exposition then rising on the marshes of Jackson Park.[7] In that role, Furness would have visited the Sullivan office in its aerie in the Auditorium Building's tower, where Wright was working as head draftsman. A quarter of a century after being included in Howe's trio of modernists, Wright visited Philadelphia while designing Beth Sholom Synagogue in Elkins Park, which, in its expressionistic, truncated, pyramidal form alluded to Mount Sinai while its materiality and crocketed ridges could be directly connected to the bristling mechanistic details of Furness's works that had passed to Wright via his years with Sullivan. In conversations with Beaux Arts–trained Alfred Bendiner (1899–1964), Wright remembered anecdotes Sullivan had told him about Furness and praised the University of Pennsylvania Library (Figure 76), which he saw not as an aging Victorian relic but as "the work of an artist."[8] Sullivan, Price, and Wright offered three distinct but related architectural responses to the industrial age in the United States and all came in one way or another from the Furness office. Howe's selections for an American genealogy were clearly not by

Figure 76 Alfred Bendiner, "The University of Pennsylvania Library." Courtesy of the Architectural Archives, University of Pennsylvania.

chance. Ironically the historical narrative that he proposed went unheard, leaving the field to the now standard narrative of European innovation peripherally connected to Chicago. As Howe was writing his essay Henry Russell Hitchcock and Philip Johnson were developing their International Style thesis that rejected the American cultural frames of economy of means rooted in the engineer's incorporation of new materials and systems in the service of flamboyance of expression of identity and purpose. Their shotgun marriage of the streams of modernism excluded Frank Lloyd Wright in large measure because he represented neither the social goals of European modernism, intent on demolishing the social order that had produced World War I, nor the ascetic simplification that affirmed modern production methods at the expense of individuality.

The Criticism

Furness's experience anticipated the future rejection of the American contribution to modern design. Despite his unequalled record of success across the heart of the industrialized nation from the New Jersey side of the Hudson River, south to Washington, D.C., and west beyond Pittsburgh, from the 1880s his designs were largely excluded from the national architectural press, and by the 1890s he was under attack by critics from New York and Boston who aimed their broadsides at his methods and results. Insofar as the nineteenth century was a battle between innovation and tradition, Furness's architecture was attacked by advocates for historical norms and traditional architectural strategies. In 1893 Montgomery Schuyler, the critic for *The Architectural Record*, only avoided a direct criticism of Furness in his essay "Architectural Aberrations—the Hale Building" by using the euphemism "Chestnut Street" as a veiled reference to Furness's highly original banks and commercial buildings in Philadelphia's downtown.[9] Nearly a decade later in 1902 Bostonian Ralph Adams Cram blasted him specifically when he targeted the "Furnissic Revolt" that was at the core of what he described as the "Philadelphia reign of architectural terror."[10] Later in the same decade, Schuyler eviscerated the University of Pennsylvania Library in his article on the university campus, which in turn led a member of the university's architectural faculty to characterize Furness's design for Penn's library as a "fortified greenhouse than which nothing more grotesque can be imagined."[11] The rage of the national press against Furness and his works suggests that more was at stake than simple allegiance to a school or style. Clearly Furness's designs were incomprehensible to critics from other American cities and eventually even to those from his own city, striking a nerve for their rejection of norms, that to Schuyler, Cram, and their peers underlay proper architecture.

When Frank Furness died in the summer of 1912 the regional architectural profession, with the notable exception of his own pupils, had reverted to the national norms with a Beaux Arts–trained dean heading the University of Pennsylvania's architecture program. In this context Furness's buildings were incomprehensible to obituary writers in his native city who referred to his youthful heroism as a cavalry officer in the Civil War but largely ignored his life's work as an architect.[12] In the 1930s, when the successor office, Furness, Casey & Kleinfelder, finally closed its doors, the firm's ink-on-linen drawings were of so little interest that they were thrown out with the trash. Out of step, first with the new historicism and Beaux Arts classicism of the late nineteenth century, then with the streamlined elegance of Art Deco, and finally with the minimal aesthetic of European international modernism, Furness's often astonishing architecture was forgotten. By the 1950s, just as his career was being rediscovered as a Philadelphia antecedent to modern design, his best buildings were being smashed by the wrecker's iron ball.

Context matters. Viewed against the light hues and soaring spires of the jazz age and later the white abstract planes of modern designs, Furness's dark, top-heavy, and complicated buildings were relics from a distant and in many ways alien past, seemingly as irrelevant as a Victorian bustle or a penny-farthing bicycle. However, to anyone looking beyond the self-imposed boundaries of high architecture, Furness was profoundly relevant. Even Cram glimpsed in Furness "a live American" rather than a "dead archaeologist," while New Yorker Lewis Mumford, a generation later, praised Furness for his "bold, unabashed, ugly, and yet somehow healthily pregnant architecture."[13] Neither critic grasped the intention of Furness's original approach to design, but they did sense an original approach that was more about the American nation, its experiences, and the dramatic changes that were remaking its civilization than the borrowed forms from history that typified the architecture of the day.

Thorsten Veblen on the Culture of Business

The focus of the critics and later the historians on norms and conventions missed the big story—the effects of the conflict between the rising engineering-based work cultures and the parallel corporate transactional culture. This formed an obvious topic for midwestern sociologist Thorsten Veblen. In *The Theory of Busi-*

ness Enterprise (1904) Veblen observed that the new culture arising in industry and mechanical and technical innovation led to different attitudes toward process and above all resulted in a different attitude toward the past and old cultural forms. Three generations before, Thomas Carlyle had posited a new "Mechanical Age" with dark warnings about what it might mean to old cultural forms and values.[14] Instead of fretting over the loss of stable orders, Veblen as a sociologist accepted the new culture and analyzed its effects: "The machine process gives no insight into questions of good and evil, merit and demerit, except in point of material causation . . . [through] mechanically enforced law and order as may be stated in terms of pressure, temperature, velocity, tensile strength, etc. . . . It knows neither manners or breeding and can make no use of any of the attributes of worth. Its scheme of knowledge and of inference is based on the laws of material causation, not on those of immemorial custom, authenticity, or authoritative enactment. Its metaphysical basis is the law of cause and effect."[15] As could be expected, so different a cultural frame led to "appreciable and widening differences between the habits of life of the two classes; and this carries with it a widening difference in the discipline to which the two classes [mercantile and industrial] are subjected. . . . There results a difference in the point of view, in the facts dwelt upon, in the methods of argument, in the grounds of validity appealed to . . . *so that the two classes come to have an increasing difficulty in understanding one another and appreciating one another's convictions, ideals, capacities and shortcomings*" (my emphasis).[16]

The "appreciable and widening differences" explain the demise of the new architectural culture of industrial Philadelphia and other industrial and logistical centers because the publications of the profession were centered in the historical and financial cultural capitals where the old values held. Only the *Inland Architect*, which was published in Chicago, had a taste for the new. Veblen's cultural explanation captured how and why Frank Furness's innovations were supported in his home base and why his students continued to find support through the industrial Midwest, in William Price's satellite offices in Indianapolis and Chicago, and in the work of Sullivan and Wright and their followers. The new architecture of the industrial age would not find its literary voice until Louis Sullivan, Frank Lloyd Wright, and eventually, albeit with the differing impetus of World War I, the European modernists made their case for an architecture of facts and not of nostalgia.

Leonard Eaton's analysis of Frank Lloyd Wright's clients closed by comparing the musical tastes of Chicago, which favored Wagner, to the traditional tastes of Boston, led by Harvard musicologist John Knowles Paine, who declared "that the future of music lay in the forms of Bach, Mozart, Handel, and Beethoven. In 1895 Daniel Gregory Mason, leader of the Boston school of composers, wrote in his journal, 'Thank God Wagner is dead and Brahms alive. And here's to the great classical revival of the twentieth century in America.'"[17] The future would play out in a different manner. Eaton observed that some of Wright's clients were attracted to him simply because they and he were in Oak Park, as well as because of his own "immense personal charm." Eaton noted that Wright's manner "made a special appeal to the independent, technologically minded businessman." A similar conclusion could be made of Furness's work two generations before, serving the Philadelphia industrial community. Eaton concluded by comparing the industrialist with the modern corporate manager, who was "less likely to be intimately involved in the industrial process than he was in the early twentieth century. He will probably be expert in marketing, in finance, or in some other business specialty. Hence he will lack the amazing open-mindedness which characterized so many of Wright's clients. Like H. P. Marquand's Willis Wayde, the prototype of the contemporary corporate tycoon, he will live in a traditional mansion and collect antique furniture."[18]

Furness's clients, like Wright's, were self-made, open-minded, innovators who were focused on the future rather than the past, members of "liberal" religions, and for the moment they intended to assert their own identity in a time of rapid cultural change. If Coleman Sellers explained the engineers' culture of innovation that expected new forms to meet new purposes, Thorsten Veblen provided an explanation for the conflict between the modern industrialist and those guided by "immemorial custom, authenticity, or authoritative enactment."

Sullivan's Experience

When Louis Sullivan arrived at Furness's office in the spring of 1873, the rise of the new industrial culture was evident across Philadelphia but its challenge to the old cultural centers was yet to be perceived. Furness's impact on Sullivan can be gauged from the future Chicagoan's appropriation of details and motifs from the cluster of his mentor's Neo-Grec, machine-aesthetic-influenced domestic commissions in the Rittenhouse neighborhood. These certainly included the row of yellow-sandstone-fronted houses on the 2100 block of Spruce Street and the Bloomfield Moore house that was nearing completion on South Broad Street. This last was the most completely decorated and fully formed of the Furness projects, with a striking polychromed exterior and a fully developed interior that was richly overlaid with carved, incised, and painted detail. Unfortunately, there are no known images of the Broad Street façade of the house, though Sullivan's account of it, "like a flower by the roadside," suggests an array of Furness's typical floral ornaments of the period.[19] Just as we may hear snatches of the office conversation in the writings of Sullivan and Price perhaps we can find aspects of the demolished Moore house in Sullivan's early Chicago domestic work, particularly the Blumenfeld Flats of 1884.

The interior views of the Moore house show a horror vacui design that attracted the decoratively minded Sullivan. Most of these elements were carefully drawn and modeled in Furness's sketchbooks, attesting both to his skill as a renderer and the personal attention that went into the most important projects. The dining room was accented by a stenciled ceiling band and featured a mantel, supported on each side by carved figures of herons spearing fish, which were detailed in the notebooks. Indeed, edible creatures and predators devouring them formed an ongoing theme of many contemporary Furness-designed dining rooms, celebrating the myriad confusions of family life—perhaps a reminder of Furness's own family experience, with children and dogs running around underfoot. Stylized rabbits, lobsters, and other game inlaid in dark walnut under a light wood field embellished the paneling that Furness designed for the dining room in Horace's Washington Square house.[20] He did similar work for the interior of the New York home of Theodore Roosevelt, Sr. There cartoonish lobsters graced the dining room paneling and herons spearing frogs formed the braced legs of the great dining table.[21] Tellingly all of these projects were under construction while Sullivan was in the office and affected his earliest independent designs.

In comparison with the later students, Sullivan was in the office during the period of its most lush ornamentation as Furness combined the richness and plasticity of late Second Empire ornament with the geometry of the Neo-Grec. It is this decorative impulse and the will to make buildings without reference to history that Sullivan learned from Furness and that he revisited in his last commissions in the twentieth-century banks of the American Midwest. Nowhere was Sullivan's affection for Furness more obvious than in the group of drawings that he carefully shepherded from his time in Philadelphia and passed on to Frank Lloyd Wright, who, in turn, donated then to Columbia University's Avery Architectural Library.[22] As evidenced by the drawings, Sullivan absorbed the Furness ornamental style in all of its manifestations, from cartoonish whimsies that could be incised by steam-powered sand-blasting in William Struthers's stone yard to carefully drawn natural studies that, in turn, could be brought to life as a three-dimensional element that enlivened a façade.

The second design strategy that influenced Sullivan was the way Furness fused Victorian Gothic and Neo Grec elements to create a potent, hybrid American manner, as exemplified in buildings such as the Pennsylvania Academy of the Fine Arts and the Guarantee Trust and Savings Deposit Company offices. Furness's first explorations of this mode had been generally monochromatic, as in the Northern Savings Fund and Safe Deposit Company building on Spring Garden Street. By 1873, when Sullivan was in the office, Furness had countered the previous year's strategy with full-blown polychromy conveyed by strident contrasts of stone and brick. The sandstones were sawn into smooth surfaces that could carry drilled, incised, and sand-blasted ornament or they could be strongly shaped into rough hammered textures while the brick could carry an array of diagonal and vertical patterns. The results were compelling architectural drama that made any building touched by the Furness firm stand out.

While in Philadelphia Sullivan certainly would have seen the recently completed Philadelphia Warehouse Company building on Dock Street (Figure 77), one of Furness's strongest early projects. Its stylized and out-of-scale acroterion breaking through the cornice and its main entrance on a beveled façade gave a robust presence to an otherwise small building. As was common in a Furness building of the period, all the surfaces were designed to catch the eye, in the light-catching planes of the façade, the bold textures at the foundation, or the delicate and repetitive ornaments at the top, as on both the Academy and the nearly complete Guarantee Trust and Safe Deposit building. The giant acroterion above the entrance was incorporated nearly whole cloth into several Sullivan designs including the 1884 Ann Halsted Row (Figure 78) and the Leon Mannheimer residence (Figure 79).[23] Clearly Sullivan absorbed what Furness was doing at both the tiny scale of detail drawings and at the larger scales of building details and forms.

The economic crash in the fall of 1873, which forced Furness to let Sullivan go, gave the youth the opportunity to gain additional education. Perhaps he heard Furness long for the missed opportunity of the École des Beaux Arts, which he had given up to serve in the Civil War and then as he settled into his marriage.[24] Though as Sullivan remembered, Furness had little patience with schools as a source of training, Furness's account of his study with Hunt and Hunt's training at the École would have made Paris a reasonable goal for Sullivan. Before going to Paris, Sullivan visited his family in its new Chicago home. While there he worked for six months in the office of engineer William LeBaron Jenney, who was riding the wave of reconstruction work across the burnt area of the city. He spent roughly the same amount of time with Jenney that he had

Figure 77 Furness & Hewitt,
Philadelphia Warehouse
Company, 1872. *Portfolio of the
Philadelphia Sketch Club*, vol. 1
(Philadelphia: Taylor & Smith,
1874).

Figure 78 Adler & Sullivan, Ann Halsted Townhouses, Chicago, 1884. Elevation drawing, Whayne Griffen, 1967. Courtesy of the Library of Congress, Prints & Photographs Division, HABS, HABS Chicago Project IV–1967.

Figure 79 Adler & Sullivan, Leon Mannheimer house, Chicago, 1884. Photograph by George E. Thomas, 2015.

spent in the Furness office, but the effect on Sullivan was drastically different. Where he was grateful to Furness for "his entry into the practical world in an office where standards were so high—where talent was so manifestly taken for granted, and the atmosphere the free and easy one of a true workshop savoring of the guild where craftsmanship was paramount and personal," he had a dreary time with Jenney, who was more interested in being a clubman than an artist and whose office was more about production than ideas and aesthetics.[25] Despite the years of work that the Chicago fire ensured, Sullivan left Jenney and returned east to cross the Atlantic to Paris. Perhaps he passed through Philadelphia on his way and saw the fruits of his efforts with the completed Guarantee Trust and the Academy under roof or he may have seen these buildings on his return trip to the west in the late spring of 1875 after his year at the École.[26]

After Paris when Sullivan returned to Chicago, he gradually gained the confidence of Dankmar Adler, with whom he would partner for some fifteen years. Sullivan's hand was immediately apparent because he brought to Chicago the decorative strategies that had characterized the Furness office in Philadelphia before the Centennial. In an age when travel was arduous and with only one architectural journal of consequence in the nation, borrowing from a distant source was less likely to be noticed, though anyone who had visited Philadelphia for the Centennial could not have missed the points of similarity between Sullivan's efforts and those of his mentor. In his first decade in Chicago, Sullivan incorporated Furness's design ideas at both the scale of the building and at the level of ornamental detail. This fealty is obvious in Sullivan's Zion Temple of 1885, which owed much to Furness's Rodef Shalom Synagogue of 1868–1869 (see Figure 15). The horseshoe arches over the doors on either side of the central block, the clustered groups of small arcaded windows above the doors, the finishing onion domes atop the towers, and the ecclesiastical rose window in the center of the façade are all found on both buildings.

Sullivan's closest surviving approximation of Furness's early method is the Jewelers Building of 1881, which directly continued his mentor's strategy of strident discontinuities of architectural polychromy with panels of yellow sandstone interrupting brick piers (see Figure 7). Crisply drilled or sandblasted ornament accents the yellow sandstone, again recalling the details Furness used in the Guarantee Trust (see Figure 9), the Academy, and the Philadelphia Warehouse Company building. Here, in the cacophony of State Street, in another commercial-industrial center, the point of the design was to stand out, to catch the eye, to elbow its neighbors out of the way, just as it had been for Furness's Chestnut Street banks. From Furness, Sullivan learned to juxtapose harsh contrasts of hue and tone with eye-catching ornament to beguile the senses if attention wandered. Every aspect of the Jewelers Building has direct roots in what Sullivan saw in Philadelphia. As Sullivan began to create his own architectural identity, his domestic projects sometimes showed hints of the designs of the Englishman R. Norman Shaw, together with bits of the Victorian Queen Anne, but until Henry Hobson Richardson's Glessner House and the Marshall Field Wholesale Store were under way in Chicago, Furness remained his central resource. In Frank Furness's office, Sullivan had learned the logic of the plan, the power of identity, the value of a personal ornamental style, and the expression of the forces and materials of modern life, ideas that reappeared in the Midwestern banks of the early twentieth century.[27]

William L. Price's Experience

In 1878, after training in the office of fellow Quaker and Furness's rival Addison Hutton, William Lightfoot Price entered Furness's office at the moment when the construction of his early commercial masterpiece, the Provident Life and Trust offices, was under way.[28] Price's father was an officer in the company's life insurance division and presumably used that connection to place his sons, Francis (who after working for Furness called himself Frank) and William, in the Furness office. William Price was two years older than Sullivan had been when he joined the office, but he was equally receptive to the ideas and values that Furness presented. Furness was everything that Will Price's first teacher, Addison Hutton, and his Quaker ancestors were not—colorful, expressive, and, as we have seen, convinced of the power of architecture to communicate the forces of modern life. The office was still in the same rooms at Third and Chestnut where Sullivan had worked, but it was a very different office. Both of the Hewitts—George with his pincers, collecting the Gothic bits for his more historicizing designs, and William, misremembered as "John" by Sullivan, who had taught Sullivan "touch" in drawing—had departed in 1875, making the office entirely Furness's tool. Instead of serving two masters, it now served one. When Will Price arrived, Henry Pettit was off in Europe supervising the American exhibits for the 1878 French Exhibition Universelle. Allen Evans would have been a new but decidedly secondary force in the office.[29] He had worked for Samuel Sloan and joined the Furness office as a draftsman shortly after the departure of the Hewitt brothers. Evans brought an English lifestyle as a cricket-playing clubman and, we learn from the Weygandt diaries, was a skilled furniture designer. In 1881 Evans would be elevated to partner. Around the same time Will Price left to join his older brother, Frank, in their own office.

While Price was in the office, Furness returned to simpler coloring and fewer stylistic references to either the Victorian Gothic or the neo-Grec, relying instead on strongly textured surfaces and machined forms that would have been strengthened as they accumulated the grimy patina of the Victorian city. The Provident Life and Trust was nearing completion when Price arrived and marked a high point of the Furnessic manner. This was Furness at his most strident in combining motifs that were half plant, half fortress, with giant leafy arms appearing to support the cornice while the mass of its tower projected out over the entrance like the portcullis of a medieval castle. The foreboding street presence of this relatively small building was countered by the brilliantly lighted, tile-clad interior. When Price was preparing to leave Furness's office, the three-story-high banking room of the Penn National Bank at Seventh and Market Streets, on the site where Jefferson had written the Declaration of Independence, was nearing completion (Figure 80). Like the Provident it was lighted by a giant skylight atop the building but its façade was accented with oversized, slightly elongated Palladian windows recalling the window above the tower door on Independence Hall. A generation later, in 1903, this same feature, supersized in the Furness manner, would reappear in the giant Palladian motif that formed the entire street-level façade of Price's first essay in reinforced concrete for the Jacob Reed's Sons Store on the 1400 block of Chestnut Street. From Furness, Price learned to transform the familiar by changing its scale, undermining its original meaning in the process. Similar changes of scale, like oversized and bold type in a Victorian advertisement, would enliven the architecture of Robert Venturi and Denise Scott Brown and was central to the methods of pop artists Claes Oldenburg, Roy Lichtenstein, and Andy Warhol.

Price worked in the Furness office while the firm's energy was focused on reshaping the Philadelphia and Reading Railroad's identity. Where Furness's early designs, such as his banks, conformed to the symmetrical, center-entrance typology of the day, his plans for the railroad buildings were intended to be economical and practical, even as they made evident the route through the building to the trains. The young Will Price absorbed the energy and sense of purpose embodied in these small buildings, taking with him the idea that the plan and elevation should directly describe the role of the building. Small houses in the Drexel & Co. development in Wayne on the Main Line of the Pennsylvania Railroad, and, later, the ambitious Kenilworth Inn that served the Vanderbilt empire outside of Asheville, North Carolina, demonstrate the lingering effects of the training that the Price brothers earned in the Furness office. Notably, even as the brothers grafted historical details to their buildings, the Furnessic American rootstock was still in

Figure 80 Furness & Evans, Penn
National Bank, 1882. Courtesy of
the Free Library of Philadelphia.

evidence because each use and function was given its own form and fenestration, and the logistics of use still determined the plan and the elevations. When Price eventually turned away from historicism in the early twentieth century, he did so with a memorable statement that, like Sullivan's "form ever follows function," must have come directly from the office dialog of the late 1870s. Wrote Price: "There is only one thing worse than ignoring precedent and that is following it."[30]

In 1903, Price formed a new partnership with architect and real estate entrepreneur Martin Hawley McLanahan (1865–1929) that gave him the opportunity to work at the scale of the new mass culture of the booming industrial society. Price's time in the Furness office led him to pare away the extraneous historical ornament of his 1890s work to capture the possibilities of new construction materials, particularly reinforced concrete, enabling him to build on Furness's goal of an architecture that expressed its own time and its own purpose. As an editor and frequent contributor to the *Artsman*, a journal published for several years as the voice for the Rose Valley Arts and Crafts community that he had founded in 1901, Price quoted Whitman and Ralph Waldo Emerson as the American testaments that should shape and guide the nation and its architecture. The continuity from Emerson and Whitman to Furness and on to Price was reinforced by Price's colleague in the *Artsman*, Horace Traubel, who had been Whitman's amanuensis recording the poet's every word in his last years in Camden, New Jersey.

As the twentieth century began and after a decade in the historical wilderness, Price returned to composing designs that drew on the poetry of contemporary life. Like Furness thirty years before, Price found clients who demanded an architecture that represented their world and their identity. His chief client was the Pennsylvania Railroad, which despite commissioning Beaux Arts stations in major cities was still receptive to modern designs in the industrial hinterlands. Tellingly as Philadelphia became more conservative, many of Price's most original commissions came from his satellite office in Indianapolis, which retained an industrial clientele open to new ideas and expression as the industrialists and engineers of Philadelphia had been a generation earlier. A decade later, the same Indianapolis clients would take Price's firm south to their automobile resort in Miami Beach, where Price's American modern style was incorporated into the Aquarium, apartment houses, and hotels, all of which were completed long before the so-called Art Deco exhibit in Paris in 1925. Price & McLanahan's Flamingo Hotel for Carl Fisher, on the shores of Biscayne Bay, with its citrus orange dome and vertical bays embodied the energy of the Furness commercial manner of half a century earlier (Figure 81). Price's exploration of modern materials, particularly reinforced concrete, again reflected the industrial culture of the city and the values of Frank Furness.

Figure 81 Price & McLanahan, perspective sketch, Flamingo Hotel, Miami, Florida. Photogravure of lost pastel, 1919. George E. Thomas Collection, Athenaeum of Philadelphia.

George Howe's Experience

Howe's experience in the Furness office differed from that of Sullivan and Price and yet it was similar. After graduating from Harvard and studying at the École des Beaux Arts, Howe moved to Philadelphia, his wife's native city, where he entered Frank Furness's office in June 1913. Furness had died in the summer of 1912 but his physical presence was not required to pass on to Howe the essence of the practice. After nearly two generations of Furness's direction, the office had been infused with his mind, his intellect, and his spirit. His design method that directly attacked a problem through rational analysis, beginning with the plan, then relating spaces and purposes to fenestration, which in turn drove building forms, and finally, incorporating in an architecturally expressive manner the new materials of the industrial age, was evidenced in the buildings that continued to flow through the office. Out of step with the rising tide of historicism, the Furness office was typically excluded from the contemporary aesthetic conversation in Philadelphia, rarely appearing in the T-Square club exhibits and annual publications. In Howe's account, it was an "ancient and honorable office more noted for its probity than its artistic gifts."[31] In contrasting probity with artistic gifts and, by extension, style and perhaps even fashion, Howe captured the essence of the Furness office over its last thirty years as the honest expression of logistical planning and the representation of purpose over the artifice of style.

For Howe, the experience must have been made even more remarkable by the sheer physical evidence of Furness's impact on his city. The west side of City Hall was literally surrounded by Furness's works, including the Morris Building, a skyscraper for the Girard Bank offices (1909–1910) facing Chestnut Street; the main offices of the Girard Trust (1905) at the prominent corner of Broad and Chestnut streets; the West End Trust (1898), which towered above the corner of South Penn Square and Broad Street; and the Arcade Building (1901), the Furness-designed bridge across Market Street (1902), leading to the titanic Broad Street Station (1892–1893) with its vast train shed and viaduct that extended west across the city nearly to the Schuylkill River. Just north of the station was the Pennsylvania Academy of the Fine Arts (1871–1876), still a powerful presence at Broad and Cherry Streets despite being coated with forty years of soot.[32] Along Market Street and throughout the old business district, around Rittenhouse Square and on its neighboring streets, in Chestnut Hill where Howe built his own house, and all over the Main Line were the evidences of Furness's influence—some five hundred buildings just in the Philadelphia region alone. In short, the Philadelphia to which George Howe moved was in every way Frank Furness's city. When Allen Evans offered Howe a partnership in November 1913, it was into an office that was still designing houses for presidents of the Pennsylvania Railroad and working across much of the vast territory of the city's great railroads, each of which had been given its identity by Furness.[33]

With his advanced training, Howe was immediately given the task of supervising the detailing and working drawings for the office's most progressive skyscraper, a twenty-one-story addition to the Arcade Building that would house the Pennsylvania Railroad's expanding workforce (Figure 82).[34] When it was completed in 1914 it was the city's tallest office building reaching 304 feet to the top of its square, copper-clad dome. Sixteen years later when Howe was designing the new offices and banking room for the Philadelphia Savings Fund Society at Twelfth and Market Streets (Figure 83), themes from Furness's architecture infused his own scheme. The relationship between function and material that was at the heart of the Furness mature method was adopted by Howe, who described the materials of the exterior of the new PSFS tower being chosen to "carry out the structural articulations" with the idea that "each color is assigned a distinct functional subdivision of the composition." Robert Stern pointed out the similarities between PSFS and the detailing of Furness's Broad Street Station and quoted John Harbeson's thoughtful piece on "Philadelphia's Victorian Architecture, 1860–1890," which gave high praise to Furness for his ability to see materials independent of detail, for his ability to plan spatial sequences based on traffic flow rather than preconceived formal schemes, and for his influence on modern architecture.[35]

These less-studied late buildings by the Furness office clarify the question of whether Howe or his Swiss partner, William Lescaze, was lead designer for PSFS. The evidence of the method gained in his training in the Furness office as well as Howe's personal connection to the bank's president, James Willcox (president 1924–1934), argue that it was Howe, the Philadelphian, who was central to the final design and not the European, Lescaze. On this question, Howe's daughter, Helen Howe West, was absolutely clear. In her biography of her father, she quoted at length from a letter from the publisher of the *Philadelphia Evening Bulletin* and a frequent Howe client, Robert McLean, who left no doubt as to the skyscraper's principal author—George Howe.[36] The greatest irony of forgetting the roots of Howe's lineage reaching back to Frank Furness and the city's industrial culture was that when Philadelphians celebrated their best modern building, it was more logical to assign it to European theory and designers than to understand its roots in Philadelphia's industrial culture.

Figure 82 Furness, Evans & Co.,
Arcade Building, Fifteenth and
Market Streets, Philadelphia, 1901,
1913. Photograph c. 1962. Courtesy
of the Library of Congress, Prints &
Photographs Division, HABS, HABS
PA,51-PHILA,676–1.

Figure 83 Howe & Lescaze, Philadelphia Savings Fund Society, Philadelphia. Photograph by George E. Thomas, 2000.

Figure 84 Louis I. Kahn, Alfred Newton Richards Medical Research Laboratories, 1956. Photograph by George E. Thomas, 1975.

Howe's ongoing debt to the Furness method is also apparent in a building whose authorship is unquestionable—his second contextual modern design, the country home known as Square Shadows, for William Stix Wasserman (1901–1979). Built outside of Philadelphia's Chestnut Hill in 1932–1934, it marked a return to a Philadelphia palette of materials. The Wasserman house's load-bearing walls were of local stone, accented with red brick. Reinforced concrete slabs, evident as light-hued bands, spanned from walls to beams carried on steel pipe columns. These materials recalled the work of the region's mill builders who spanned openings in rubble stone walls with brick arches at window heads. Furness had adopted this economical manner for monumental suburban structures such as the Bryn Mawr Hotel of 1890 and for smaller charities like the Gorgas Home for Indigent Women, which housed the widows of workmen from the Manayunk mills. In the factuality of its materials, the Wasserman house contrasts with Howe and Lescaze's earlier projects like the Oak Lane Country Day School that were derived from the white abstractions of Euromodernism. Indeed, the wide gap between Howe's and Lescaze's architectural sensibilities recalled Sullivan's description of the conflicting methods of the Furness office of half a century before. As with Furness & Hewitt, so with Howe & Lescaze, a split resulted, with Lescaze moving to New York, where his work explored exuberant European minimalism to which he later added strident patterning of brick. Howe remained in Philadelphia and continued to express the facts of a building.

During the Depression, Howe formed partnerships with several young Philadelphia architects. One was Louis Kahn, who absorbed much of Howe's expression of the regional representation of physicality, as seen in his best work in the late 1950s, culminating with the Richards Medical Research Laboratories on the University of Pennsylvania campus (Figure 84). The Richards building was designed while Kahn was teaching in Penn's architectural program in a studio in the upper reaches of Furness's University of Pennsylvania Library. It shares with Furness's library the insistent and particularized expression of the facts of function, materials, and construction, synthesized into a powerful work of art. Kahn's laboratory carried on Furness's design lineage, expressing ideas that reach back to the Pennsylvania Academy of the Fine Arts and the forgotten engineering culture of Philadelphia.

Finding Frank Furness

When John Ford's elegy for the American western, *The Man Who Shot Liberty Valance*, appeared on American movie screens in the spring of 1962, ambivalence about the already dated western was central to its purpose. The movie captured the inherent conflict between tradition and the future as the dynamism of John Kennedy's "New Frontier" undermined the cultural certainty that had united the nation during the difficult times of the Depression and World War II and persisted as a gentle afterglow in the Eisenhower years. Toward the end of the film, the lawyer and U.S. senator, played by Jimmy Stewart, who had led his town from lawless frontier village to law-abiding community, learned that it was not he who had fired the shot that killed the town-terrorizing villain. Instead, it was John Wayne, in a variation of his usual role, who had fired the shot that killed the villain and saved the lawyer's life. By receding into the darkness and not taking credit, Wayne's character created the town's legend of the law-abiding lawyer that enabled it to turn from its gun-slinging past toward its picket-fence-building future. The gun-wielding western archetypical hero had saved the day, but the legend that defined the town's history gave the heroic role to the pacifist lawyer forced to defend himself. When, many years later, the town lawyer-turned-senator was confronted by the actual facts and offered to set the record straight, he was advised: "When the legend becomes fact, print the legend." With its founding legend preserved, the town stayed on course toward modern civilized life.[37]

The movie was first shown as the Cold War was at its height, backyard bomb shelters were in the news, and *Sputnik*, five years earlier, marked the dual realization that no place was truly safe and that other nations might challenge American technical supremacy. Six months after the movie was first screened in April 1962, the Cuban missile crisis caused American schoolchildren to cower under their desks while college boys, watching the lone TV in the living rooms of their fraternity houses, wondered about the logic of continuing their studies if the world was about to end. The modern culture wars roared to life as rock 'n roll smashed music standards and celebrity culture rose to the fore, inverting social orders that heretofore had kept the mature white male in charge. Pierre Bourdieu's theory of distinction that presumed the permanence of cultural knowledge systems was no more effective in stopping cultural change than John Ruskin's attempts to hold back the rising tide of the industrial culture a century and a quarter before.[38] "Never trust anyone over thirty" became the watchword of a generation in flux. The past was truly past and its values and certainties were finished as well.

The classic westerns that Ford had done so much to create were morality plays, set in iconic Monument Valley landscapes, populated by inner-directed characters, played by larger-than-life actors, such as John Wayne and Jimmy Stewart. In their place came Marlon Brando in *The Appaloosa* and Clint Eastwood and the "spaghetti westerns" filmed in Italy, with heroes scarcely distinguishable from villains. The age of certainty that had provided satisfying big historical narratives and happy endings that upheld the dominant social values was replaced by doubt and complication, the mood of the late 1960s. In architecture as in other realms, 1960s cultural relativism was paralleled by situational history as the architectural heroes of high modernism, Mies van der Rohe and Le Corbusier, gave way to more complicated antiheroes led by Robert Venturi, Denise Scott Brown, and the shape-changing Frank Gehry and Rem Koolhaas.

Like the narrative of the western town "saved" by Jimmy Stewart, the history of modern architecture also has been clouded by a powerful but factually misleading founding legend. It, too, was purposeful, a form of propaganda that provided a supportive genealogy that rooted modern architecture in design theories that arose in Europe around World War I. Championed by Henry Russell Hitchcock and Philip Johnson, their constricted view of modern architecture became the basis for what might be termed MoMA modernism after the Museum of Modern Art, the site of the first curated selection of contemporary architecture in 1932. Their framework excluded from the exhibit almost all American buildings including those of Frank Lloyd Wright and the California modernists. Howe & Lescaze's Philadelphia Savings Fund Society skyscraper barely made the text because in the context of Euromodernism, it was too contextual, too expressive of its multiple functions. Hitchcock's later exhibits focused on *Early Modern Architecture: Chicago, 1870–1910*, portraying the buildings of Frank Lloyd Wright and Louis Sullivan as purgatives to the historical revivals of the Beaux Arts style and academic training that shaped fin-de-siècle architectural practice. An exhibit on the by then highly regarded PSFS building followed. Almost inexplicably, the next exhibit focused on Henry Hobson Richardson.[39] The irony of rooting antihistorical modern architecture in Richardson's antimodern historicism underlies the paradox of twentieth-century architectural history.[40] But this now standard history had the advantage of connecting post–World War I Euromodernism to the New England and New York zones that have been most receptive to the American twentieth-century avant-garde.

Sigfried Giedion's *Mechanization Takes Command* questioned the origins of the modern movement in a pointed corrective to Hitchcock and Johnson's thesis. Instead of focusing on elitist avant-garde European modernisms or social-reformist modernism aimed at breaking the hold of old traditions and patterns and replacing them with modern efficiency, Giedion took a cultural stance, looking for specific sources of modern design in what he called "anonymous history." The Swiss historian argued that "the present role of mechanization can nowhere be observed better than in the United States, where the new methods of production were first applied and where mechanization is inextricably woven into the patterns of thought and customs."[41] Giedion found important developments in Philadelphia, where Oliver Evans's machines powered entire mills, where William Sellers designed the standardized screw thread and the ergonomically shaped machine, and where Frederick Winslow Taylor first analyzed the individual tasks that would make the worker an efficient part of industrial process. While he missed the Franklin Institute, Giedion alone managed to find Philadelphia and its wealth of innovation.

The standard narrative of modern architecture has survived for three-quarters of a century, distracting attention from the broader sources of modern design that Giedion discovered.[42] The blinders at MoMA were nowhere more evident than in its 1968 exhibition, *The Machine as Seen at the End of the Mechanical Age*. The objects selected included none of the American–Philadelphia-made machines of the Centennial that had unleashed modern design. Instead the focus was on the European avant-garde, and the "machinesque" as artists created machinelike sculptures and mechanical amusements. Rube Goldberg's fancies appear, as do the usual stills from Charlie Chaplin's *Modern Times*, but the only hint of the American transformation of machine design is Frenchman Georges Melias's *Set for Impossible Voyage* (1904), which clearly depicts an industrial exhibition with a Corliss-type engine in the foreground and locomotives and other machinery in the distance in a steel-framed hall.[43] Anthony Granatelli's STP Lotus Turbocar of 1968 was the only American automobile in the exhibit. Henry Ford's Model T that made Americans and the world mobile was ignored as were the streamlined automobiles and locomotives of Raymond Loewy and Walter Dorwin Teague. The machines that were selected were made in the Europe that was the setting of Federico Fellini's *Amarcord,* where machines were playthings for the wealthy. In the United States, machines had been facts of life for a century. The deeper problem with MoMA modernism was its restriction to one stream that could quickly run dry, as happened in the 1950s when corporate modernists appropriated the style to represent the corporate values of business efficiency.[44] Replicated in endless lines of clones that deadened American downtowns, high modernism turned a revolutionary architecture, aimed at expressing modern industrial life and contemporary methods and values, into a self-referential monoculture.

In fact there always were fissures in the modern narrative. Nearly a decade before the 1932 Museum of Modern Art exhibit, Lewis Mumford, working from a broadly cultural rather than an avant-garde connoisseurship perspective, made the case for American origins for modern designs. In his 1927 preface to a portfolio of plates on contemporary American architecture, Mumford suggested that the reasons behind the differing American and European strategies for modern design lay in the separate cultures that produced them. The works of the European moderns, Mumford wrote, were preconceived and rooted in "a program of modernism," an intellectual construct, more an avant-garde abstraction than an expression of constructive reality.[45] To Mumford, Americans found their method in "a straightforward facing of the problems of function," recalling the European engineers' views about American machines in the 1860s and 1870s. Americans were "modern in spite of themselves," but at the same time, their buildings were also "crystallizations of what is best in the age."[46] And because he looked at building typologies as well as surface style, Mumford grasped that the modern American buildings were about work, "office buildings, the lofts, the factories and the hotels." A quarter of a century later Mumford returned to the question of the origins of modern architecture in his introductory essay for *The Roots of Modern Architecture*. Again he argued that modern architecture was rooted in the technologically engaged United States in its workplaces and houses at least as much as in the European fashionable avant-garde.[47] Ironically, even as he was teaching at the University of Pennsylvania, he could only see Furness through the established historical narrative, as a Victorian who "turned ugliness into a positive principle" because "nothing could shock the Philadelphians of his era."[48]

Toward a Critical Historical Regionalism

As Reyner Banham pointed out in 1971, historians when confronted with subjects that conflict with their established narratives "are too prone to behave like Socrates in Paul Valéry's *Eupolinos*, to reject the inscrutable, to hurl the unknown into the ocean."[49] For more than a century, Furness has been thrown into whatever ocean was available, yet because of Louis Sullivan's praise in the 1920s, he has been rediscovered as tides of taste changed. Clearly culturally based regional rifts divided the nation and in turn shaped design and criticism into the early twentieth century, partly explaining why Furness was excluded from the historical narrative. Furness was not alone. Historians have focused on the architecture that could best be connected to European international modernism.[50] This has significantly distorted the history, resulting in the presumption that modern "Chicago construction" was invented in Chicago, despite Joseph Wilson's comment that he had put together all of the elements of steel-framed construction in the industrial ecology of Philadelphia, beginning with the first block of Broad Street Station in 1880.[51] Similarly, the style now called Art Deco is claimed to have originated in the French Exposition Internationale des Arts Décoratif et Industrielle Modernes of 1925, despite the style's obvious existence in the streamlined architecture of Raymond Hood's American Radiator Building of 1923, which in turn was based not on some European source but rather on Price & McLanahan's Traymore Hotel in Atlantic City of 1914–1915 and the same firm's later work in Miami Beach immediately after World War I. This has meant that Frank Furness, Joseph Wilson, William L. Price, Ralph B. Bencker, and others in the Philadelphia cohort were written out of history, reappearing only peripherally, as in the case of Carl Condit's appraisal of their innovative engineering solutions in *American Building Art* or Peter Collins's *Concrete, the Vision of a New Architecture*, which rediscovered Price & McLanahan's Atlantic City hotels. The role of earlier Philadelphia architects in laying the foundations for the post–World War II Philadelphia School was overlooked as well. It was better to make Louis Kahn a Euromodernist than to connect him to the industrial culture of the place where he lived and practiced.[52] Similarly, California moderns were excluded from the larger historical narrative despite Esther McCoy's, Reyner Banham's, and most recently Alan Hess's acutely focused efforts on behalf of the distinctive car-centered designs of the West Coast. Insofar as the historical narrative was rigidly conceived, it functioned in the manner of Pierre Bourdieu's theory of "habitus" and cultural and social capital, framing a conceptual permanence that was restricted to limited categories of known and culturally conveyed objects and ideas.

Regional Alternatives

A generation after Mumford wrote his introduction to *Roots of Contemporary Architecture*, Kenneth Frampton's essay "Towards a Critical Regionalism: Six Points for an Architecture of Regionalism" took aim at the concept of universal modernism that was sustained by the "Enlightenment myth of progress." To Frampton, after World War II architecture had reached two seemingly insoluble design impasses. The first, which he labeled "the optimization of advanced technology," was manifested in the glittering, glass-sheathed, corporate modern office buildings. The second became evident in the then nascent and now unfortunately pervasive "nostalgic historicism or the glibly decorative" mode of so-called postmodern. Frampton predicted that the vacuous formalism of high modern would lead to the "reactionary, unrealistic impulse to return to the architectonic forms of the preindustrial age,"[53] a prediction that came all too true in the 1990s in the Potemkin villages of gated suburbanism and the faux Beaux Arts apartment towers of the superrich.

Because he was not cognizant of the distinct industrial culture that joined Philadelphia architects from Furness to Venturi, Vincent Scully's introduction to David B. Brownlee and David De Long's *Louis I. Kahn: In the Realm of Architecture* tragically undercut the originality of Kahn and his generation by tying their work to revivals and classical traditions. It was the fate that Frampton had feared. To Scully, Kahn and his generation were revivalists:

> They effectively bring the International Style to a close and open the way
> to a much solider modernism, one in which the revival of the vernacular
> and classical traditions of architecture, and the corollary mass movement

for historic preservation, would eventually come to play a central role. Kahn's greatest early associate, Robert Venturi, was to initiate these revivals of the urban tradition and to direct architecture toward a gentle contextuality unsympathetic to Kahn. Aldo Rossi in Italy was to move in a similar direction, creating a haunting poetry of urban types out of a vision of Italian vernacular and classical traditions not so different from that Kahn revealed in his pastels of Italian squares in 1950–51 and in some of his greatest buildings thereafter. Indeed, Kahn changed architecture for the better in every way, to some considerable degree changed the built environment as a whole and, beyond his knowledge or intention, made us value the fabric of the traditional city once more.[54]

It is hard to imagine Kahn abandoning the barricades of American Communism in the 1930s for the gated communities of Andrés Duany and the tea circles of the modern preservation movement.[55] And we know from his texts what Robert Venturi thinks about the revivalists and historic preservationists.[56]

To escape the conundrum that avant-garde had pushed high minimalism to an end point not unlike that which Arthur Danto proclaimed as "the end of art," Frampton in his essay proposed an "arrière-garde" that would reopen the foundational questions of modern theory for contemporary design. One strategy was to reengage with the multiple moderns that were dismissed at the outset by Hitchcock and Johnson, not to find additional sources for postmodern revivals but rather to get at the goals and processes that underlay the new designs and thereby to reengage design with contemporary life.[57] Turned around, Frampton's essay suggests a parallel strategy for historians, one that demands from historians more curiosity than Paul Valéry's Socrates and a deeper pursuit of context than modern historians have found.

Architectural history has not been alone in distorting its history through the alien theories of European avant-gardism. A parallel can be found in the history of jazz, which, like the various architectural modes, has regional and outsider narratives that were long ignored by academic culture. From the perspective of 1920s elite culture, jazz was criticized as brutally as Furness's architecture had been by the architectural press. In an article in the *Ladies' Home Journal*, Dr. Henry van Dyke, Princeton English professor, Presbyterian hymn writer, and advocate for traditional culture, defined jazz as "not music at all. It is merely an irritation of the nerves of hearing, a sensual teasing of the strings of physical passion. Its fault lies not in syncopation, for that is a legitimate device when sparingly used. But 'jazz' is an unmitigated cacophony, a combination of disagreeable sounds in complicated discords, a willful ugliness and a deliberate vulgarity."[58]

"Willful ugliness and a deliberate vulgarity" are good paraphrases of the academic criticism that was leveled at Furness by even so astute a critic as Lewis Mumford. Jazz is now studied for its culturally rooted narratives, but the commentary on Furness continues to miss his role in shaping the industrial culture that formed the base of the Philadelphia region and that extended west to Chicago and St. Louis. When, in 1970, David Gebhard in his essay "The Moderne in the U.S. 1920–1941," ventured to assert an American origin for "moderne" design, he too ran into the barrier of the terra incognita before the early 1920s.[59] Similarly Reyner Banham missed the Philadelphia innovations when he titled his history of early twentieth-century modernism *Theory and Design in the First Machine Age*, by which he meant the architecture of the 1920s and not Furness's machine-influenced buildings of the 1870s and 1880s.

Regionalism has liabilities, being portrayed as local, parochial, and therefore minor in contrast with the universal and important. Nearly thirty years before Frampton's essay, Paul Rudolph, who had learned to meet the demands of heat and humidity in his early training and work in Sarasota, Florida, reflected on the importance of place specificity of architecture, which also had been written out of the theoretical frame by the universalist Euromods: "The great architectural movements of the past have been precisely formulated in a given area, then adapted and spread to other regions, suiting themselves more or less to the particular way of life of the new area. We now face such a period. If adaptations, enlargement and enrichment of basic principles of twentieth-century architecture were carried out, always relating it to the main stream of architecture and the particular region, the world would again be able to create magnificent cities. Unfortunately, this has not yet come to pass. We continue to ignore the particular."[60]

Robert Venturi's later *Complexity and Contradiction in Architecture* (1966) working back and forth between examples and wry commentary made the parallel argument that expression of modern life required the full richness of architectural communication that had been abandoned to the arbitrary mechanistic minimalism of the International Style. Exploring the language of design, Venturi illustrated examples from the history of architecture, not as sources to be emulated but rather as methods of expression to be understood. Richness of communication need not mean postmodernists' out-of-context quotes, revivalists' whole cloth adaptation of old forms, or preservationists' embalming of a building from the past. Kahn, Venturi, Ehrman Mitchell, and Romaldo Giurgola in Philadelphia, as well as Edward Durell Stone, Eero Saarinen, and Paul

Rudolph were the opening wave of an American tide of designers who reopened the great issues of modernity before its reduction to formula. Each resisted the formulaic high modern but tellingly it took the broad cultural frame that Denise Scott Brown brought to urban and formal research in *Learning from Las Vegas* to grasp the potency of modern media-driven culture. Las Vegas should have been a clue. Innovation arises not just from climate; it arises from cultures of originality that can be found wherever identity is encouraged—in resorts, in intellectual centers such as universities, in new industrial centers.

Not coincidently Furness was rediscovered when the ferment of the Philadelphia School was at its peak. The Philadelphia Museum of Art's 1973 exhibit *The Architecture of Frank Furness* coincided with Kahn's emergence on the international stage. Simultaneously Robert Venturi and Romaldo Giurgola were winning national and international competitions. It was a special moment, one that marked the high-water mark of the school's impact before globalization and media connectivity eroded the remaining foundations of the industrial culture that had sustained and informed the Philadelphians. Despite the major exhibit at the Philadelphia Museum of Art, no one made the connection between the architecture created by Furness and his peers in Philadelphia after the Civil War and the so-called international modernism with its abstract white surfaces and sleek pipe railings of post–World War I Europe. Indeed it is still hard for most to see a direct visual connection between Furness's flamboyantly colored and decorated Pennsylvania Academy of the Fine Arts or his towered and functionally expressive University of Pennsylvania Library, with its hot colors, strongly textured surfaces, and medievalizing ornament, and the cool, minimalist, and efficient-looking architecture that embodied modernism in most of the histories.

Nonetheless, there is an obvious link between the two modes of design, one looking forward, the other backward. The career of Frederick Winslow Taylor, the initiator of industrial efficiency, which underpinned the transformative goals of European modernism, was invented in Frank Furness's Philadelphia and its industrial culture. The essential connection between the two types of architecture lies in their relationship to the machine. The machines that engaged Furness were the focus of the Centennial Exhibition, where they won the principal awards and provided the physical model of new forms for new purposes that Sellers had described in 1874. Europeans saw in the same machines and their products the elimination of extraneous detail that became their means to transform European architecture in the next century. In the case of the Europeans who had been shocked into total transformation of their culture by the horror of

World War I, Taylorism, the process of total redesign that ended craft culture and supplanted traditional hierarchy, was a powerful antidote to the hand of the past that still controlled the present. The aestheticized machine, shorn of ornament, shaped to purpose, and expressive of function, became a model for two types of design, one expressive, the other systematic, both of which reflected the application of Taylor's methods and goals.

Furness, working fifty years before the European moderns, drew on the machine's mid-nineteenth-century manifestation of dynamic power that extended human strength, sped locomotives along rail lines, and powered mills. Products of their own time, Furness's buildings were like the machines that inspired him. His buildings were also manifestations of the particular Victorian civilization in which he lived, valuing the economy of production in the complicated silhouettes, rich details, and dynamic compositions. Their purposeful expression of function and their striking energy captured their specific moment in the age of the great machines of Centennial-era Philadelphia. As Furness combined the aesthetics of the Philadelphia machine, the functional planning of factories, the experimental culture of industry, and the organic connection between form and function as constituent elements of his art, he set off the line of architectural evolution that extends to our present day. Today the implied energy of his buildings, like the great machines of his time, still attracts our eye in ways that those of other Victorian designers do not.

Grounded in ideas that went back to the great machine designers of post–Civil War America, Furness's best buildings exemplified Coleman Sellers's thesis that new purposes needed new forms. Furness and his pupils were right. The innovative architects of the twentieth century found new architectural forms using methods that were first discovered by Furness. Other architects working in other cultures and places took the implication of the modern machine as process to create the great abstractions of post–World War II modernism. Given Furness's role in initiating the genealogy of American modernism, the industrial ecology of Philadelphia offers a logical starting point to reexamine the culture where modern machine design began as well as a critical origin for the beginning of modern architecture. Recently historians have returned to context, particularly as an antidote to the anticontextual, antihistorical modern of the pre–World War II years. It turned out of course that even universal modern architecture had contexts and histories and that it was better explained from the ecological perspective than the standard narrative of artistic genius operating alone. *Mies in Berlin* by Barry Bergdoll and more recently *Louis Kahn's Situated Modernism* by

Sarah Williams Goldhagen both make the point that great architecture arises from the place where it is made, and reflects the culture and people who commission it, thereby representing the conversations and ideas of its time.

To truly understand the particular requires that historians extend beyond the standard narrative to dig deeply into the time and place that supported and encouraged the new in design rather than simply reducing the discussion to the personality of the architect. Instead of the standard modernist pose that there is no American or European mathematics, and by inference, specific cultures, it is important to understand the identity and meaning of cultural regions. Insofar as history is written in the present with the goal of shaping the future, the inventions of Furness and his generation should cause us to ask where the new cultures and their values are arising that will provide the basis for the architecture of the future. Will a technodesign method arise that represents our allegiance to the miniaturized electronic circuitry that is the basis for our modern lives? Will nostalgia and historic preservation regulations shape a permanent nostalgia, a faux history that denies us a future? Will the future of architecture devolve into a cinematic Harry Potter nostalgic mode that can be digitally manifested in a greenboard world? Or will architects continue to have the opportunity to make telling forms and shapes that crystallize experiences and connect us to the energy and dynamism of modern life?

Ralph Waldo Emerson argued in his essay "Prospects" that each person was responsible for his or her own place. It was a command that Frank Furness and his followers clearly heard and understood: "Build, therefore, your own world. As fast as you conform your life to the pure idea in your mind, that will unfold its great proportions."[61] To the extent that Emerson's command still resonates, Furness's architecture stands out for its daring, its willingness to take risks, its engagement with the life of its time. But to happen, it required his father's transcendentalism coupled with Philadelphia industrialists as clients who were willing to turn machine design from precedent to progressive evolution. Architects and historians would do well to closely examine context to better understand the architecture of Frank Furness and the other innovators who have together shaped modern architecture.

NOTES

PROLOGUE

Note to epigraph: Coleman Sellers, "American Machines," *Executive Documents: Published by Order of the United States Senate, 2nd Session, 46th Congress, 1879–'80*, vol. 7, part 3, "Art and Industry" (Washington, DC: Government Printing Office, 1898): 34–40, quote on 40.

1. "Correspondence," *American Architect and Building News* 1 (October 14, 1876), 334–336.

2. For the clearest account of steampunk, see http://www.ministryofpeculiaroccurrences .com/what-is-steampunk/ (accessed March 2014).

3. For a contemporary leading architect's reaction to the preservation movement, see Robert Venturi, "The Preservation Game at Penn," *Iconography and Electronics upon a Generic Architecture: A View from the Drafting Room* (Cambridge, MA: MIT Press, 1996), 145–148.

4. J. Mordaunt Crook, *The Dilemma of Style: Architectural Ideas from the Picturesque to the Post-Modern* (Chicago: University of Chicago Press, 1987), 142. Crook referred to the 1949 essay by Harry Goodhardt-Rendel, who coined the phrase using the imagery of the rogue elephant in contrast to the working herd to convey the "attack" qualities of the most extreme British modern Gothic architects of the mid-nineteenth century. Nikolaus Pevsner was particularly critical of Townsend and was not fond of Furness, referring to his then recently restored Pennsylvania Academy of the Fine Arts as "vintage Furness of the grossest caliber" in *A History of Building Types* (Princeton, NJ: Princeton University Press, 1976), 131. Examples of Keeling's works were collected by William Robert Ware while he was teaching at MIT after 1868 and may well have been seen and studied by Louis Sullivan. See http://web .mit.edu/museum/ware/keeling36.html (accessed July 2013).

5. Albert Kelsey quoted in "Men and Things," *Philadelphia Evening Bulletin*, April 18, 1924, p. 8, col. 5.

6. The Metropolitan Museum's 2013 exhibit "Impressionism, Fashion, and Modernity" brilliantly evoked the new society and the changing role of art and artist. For the introduc-

tory text, see http://www.metmuseum.org/exhibitions/listings/2013/impressionism-fashion
-modernity/introduction (accessed May 2013).

7. Doyle's second Sherlock Holmes novel, *The Sign of the Four,* was first serialized in Philadelphia's *Lippincott's Magazine* beginning in February 1890. See http://babel.hathitrust.org
/cgi/pt?id=mdp.39015023962569;view=1up;seq=169 (accessed March 2014).

8. The Philadelphia Museum of Art's 2015 exhibit *Paul Durand-Ruel and the New Painting* discovers the connections between the dealer, the new art of the Impressionists, and the American industrialists who were among the first purchasers of the art.

9. The Merchants Club was succeeded by the Commercial Club of Chicago in funding and directing Daniel Burnham's 1909 *Plan of Chicago.* Again instead of following tradition, its members were free to push the city in a modern direction dictated by the values of its business culture.

10. Sigfried Giedion, *Mechanization Takes Command* (New York: Oxford University Press, 1948), 4–11; Evans is treated on 79–87; Frederick Winslow Taylor is treated on 96–101f.

11. Giedion discusses Frederick Winslow Taylor and the rise of scientific management without connecting it to the Philadelphia culture from which it came on 96–101. John Kouwenhoven's *Made in America* (Garden City, NY: Doubleday, 1949), 50, advanced the Giedion narrative but also missed the specific Philadelphia roots in his remarks about the machine design at the Philadelphia Centennial.

12. John Coolidge, *Mill and Mansion: Architecture and Society in Lowell, Massachusetts, 1820–1865* (New York: Columbia University Press, 1942, reprinted 1992), 40–43.

13. There may be links between shipbuilders and the framing and flat-planked and caulked façade techniques in churches and houses in the vicinity of the shipbuilding and iron center of Bath, Maine, but the classically detailed exteriors are stylistically like others in New England. John Calvin Stevens's commercial Sagadahoc Block (1895) in Bath uses exposed, riveted steel lintels to carry the upper masonry above street-level shop fronts, perhaps reflecting the presence of and the values of the principal business of the city, the Bath Iron Works. But these are few and far between, with most of Bath's buildings reflecting the general trends of New England, Boston-centric, historically based architecture.

14. Many of Frank Furness's patents are online at www.frankfurness.org (accessed April 2013).

15. Albert Kelsey used the phrase in his criticism of the University of Pennsylvania's reversion to historical revivals for its campus architecture after Furness; *Architectural Annual,* vol. 2 (Philadelphia: Architectural Annual, 1901), 179. A similar phrase was used by Horace Howard Furness when he demanded of Penn's provost Charles Custis Harrison why he had replaced Furness with Cope & Stewardson when he had a "poem in brick" in Furness's library. Charles Custis Harrison, "Memoirs," 1925–1927, pp. 40–42, typescript, Harrison Papers, UPA 6-2H box 5, folder 17., University of Pennsylvania Archives; this is the later and revised version of his earlier "Autobiography," also in the same University Archives folder.

16. R. L. Polk, *District of Columbia, City Directory* (Washington, DC: R. L. Polk & Co., 1935), 775. See Ancestry.com, *U.S. City Directories, 1821–1989,* 2011 (accessed March 2015).

17. David Lowenthal, *The Past Is a Foreign Country* (New York: Cambridge University Press, 1985), especially introduction and first chapter, 1–34.

18. Reyner Banham, *Los Angeles: The Architecture of Four Ecologies* (London: Allen Lane/Penguin Press, 1971), 23.

19. Louis Sullivan, *Autobiography of an Idea* (1924; reprint, New York: Dover, 1956), 190–196.

20. For a cultural overview of American regions, see David Hackett Fischer, *Albion's Seed: Four British Folkways in America* (New York: Oxford University Press, 1989) 419 ff. and especially 530–538, "Delaware Valley Learning Ways: Quakers Ideas of Learning and the Light Within." These ideas are applied to architecture in George E. Thomas et al., *Buildings of the United States: Philadelphia and Eastern Pennsylvania* (Charlottesville: University of Virginia Press, 2010), 1–35.

21. The count of Furness's projects reached 679 in George E. Thomas et al., *Frank Furness: The Complete Works* (New York: Princeton Architectural Press, 1991, revised 1996). Since the last edition, another 45 to 50 commissions have been discovered. The Library Company of Philadelphia recently acquired a scrapbook of photographs of some 50 stations for the Philadelphia Division of the Baltimore and Ohio Railroad built from Furness's designs between 1886 and 1887 which further enlarges our list. Other newly discovered individual projects include a library commissioned in 1876 and built as an addition to the Cincinnati home of Albert Goshorn, the director of the Centennial. A barn at Clement Griscom's Soapstone Farm near Philadelphia had the Furness hallmarks. In 2013 James Duffin at the University of Pennsylvania Archives convincingly documented the important Lebanon Trust and Safe Deposit Bank in Lebanon, PA, from the early 1880s. The 1883 contract with Furness for the Deborah M. Cresswell residence on Union Avenue, now Latches Lane in Montgomery County (demolished), is mentioned in the court case of *Bugger v. Cresswell*. Carol Benenson Perloff has identified the Moorhead Kennedy house in Chambersburg, PA, a 1900 commission. Furness reached into the Midwest with interior designs for James J. Hill's Minneapolis mansion. See Barbara Ann Caron, "James Hill House, Symbol of Status and Security," *Minnesota History* 55, no. 6 (Summer 1997): 234–249. Another likely project is the early 1880s office building for the Pencoyd Iron Works, in West Manayunk, Lower Merion. Michael Lewis continues to discover commissions as well including the early, monumental brownstone row at 42nd and Spruce Streets for banker Clarence Clark. While a couple of the Reading, PA, attributions have been convincingly documented to a Furness pupil, there are doubtless more commissions to be discovered dating prior to 1886 when the *Philadelphia Builder's Guide and Real Estate Record* was first published, so that a number approaching 800 seems likely.

CHAPTER 1

1. Louis Sullivan, *Autobiography of an Idea* (1924; reprint, New York: Dover, 1956), 190–196. Beginning in 1922 the *Autobiography* was published serially in the *Journal of the American Institute of Architects*. Essays were commissioned by the *Journal*'s editor, Charles Whitaker, who would later write *The Story of Architecture: From Ramses to Rockefeller* (New York: Random House, 1934), which would contain effusive praise for Sullivan and for another member of the Furness genealogy, William Price.

2. It is possible that the office building at Third and Chestnut Streets was an early work of the Furness office. Most of his offices were in buildings of his design, doubtless as a form of advertising but perhaps also a quid-pro-quo of work for rent.

3. Sullivan, *Autobiography*, 193.

4. Ibid., 193.

5. Henry Russell Hitchcock, *The Architecture of H. H. Richardson and His Times* (1936; reprint, Cambridge, MA: MIT Press, 1966), 331–332. The 1966 text revised his earlier assessment referencing Sullivan's "almost incredible corruption of form, inspired by the bold vagaries of his master, Frank Furness," that appeared in the 1936 edition on 293. By the later edition, with Sullivan taking a larger role in the creation of modern architecture, Richardson

eliminated Furness's role as "master" and proposed that Sullivan was less "inspired" than "encouraged" by the Furness method.

6. Louis Sullivan, "An Oasis," in *Kindergarten Chats* (1918; reprint, New York: Dover, 1979), 29–30. The essays were published weekly between February 16, 1901, and February 8, 1902, in the *Interstate Architect and Builder*, a short-lived Cleveland-based publication that was taken over in 1902 by the *National Builder*.

7. For a discussion of the actual appearance of the Marshall Field Wholesale Store, see James F. O'Gorman, "The Marshall Field Wholesale Store: Materials Toward a Monograph," *Journal of the Society of Architectural Historians* 37, no. 3 (October 1978): 175–194. He concluded that it would have been better described as "U-shaped and red."

8. It is probably the Guarantee Trust and Safe Deposit Building but it could also have been the Union Banking Company, which was built at the same time also on Chestnut Street. Sullivan, *Autobiography*, 193.

9. "Fearless Frank Furness," *Architectural Forum* (June 1960): 108–115.

10. Alfred H. Barr, Jr., *Defining Modern Art: Selected Writings of Alfred H. Barr, Jr.*, ed. Irving Sandler and Amy Newman (New York: Harry N. Abrams, 1986), 74–75. Barr was MOMA's director during its formative period and helped shape the narrative of Euromodernism that became the context in which Furness was rediscovered.

11. The richest account of Frank Furness's personality is Michael Lewis, *Frank Furness: Architecture and the Violent Mind* (New York: W. W. Norton, 2001), which mines family correspondence and gives a sense of the person. The best contemporary descriptions are by Louis Sullivan and Albert Kelsey, both cited in note 12.

12. The family connection between Owen Wister and Frank Furness is detailed by Lynne Tatlock, "Domesticated Romance and Capitalist Enterprise: Annis Lee Wister's Americanization of German Fiction," in *German Culture in Nineteenth Century America: Reception, Adaptation, Transformation*, ed. Lynne Tatlock and Matt Erlin (Rochester, NY: Camden House, 2005), 156. The connections to Theodore Roosevelt are discussed later p. 258, n. 21. Kelsey's description was included in the column "Men and Things," published in response to Sullivan's praise for Furness in his *Autobiography*, *Philadelphia Evening Bulletin*, April 18, 1924, p. 8, col. 5.

13. Walt Whitman's "To a Historian" had its beginning in "Chants Democratic" in the 1860 edition of *Leaves of Grass* (Boston: Thayer & Eldridge), ending with the line "I project the ideal man, the American of the future," on 181. By the 1867 edition (New York: W. E. Chapin & Co.), on 31, it had been rephrased "I project the history of the future." For a perceptive review of Whitman's 1867 edition, see J[ohn] B[urroughs], "Literary Review," *Boston Commonwealth* (November 10, 1867), 1–2.

14. William Henry Furness's most direct sermon on the topic, "The Blessings of Abolition," was delivered in early July 1860, referencing the book of Isaiah and the nation's coming Independence Day. In his view, because the nation had the inherent injustice of slavery at its core, civil war was likely: "I know that darkness and disunion come, and can only come, not from righting the wronged, but from wronging the weak; not from obeying, but from disobeying the law of equal justice." W. H. Furness, "The Blessings of Abolition: A Discourse Delivered in the First Congregational Unitarian Church, Sunday July 1, 1860" (Philadelphia: privately published, 1860), 4. For the Reverend Furness's long devotion to the cause, see also Len Gougeon, *Virtue's Hero: Emerson, Antislavery, and Reform* (Athens: University of Georgia Press, 1990), 140–142.

15. A rich source on the family and its myriad connections across American culture is James M. Gibson, *The Philadelphia Shakespeare Story: Horace Howard Furness and the Vari-*

orum Shakespeare (New York: AMS Press, 1990). This assembles from the family letters and papers a chronology centered on Frank's brother, Horace Howard Furness, but capturing the range of the family enterprises. See also *The Letters of Horace Howard Furness in Two Volumes*, ed. H.[orace] H.[oward] F.[urness] J.[r.] (New York: Houghton Mifflin, 1922).

16. William Henry Furness, "The Sources of False Doctrine," *Discourses* (Philadelphia: G. Collins, 1855), 186 ff. The passage in question begins on 199 and continues: "They love to cling to some outward support, to lean upon the arm of another even when that other is a weak fallible being liable to go astray like themselves. This disposition also is in its origin a wise and salutary part of our nature. We come into existence utterly helpless and dependent. We rely for life itself upon the protection of others. Reason dawns slowly and since we need the guidance of others it is happy."

17. David Riesman, Nathan Glazer, and Reuel Denney, *The Lonely Crowd: A Study of the Changing American Character* (New Haven, CT: Yale University Press, 1950), particularly chapter 1, "Some Types of Character and Society," 13 ff.

18. Horace Howard Furness, ed., *Records of a Lifelong Friendship, 1807–1882: Ralph Waldo Emerson and William Henry Furness* (Boston: Houghton Mifflin, 1910). This book includes photographs of the two men together with a third friend, Samuel Bradford, who joined the group at age six and remained a friend through life; Bradford became the Treasurer of the Philadelphia and Reading Railroad, another important Furness client (ix). This volume also includes Emerson's effusive praise of Walt Whitman's *Leaves of Grass*: "that wonderful book with all its formlessness and faults" (Emerson to W. H. Furness, October 1, 1855), 107.

19. Ralph Waldo Emerson "Success," in *Society and Solitude* (Cambridge, MA: [Harvard] University Press, 1870; Boston, James R. Osgood, 1876), 233.

20. Emerson gave young Frank a stereopticon viewer with scenes of the American West that his father reported held his interest for "an unusually long time." W. H. Furness to Emerson, August 25, 1854, (97) and October 18, 1854, (101), in H. H. Furness, ed., *Records of a Lifelong Friendship.*

21. William Henry Furness, "The Architect an Artist," Address to American Institute of Architects, *Penn Monthly* 2, no. 6 (June 1871): 308.

22. Ibid., 300.

23. Each of these railroads was strikingly different in aspiration and character. The Philadelphia and Reading was a powerful coal hauler and regional railroad serving the three states that make up metropolitan Philadelphia; the Baltimore and Ohio aimed to create a prestige passenger division connecting New York and Washington, D.C.; and the Pennsylvania was the most powerful railroad in the nation, establishing the national industrial standards and, through its own vast array of tracks and its subsidiaries, spanning the continent.

24. In building a Unitarian congregation in Philadelphia far from its intellectual and cultural roots in Boston, William Henry Furness had to attract congregants from other religions, making them the equivalent of what Quakers call "convinced" members who arrive at the choice of a religion as an adult rather than "birthright" members who merely follow their family.

25. These remarks are condensed from two twentieth-century drafts by Charles Harrison, one entitled "Autobiography" and the other, more edited manuscript entitled "Memoirs." The remark about Furness is in the "Autobiography" in a section entitled "Flotsam and Jetsam" (Harrison Papers, UPA 6.2H box 5, folder 17, University of Pennsylvania Archives). In fact Harrison knew perfectly well how Furness received commissions. Furness had designed his country house, Happy Creek Farm, as well as his office, the Franklin Building, and multiple buildings on the Penn campus including the library and the Veterinary School that

were built while Harrison was on the board of trustees. When Harrison turned to the historicists Cope & Stewardson, he was looking to rebrand the university. See George E. Thomas, "Building Penn's Brand," *Pennsylvania Gazette* 101, no. 1 (September–October 2002), 28–33.

26. Alan Hess, *Googie: Fifties Coffee Shop Architecture* (San Francisco: Chronicle Books, 1986; revised as *Googie Redux: Ultramodern Roadside Architecture*, 2004), surveys the exuberant design of the informal architecture from the golden age of the automobile.

27. For an overview of Emerson's career, see Cynthia Zaitzevsky, *The Architecture of William Ralph Emerson* (Cambridge, MA: Fogg Art Museum, 1969). Her genealogical note clarifies his relation with Ralph Waldo Emerson on 88–89.

28. Priestley was a founder of the city's Unitarian congregation but in pursuit of his own utopian vision removed to the distant country at the Forks of the Susquehanna, now Northumberland, PA. Priestley's son, William, moved to St. James Parish, Louisiana. William's daughter Catherine was Henry Hobson Richardson's mother. Because of the family connection, Richardson's office was selected in 1889 by the Philadelphia Unitarian congregation to design the monument to Priestley in the Unitarian church that Furness had designed.

29. David B. Dearinger, "William Henry Furness, Jr.," in *Paintings and Sculpture in the Collection of the National Academy of Design* (Manchester, VT: Hudson Hills Press, 2004), 219.

30. Lynne Tatlock, *German Writing, American Reading: Women and the Import of Fiction, 1866–1917* (Columbus: Ohio State University Press, 2012). See in particular the chapter "German Fiction Clothed in 'So Brilliant a Garb': Annis Lee Wister (1830–1908)," 216–234.

31. George E. Thomas et al., *Frank Furness: The Complete Works* (New York: Princeton Architectural Press, 1991; revised, 1996), 351.

32. Emerson expected Frank to be sent to Harvard College; letter 42, Emerson to W. H. Furness, Concord, August 22, 1854: "And you have given away Annie, & sent William abroad; & now Horace; and when Frank comes to College, I think your ties must be looser." H. H. Furness, *Records of a Lifelong Friendship*, 95. Lewis in *Frank Furness: Architecture and the Violent Mind* references Furness's early schooling as provided by a "Mr. Gary" on 13. This is probably a phonetic misspelling of John F. Geary's name. He ran a private seminary at 364 Chestnut Street, the old numbering system, near Broad Street. Geary's school is listed in *A. McElroy's Philadelphia Directory for the Year 1853* (Philadelphia: Edward C. & John Biddle & Co., 1853), 146. The school was coeducational. See Finding Aid to the William B. Pennebaker Watermark Collection, 1710–ca. 1936, Winterthur Museum and Library, "Receipted bill from John F. Geary, for tuition for Miss D[illegible], Philadelphia, January 30, 1854. embossed: Southworth Superfine," http://findingaid.winterthur.org/html/col068.xml (accessed February 2014).

33. Furness's account of his training and of his experiences with Hunt, "A Few Personal Reminiscences of His Old Teacher by One of His Old Pupils" (1895), transcribed from a twenty-eight-page edited typescript in the collection of George Wood Furness, is reprinted in Thomas et al., *Frank Furness: The Complete Works*, 351–356. Furness used the phrase "learning the instruments" in his essay "Hints to Designers" (*Lippincott's Magazine* 21 [May 1878]: 612–614) as an example of the standard teaching practice that "cramped" the mind and hand. See "Hints," 612. For a broad account of Hunt's career, see Paul R. Baker, *Richard Morris Hunt* (Cambridge, MA: MIT Press, 1980), especially chapter 7, "The Tenth Street Studios." Hunt's work in Paris, including his work on the design for the Bibliothèque wing of the Louvre under the direction of Hector Lefuel, is noted in "Commencement Honors to Hunt," *Harvard Graduate's Magazine* 1, no. 1 (1892–1893), 93.

34. Annette Blaugrund, "The Tenth Street Studio Building: A Roster, 1857–1895," *American Art Journal* 14, no. 2 (Spring 1982): 64 ff. Given that Homer later drew and painted multiple images of Furness's regiment, the Sixth Pennsylvania Cavalry, it is likely that the two knew each other in New York City. Bierstadt was a founding member with Furness and Theodore Roosevelt of the Boone and Crockett Club in 1887.

35. Louis Sullivan would enjoy a similar array of experiences from his native Boston to Philadelphia and then to Chicago and Paris before returning to Chicago.

36. Frank Furness, "A Few Personal Reminiscences," in Thomas et al., *Frank Furness: The Complete Works*, 356 ff.

37. Bureau of the Census, United States census (Washington, DC: U.S. Printing Office, 1860), New York, Third District, Fifteenth Ward, 264. Others in the household were artists Sanford Gifford and Charles Moore (the future Princeton College art historian), together with other architects, engineers, painters, and a housekeeper, a cook, and a porter. The adjacent building held another ten students together with three servants, suggesting a student neighborhood in the immediate vicinity of New York University and Washington Square. The Third District, Fifteenth Ward was bounded on the north by St. Mark's Place, on the east by Fourth Avenue, on the south by East Third Street, and on the west by University Place. This would have been an easy walk to the Tenth Street Studio Building.

38. Rev. S. L. Gracey, *Annals of the Sixth Pennsylvania Cavalry* ([Philadelphia]: E. H. Butler, 1868). Gracey was the chaplain of the regiment. His account of the Battle of Trevilian Station (see n. 41 below) begins on 259. The first mention of Furness is in a list of officers on December 6, 1861, where he is noted as second lieutenant in I Company. Future clients were among the officers, including William West Frazier and Rudolph Ellis. An anecdote about Furness drawing a cartoon showing the advantage of the lance over the saber, with their lances skewering many of the enemy, is recounted on 361–362. The regimental list is online and conflicts with some of the dates given by Gracey. The online register lists Furness as enrolled May 18, 1862, with the endorsement of the governor of Pennsylvania and mustered into service two months later in July when the regiment was in Washington, DC. See http://www.phmc.state.pa.us/bah/dam/rg/di/r19–65RegisterPaVolunteers/r19–65Regt070/r19–65Regt070%20pg%2071.pdf (accessed April 2014).

39. In December 1862, his brother Horace, in his wartime work with the Sanitary Commission, found Frank with General George B. McClellan's army and described him as "jolly hearted & contented & glorying in his present life[.] He sent his dear love to all at home & is full of anecdote." Horace Howard Furness to Helen Rogers Furness from Falmouth, VA, December 20, 1862, *Letters of Horace Howard Furness*, ed. Horace Howard Furness Jayne, vol. 1 (Boston: Houghton Mifflin, 1922), 131.

40. The Lancers, crossing into Virginia, mounted and holding their lances, were sketched by Winslow Homer. Cooper-Hewitt, National Design Museum, Smithsonian Institution, gift of Charles Savage Homer, Jr. (1912-12-137).

41. The Medal of Honor citation read: "On this occasion, a detachment occupying an exposed and isolated outpost having expended its ammunition, Captain Furness, carrying a box of ammunition on his head, ran to the outpost across an open space that was swept by a fierce fire from the enemy. This ammunition together with that carried by another officer who had responded to Captain Furness' call for volunteers, enabled the detachment to hold its position until nightfall, thus saving the main line from severe loss." Furness was awarded the medal in 1899, a date in keeping with other members of the Pennsylvania cavalry, several

of whom received the Medal of Honor after 1889. See http://www.history.army.mil/html/moh/civwaral.html (accessed February 2013).

42. Michael P. McCarthy, "Traditions in Conflict: The Philadelphia City Hall Site Controversy," *Pennsylvania History* 57, no. 4 (October 1990): 301–317.

43. For an overview of the Philadelphia economy, see Domenic Vitiello, *The Philadelphia Stock Exchange and the City It Made* (Philadelphia: University of Pennsylvania Press, 2010) especially chapters 4, "The Workshop of the World," and 5, "Bankrolling the Union," 76–119.

44. Nikolaus Pevsner, *Pioneers of Modern Design* (New York: Museum of Modern Art, 1949; revised, 1960, revised and republished, 1975), 165.

45. Leonard K. Eaton, *Two Chicago Architects and Their Clients: Frank Lloyd Wright and Howard Van Doren Shaw* (Cambridge, MA: MIT Press, 1969), 32. Viewing Wright's and Shaw's clients individually missed the milieu that formed them but suggests close parallels with Furness's clients. The logistics-based business culture of Chicago, like that of Philadelphia's industrial culture, underlay the willingness to explore the new. Daniel Burnham's 1909 *Plan for Chicago* was supported by the Merchants' Club and its successor, the Commercial Club of Chicago. Presumably one of the values of the new plan was vehicular movement.

CHAPTER 2

Note to epigraph: William Gibson, interview, *Fresh Air*, NPR (August 31, 1993), http://en.wikiquote.org/wiki/William_Gibson (accessed December 2011).

1. Arthur Shadwell, *Industrial Efficiency: A Comparative Study of Industrial Life in England, Germany and America* (London: Longmans, Green, 1909), 303, 304.

2. Robert A. M. Stern, *George Howe: Toward a Modern American Architecture* (New Haven, CT: Yale University Press, 1975), 24. Stern overlooked the innovative Philadelphia architects such as William Price who so perturbed critics from the rest of the country in the twentieth century, seeing instead only the more conventional architects of the turn of the century. Ironically, Stern's recent buildings in Philadelphia, the banal Colonial Revival McNeil Center for Colonial History, the lumbering brick and limestone tower on Rittenhouse Square, and the even less revolutionary Museum of the American Revolution, have contributed to reinforcing his view of the city.

3. E. Digby Baltzell, *Philadelphia Gentlemen: The Making of a National Upper Class* (Glencoe, IL: Free Press, 1958; revised, Chicago: Quadrangle Books, 1971). By depending on the *Dictionary of American Biography* edited in Boston and New York as his standard for significance, Baltzell left out all the engineers who appeared on the University of Pennsylvania's board and led the city, among them William Sellers, Strickland Kneass, and John Cresson. Frank Furness made the book, as a member of the Furness family, but not for his architecture; the Wilson brothers, William Price, and Louis Kahn are ignored.

4. A foundational summary of Philadelphia's role in creating industrial America is Thomas C. Cochran, "Philadelphia: The American Industrial Center, 1750–1850," *Pennsylvania Magazine of History and Biography* 106, no. 3 (July 1982): 323–340. Cochran's explorations of Philadelphia's role in shaping the nation's industrial culture began in the 1940s and continued into the 1990s. More recently Domenic Vitiello has opened up the topic of the engineers' impact on the city in his Ph.D. thesis on William Sellers, which is summarized in his article "Engineering the Metropolis: William Sellers, Joseph M. Wilson and Industrial Philadelphia," *Pennsylvania Magazine of History and Biography* 126, no. 2 (April 2002): 272–303.

5. James Mease, *The Picture of Philadelphia as It Is in 1811* (Philadelphia: B. & T. Kite, 1811), 346–347. Evans also designed and manufactured high-pressure steam engines, con-

structed a steam-powered amphibious dredge, the *Oruktor Amphibolos*, established the principles of refrigeration using expanding vapor, and envisioned rail networks connecting the nation's regions—all before his death in 1819.

6. Philadelphia has recently begun to receive the attention it deserves for its innovative industries. See in particular John K. Brown, *Baldwin Locomotive Works, 1831–1915: A Study in American Industrial Practice* (Baltimore: Johns Hopkins University Press, 1995).

7. Pennsylvania Railroad Company, *One Hundred Years, 1846–1946: Ninety-Ninth Annual Report for the Year Ended December 31, 1945* (Philadelphia: Pennsylvania Railroad Company, 1945).

8. For a recent comment on the impact of William Sellers's system, see James Surowiecki, "Turn of the Century," *Wired* 10, no. 1 (January 2002), http://www.wired.com/wired/archive/10.01/standards_pr.html (accessed February 2012), which makes the comparison between Silicon Valley and the machine tool makers centered in the Franklin Institute.

9. Bruce Sinclair, "At the Turn of a Screw: William Sellers, the Franklin Institute and a Standard American Thread," *Technology and Culture*, 10, no. 1 (January 1969): 20–34.

10. The motto of the "Standard Railroad of the world" appears as early as the 1890s on Pennsylvania Railroad timetables but was already a corporate practice as far back as the 1870s, when the railroad led the push for uniform track standards.

11. The railroad's push for standard track gauges is discussed in the *Twenty-Third Annual Report of the Board of Directors of the Pennsylvania Railroad to the Stockholders, February 15, 1870* (Philadelphia: Pennsylvania Railroad Company, 1870), 20.

12. George E. Thomas and David B. Brownlee, *Building America's First University: An Historical and Architectural Guide to the University of Pennsylvania* (Philadelphia: University of Pennsylvania Press, 2000), 214. After being situated at the university's engineering school and later in facilities owned by the Franklin Institute, the American Society for Testing Materials commissioned its own offices near the Franklin Institute in the mid-twentieth century and more recently moved to Conshohocken in the Philadelphia suburbs, where it remains today as a vestige of the city's industrial past.

13. Robert Kanigel, *The One Best Way: Frederick Winslow Taylor and the Enigma of Efficiency* (New York: Viking Press, 1997), provides an illuminating narrative of Taylor. Unfortunately Kanigel rarely left the factory to see the city that Taylorism transformed and in the process missed the equally great innovation of the changing lifestyle as workers became consumers.

14. Charles Baudelaire, "De l'Héroïsme de la Vie Moderne," *Salon de 1846,* available online via Collection Litteratura, pp. 56–58 http://210.42.35.80/G2S/eWebEditor/uploadfile/2013120518024551 7.pdf (accessed May 2017).

15. William Henry Furness, "The Architect an Artist," *Penn Monthly* 2, no. 6 (June 1871): 295–308, quote on 300.

16. "Correspondence," *American Architect and Building News* 2, no. 60 (February 17, 1877): 58.

17. Ralph Adams Cram, "The Work of Messrs. Frank Miles Day & Brother," *Architectural Record* 15, no. 5 (May 1904): 397. Cram's misspelling is one of many nineteenth-century demonstrations of the family's pronunciation of their name with an unstressed second syllable in the manner of its origins in southwest Scotland.

18. Ibid., 398.

19. See George E. Thomas et al., "Quaker Meeting House," in *Buildings of the United States: Philadelphia and Eastern Pennsylvania* (Charlottesville: University of Virginia Press, 2010),

53, 170–171. The south-facing meetings were noted by Swedish naturalist Petr Kalm on his visit to Philadelphia in 1750 when he commented that dissenting churches "were not as careful about which direction they faced" as the traditional churches. See Petr Kalm, *Travels in North America 1770*, trans. and ed. Adolph B. Benson (New York: Dover Publications, 1987), 22. For a more conventional survey, see Emma Lapsansky, ed., *Quaker Aesthetics: Reflections on a Quaker Ethic in American Design and Consumption, 1720–1920* (Philadelphia: University of Pennsylvania Press, 2002).

20. The span exceeded the capacity of the truss and has since had to be supported by posts. On the other hand, in contrast to Quakers' meetings, which have remained largely static over centuries, Unitarians have commissioned significant works of architecture from Furness and Frank Lloyd Wright on to Louis Kahn, revealing their beliefs in expressive architectural forms and in their evocative use of light.

21. Baltzell, *Philadelphia Gentlemen,* 108–109. Baltzell lumps industrialists and engineers with "businessmen," missing the critical cultural distinction.

22. David Hackett Fischer, *Albion's Seed: Four British Folkways in America* (New York: Oxford University Press, 1989), 419ff and especially 530–538, "Delaware Learning Ways: Quakers Ideas of Learning and the Light Within."

23. Arthur Raistrick, *Quakers in Science and Industry: Being an Account of the Quaker Contributions to Science and Industry in the 17th and 18th Centuries* (New York: Philosophical Library, 1950). Quakers ended up controlling the basic industries of the British Midlands and the parallel zone in Pennsylvania.

24. Historian of science Robert Kohler of the University of Pennsylvania pointed out this source. Arnold Thackray, "Natural Knowledge in Cultural Context: The Manchester Mode," *American Historical Review* 79, no. 3 (June 1974): 676. Thackray links medical and progressive religious groups, "Dissenters" such as Quakers and the Unitarians who were excluded by British landed society but made their way to the fore in the sciences and medicine.

25. Thomas Cochran and William Miller, *The Age of Enterprise: A Social History of Industrial America* (New York: Harper & Row; revised, 1961).

26. Much of the material on the Franklin Institute was researched by Williamina Granger, my student and colleague at the University of Pennsylvania, with the notable assistance of the Institute's archivist, John Alviti, and librarian, Virginia Ward, who magically set before us the right books and files at the moment when they were most needed.

27. Wyndham D. Miles, "A Versatile Explorer, A Sketch of William H. Keating," *Minnesota History Magazine* 36 (December 1959): 294–297 (accessed December 2014). Keating's notebooks are at the American Philosophical Society in Philadelphia. For Merrick's obituary, see Daniel R. Goodwin, "Obituary Notice of Samuel Vaughan Merrick, Esq.," *Proceedings of the American Philosophical Society* 11, no. 81 (December 1870): 584–597.

28. For a history of the early institution, see Bruce Sinclair, *Philadelphia's Philosopher Mechanics: A History of the Franklin Institute, 1824–1865* (Baltimore: Johns Hopkins University Press, 1974).

29. Their names are entered in the lists of students in the drawing courses of the Franklin Institute. Archives, box: "Committee on Instruction," Drawing School, pupil records, 1836–1889. "List of Pupils—Drawing School 1836–7" lists William Henry Furness [Sr.] in attendance on October 19, 1840; vol. 2, "Pupils in Drawing School for Session 1841–1849," lists W. H. Furness [Sr.] in October 1841 in the same class with J. Vaughan Merrick; five years later William Henry Furness, Jr., was listed as attending with William Sellers in the class beginning October 3, 1846.

30. The first such institute was created in Glasgow. Philadelphia's Franklin Institute was the first of these organizations in the United States, followed by one in Baltimore. A parallel example that did not make the same leap to control of its city was the Ohio Mechanics Institute, founded in 1828, which continues as the OMI College of Applied Science, a branch of the University of Cincinnati. See http://www.omicas175.uc.edu/pdf/history.pdf (accessed February 2012). For a late nineteenth-century survey of American mechanics institutes, see *Executive Documents: Published by Order of the United States Senate, 2nd Session, 46th Congress, 1879–1880*, vol. 7, part 3, "Art and Industry" (Washington, DC: U.S. Printing Office, 1898), 209ff.

31. Quoted in William H. Wahl, *The Franklin Institute of the State of Pennsylvania for the Promotion of the Mechanic Arts: A Sketch of Its Organization and History* (Philadelphia: Published by the Institute, 1895), 14.

32. *Journal of the Franklin Institute of the State of Pennsylvania for the Promotion of the Mechanic Arts* (hereafter *Journal of the Franklin Institute*) 71, no. 1 (January 1876), published a full list of members as of January 1, 1876, which showed members in every industrialized state as well as the remarkable variety in and around Philadelphia. San Francisco was represented by three members including Charles Bache, a chemist, civil engineer, and real estate operator. Among the female members was Rachel Bodley (1831–1888), the first female professor of chemistry at the Woman's Medical College of Philadelphia.

33. In the arts alone the library collection was comprehensive, including the complete runs of the *American Architecture and Building News*, *Proceedings and Transactions of the American Society of Civil Engineers*, *American Naturalist*, *Scientific American* (Architects' and Builders' Edition), and German, English, and French journals including *Revue Générale de l'Architecture*. See Wahl, *Franklin Institute*, 94–96. The institute's library was also the depository of record for U.S. government publications and patents as well as the patent records of many European governments including Great Britain, France, and Germany. Today most issues of the *Journal of the Franklin Institute* are online through Google Books, making it easy to search through them.

34. Steven Johnson, *Where Good Ideas Come From: The Natural History of Innovation* (New York: Penguin, 2010). Paralleling Johnson's work is Thomas C. Cochran, "Role and Sanction in American Entrepreneurial History," in *Change and the Entrepreneur: Postulates and Patterns for Entrepreneurial History* (Cambridge, MA: Research Center for Entrepreneurial History, Harvard University, 1949), 153–175. See also Cochran, "The Executive Mind: The Role of Railroad Leaders, 1845–1890," *Bulletin of the Business Historical Society* 25, no. 4 (December 1951): 230–241.

35. Johnson, *Where Good Ideas Come From*, 43.

36. See Wilson Brothers & Co., *Catalogue of Work Executed* (Philadelphia: Lippincott, 1885); the Wilsons were the subject of numerous comments by Carl Condit, *American Building Art: The Nineteenth Century* (New York: Oxford University Press, 1960), 190, 202, 214–215.

37. Johnson, *Where Good Ideas Come From*, especially 59–61.

38. Philadelphia's wealth of medical sciences is evident in *A. McElroy's Philadelphia Directory for the Year 1853* (Philadelphia: 1853), 518. It listed the University of Pennsylvania's medical school at its campus on Ninth Street, the Jefferson Medical College at Tenth Street near Walnut Street, the Philadelphia College of Medicine at Fifth and Adelphi Streets, and the Medical College of Pennsylvania College at Ninth Street below Locust Street, but missed the Homeopathic Medical College (founded in 1846, later Hahnemann Medical School)

and the Female Medical College (founded in 1850, later Woman's Medical College), as well as the first college of pharmacy, founded in 1822. These were augmented by another cluster of institutions and schools devoted to industrial subjects including the Spring Garden Institute (1851). The College of Physicians, which formed an early center for medical research and professional association, was founded in 1787 and established its medical library in 1788.

39. The presence of the Institute and its courses in the sciences delayed the formation of advanced courses of study at the University of Pennsylvania but when the Department of Agriculture, Mines, Arts, and Mechanical Arts opened in 1852, the number of engineering students quickly rivaled that of the medical school. This in turn accelerated the tilt of the university toward the sciences, a condition that prevailed through much of the late nineteenth century and was encouraged by the region's great industries, which funded specific departments that benefited them. New fields of study in turn required new types of classrooms and laboratories that forced the university's move to a new campus after the Civil War. Thomas and Brownlee, *Building America's First University*. A few years after Penn founded its science program, Haverford College, a local Quaker institution of higher learning, opened a similar program in a factorylike building constructed to house its engineering and science classes. See George E. Thomas et al., *Buildings of Pennsylvania: Philadelphia and Eastern Pennsylvania* (Charlottesville: University of Virginia Press, 2010), 232.

40. The University of Pennsylvania Department of Agriculture, Mines, Arts, and Mechanic Arts led to its program in civil engineering and by 1870 to the teaching of architecture. See George E. Thomas, "Mining . . . and Other Kindred Subjects," in Ann Strong and George E. Thomas, *The Book of the School: 100 Years of the Graduate School of Fine Arts* (Philadelphia: University of Pennsylvania, Graduate School of Fine Arts, 1990), 3–12.

41. Theodore Hershberg et al., *Philadelphia: Work Space, Family and Group Experience in the Nineteenth Century* (New York: Oxford University Press, 1981), provides an overview of the social and spatial transformations of the industrial city in the years between 1840 and 1880. The destruction of the 1890 U.S. census stopped the study at the point that the new Taylorized industrial economy would have been evident.

42. *History and Description of the Opera House or American Academy of Music in Philadelphia* (Philadelphia: G. Andre, 1857), 15.

43. Conversation, autumn 2012, with Nicholas Gianopulos, P.E., who analyzed the system in 1981 as a member of the firm of Keast & Hood.

44. Coleman Sellers, "An Obituary Notice of Mr. Joseph Harrison, Jr.," *Proceedings of the American Philosophical Society* 14, no. 94 (February 1875): 347–355, quote on 350.

45. During the demolition in 2013 of an 1850s commercial building at 36 South Third Street north of Chestnut Street, I observed a cast iron beam with an arched head and flat bottom that was used to span a broad opening at the rear of the building. Its shape served as the form for a relieving jack arch of brick that carried the weight of the wall. Presumably structures such as this were incorporated in the Harrison mansion.

46. C. Ford Peatross, Pamela Scott, Diane Tepfer, and Leslie Mandelson Freudenheim, *Capital Drawings: Architectural Designs for Washington, D.C. from the Library of Congress* (Baltimore: Johns Hopkins University Press, 2005), 78–83. Meigs is listed with the University of Pennsylvania class of 1835 in W. J. Maxwell, ed., *General Alumni Catalog of the University of Pennsylvania* (Philadelphia: University of Pennsylvania, 1917), 37. Meigs's Pension Building (1882–1887), now the National Building Museum, reflected the Philadelphia industrial culture in its brick construction and its steel truss roof with industrial monitors for ventilation at the top.

47. The nearby Phoenix Iron Works in Phoenixville, PA, produced rolled wrought iron structural beams in the 1850s, and rolling mills were common before the Civil War around Philadelphia. Rolled or "mild" steel was commonly available in the Philadelphia region by the 1860s. In 1866, the Pennsylvania Railroad constructed a plant at what was later called Steelton on the banks of the Susquehanna River south of Harrisburg that was exclusively devoted to the manufacture of steel for railroad tracks. Regional architects often used railroad track as a quick substitute for steel beams, as Furness did in cantilevering the chimney of the Samuel Shipley summer house, Winden, in West Chester.

48. C. R. Grimm, "The Tower of the New City Hall at Philadelphia, Pa.," *American Society of Civil Engineers Transactions* 31(March 1894): 249 - 71 (paper no. 694).

49. Architect of the Capitol, "Capitol Construction History," (2010), http://www.aoc .gov/cc/capitol/capitol_construction.cfm (accessed September 2010). In some areas there are as many as twenty-one layers of paint, suggesting recoating every seven to ten years.

50. M. P. Wood, "Rustless Coatings for Iron and Steel," *Transactions of the American Society of Mechanical Engineers* 15 (1894): 998–1073, particularly 1054–1058. See also G. J. Binczewski, "A History of the Aluminum Cap of the Washington Monument," *Journal of Metallurgy* 47, no. 11 (1995), www.tms.org/pubs/journals/jom/9511/binczewski-9511.html (accessed January 2013). The City Hall tower was the subject of several articles in *Scientific American*. See in particular "The Tower of the New City Hall, Philadelphia—the Loftiest Statue in the World," *Scientific American* 71, no. 24 (December 15, 1894): 376. The tower aluminum covering weathered to a dull gray that did not need to be resurfaced until the 1980s. By then the lesson of the aluminum was forgotten and the modern finish is now paint, applied from a scaffold. Rust stains are now appearing.

51. Penn's board in 1875 included five ministers, three doctors, five lawyers, six industrialists and engineers; five of the earlier boards were led by the financiers and merchants. The largest professional group was the six engineers and industrialists, and the board included nine members of the Franklin Institute.

52. Edwin Hubbard and William Blanchard Towne, *The Towne Family Memorial* (Chicago: Fergus Printing Company, 1880), 88–91. The Towne family originated in New England but John Towne (b. 1787) moved from Massachusetts to western Pennsylvania where he was engaged in "steamboating." He sent his son, John Henry Towne (b. 1818), to Philadelphia to learn the business from Samuel Merrick. Towne then remained in Philadelphia, creating his own business and serving on the boards of institutions.

53. H[orace] H[oward] F[urness], *F[airman] R[ogers], 1833–1900* (Philadelphia: privately published, 1903), 12.

54. Thomas and Brownlee, *Building America's First University*, 52–61. There are other connections between Thomas Richards, the architect of the University of Pennsylvania's new West Philadelphia campus, and the sciences. His first employer, chandelier manufacturer Robert Cornelius, was an early amateur photographer and made a business of producing silvered plates for photography.

55. George E. Thomas, "Lea Institute of Hygiene," *Historic American Buildings Survey*, HABS PA-6175 (1995). http://cdn.loc.gov/master/pnp/habshaer/pa/pa3300/pa3375/data /pa3375data.pdf (accessed January 2015).

56. The engineering school was supported by the Pennsylvania Railroad. Although the school would devise ENIAC, the first integrated, operational digital computer in 1945, the increasing conservatism of Philadelphia engineering is suggested by the continued focus on shop craft with Sellers's machines at the core. The golden age of Philadelphia industrial inno-

vation was over. See John K. Brown, "When Machines Became Gray and Drawings Black and White: William Sellers and the Rationalization of Mechanical Engineering," *Journal of the Society for Industrial Archaeology* 25, no. 2 (1999): 29–54, especially 47.

57. Mid-nineteenth-century Philadelphia did not attract a large pool of unskilled immigrants like New York, Boston, and Chicago; instead it attracted young, already trained, and directed workers who were drawn to the city's industries. This gave the city its identity at the end of the century as the most "American," meaning native-born, city, which the city proudly proclaimed to set itself apart from the polyglot cities of New York, Pittsburgh, and Chicago. The new wealth of the city was evident by the end of the Civil War. See *Rich Men of Philadelphia: Income Tax of the Residents of Philadelphia, Income of 1865 and 1866* (Philadelphia: John Trenwith [1866]), which provides a listing of the incomes that were taxed for the war and offers a clear picture of the rising industrial economy. While some of the largest incomes were still derived from banking, e.g., F. A. and A. J. Drexel and John A. Browne, the new industrialists were rising quickly including coal merchants Lewis Audenreid and J. Gillingham Fell, chemical manufacturers S. A. and Clayton French and William Weightman, sugar refiner Joseph S. Lovering, boilermaker Joseph Harrison, and William Sellers, all of whom were making $100,000 or more a year—the equivalent of roughly $5 million to $10 million today. Future Furness clients appear among the superwealthy, notably paper manufacturer Bloomfield H. Moore, client for the South Broad Street house that drew Sullivan to the office. R. D. Wood, who would manufacture the lamps at the Academy, is on the list as well. By contrast the leading lawyers and professionals were making between $15,000 and $30,000 (roughly $750,000 to $1.4 million today). Horace H. Furness and his father William H. (last name misspelled phonetically as "Furnace") are both listed with incomes around $2,000 (today, $100,000 to $200,000). See http://www.archive .org/stream/incometaxofresid00tren#page/26/mode/2up (accessed September 2011).

58. For a comparison with his primary contemporaries, Theophilus Parsons Chandler and Willis G. Hale, see George E. Thomas, "Architectural Patronage and Social Stratification in Philadelphia Between 1840 and 1920," in *The Divided Metropolis: Social and Spatial Dimensions of Philadelphia, 1800 –1975*, ed. William B. Cutler and Howard Gillette (Westport, CT: Greenwood Press, 1980), 85–123. Hale primarily worked for real estate developers, especially William Weightman, whose niece he married; Chandler, trained at Harvard, found a more elite clientele with numerous historically derived churches and the majority of his business clients from finance.

59. Leonard K. Eaton, *Two Chicago Architects and Their Clients: Frank Lloyd Wright and Howard Van Doren Shaw* (Cambridge, MA: 1969), 129.

60. Philip Scranton, *Endless Novelty: Specialty Production and American Industrialization, 1865–1925* (Princeton, NJ: Princeton University Press, 1997), 27.

61. Edwin T. Freedley, *Philadelphia and its Manufactures: A Handbook Exhibiting the Development, Variety, and Statistics of the Manufacturing Industry of Philadelphia in 1857* (Philadelphia: Edward Young, 1859), especially 131–135, 314–316, quote on 328.

62. Editorial, "American Machinery Abroad," translation from the *Public Ledger,* October 4, 1873, reprinted as "Editorial: American Machinery Abroad" in *Journal of the Franklin Institute* 66, no. 5 (November 1873): 349–356, quote on 350. Reuleaux was appointed as the chair of the German panel of judges at the Centennial Exhibition and made the case in *Briefe aus Philadelphia* (Braunschweig: Druck und verlag von Friedrich Viewig und Sohn, 1877) that German machines by comparison with American machines were "cheap and shoddy." From his previous similar comments in 1867, his dismay over the state of German industrial innovation antedated the American Centennial. See Michael Lewis, "Modernism Without

Program," in *American Architectural Masterpieces*, ed. George E. Thomas (New York: Princeton Architectural Press, 1992), xvii–xxi.

63. This passage was also picked up by the Franklin Institute in its reprint "Editorial: American Machinery Abroad." The editorial made the economic argument that high wages and material costs caused Americans to look for ever-more efficient systems to keep production costs in line with other nations, accounting for the degree of American mechanization.

64. Retailer John Wanamaker purchased the freight station and would adapt it as his Grand Depot in time for the Centennial crowds, but for the moment it was available for rent.

65. Coleman Sellers, quoted in Wahl, *Franklin Institute*, 44–45. Sellers's entire speech is published as "American Machines" in *Executive Documents Printed by Order of the Senate of the United States for the Second Session of the Forty-Sixth Congress. 1879–'80*, 7, part 3 (Washington: Government Printing Office, 1898) 34–40, quote on 37–38. ,

66. Coleman Sellers, "Transmission of Power," *Journal of the Franklin Institute* 64, no. 4 (October 1872): 233 ff., and continued in 64, no. 5 (November 1872): 315. This lecture took place shortly before Sullivan was in the Furness office.

67. Ruskin's definition of architecture is stated in *The Seven Lamps of Architecture* (New York: J. Wiley, 1849), 7: "Let us, therefore, at once confine the name to that art which, taking up and admitting, as conditions of its working, the necessities and common uses of the building, impresses on its form certain characters venerable or beautiful, but otherwise unnecessary." For an overview of the aesthetics of transformation in the Sellers Company, see Brown, "When Machines Became Gray."

68. These similar ideas were raised by Ralph Waldo Emerson in his essay "Beauty" (1860), in *The Conduct of Life, Emerson's Complete Works*, vol. 6 (Boston: Houghton, Mifflin, 1892), 275. As reflected in the quote, Emerson termed this design strategy "organic." For a contemporary summary of the theories that typically differentiated between architecture and building, see Barr Ferree, "What Is Architecture?" *Architectural Record* 1, no. 2 (October–December 1891): 199–218, especially 199–200.

69. Charles Darwin was made a member of Philadelphia's American Academy of Natural Sciences in 1860 and the American Philosophical Society in 1870. The extent of discussion of his ideas in Philadelphia is not known, though Darwin's evolutionary theory was included in the discussion of bridge building in John W. Murphy, "Bridge Building Considered Normally," *Journal of the Franklin Institute* 96, no. 4 (October 1873): 242–250. The connection between engineering logic and Darwin's principle is obvious. Daniel C. Dennett, *Darwin's Dangerous Idea: Evolution and the Meanings of Life* (New York: Simon & Schuster, 1995); see especially chapter 8, "Biology Is Engineering," on 187 ff.

70. Francis A. Walker, ed., *United States Centennial Commission, International Exhibition, 1876*, vol. 7, Reports and Awards Groups 21–27, "Group XXI: Machine Tools for Metal, Wood and Stone" (Washington, DC: U.S. Government Printing Office, 1880), 14–18, quote on 14. The judges also found a similar aesthetic sensibility in the locomotives produced by Philadelphia's Baldwin Locomotive Works, suggesting a community of ideas shared among the region's designers. This is not surprising given that Baldwin's vast operation surrounded the Sellers plant in the midst of Philadelphia's industrial heartland. The judges commented, "The painting and general finish of the engine is planned with a view to quiet and harmonious effect, and is based upon the principle that the purpose for which a locomotive is used does not admit of any merely ornamental devices: but that its *beauty, so far as it may have any, should depend upon good proportions and through adaptation of the various parts to their uses*" (my emphasis). Vol. 6, "General Report of the Judges of Group XVIII," 236.

71. Horatio Greenough, *The Travels, Observations, and Experience of a Yankee Stonecutter* (1852), quoted in John Kouwenhoven, *Made in America: The Arts in Modern Civilization* (Garden City, NY: Doubleday, 1949), 106. See especially the chapter "The Practical and the Aesthetic."

72. Thomas et al., *Buildings of the United States*, 20–23.

73. Joseph M. Wilson, *The Masterpieces of the Centennial International Exhibition*, vol. 3 (Philadelphia: Gebbie & Barrie, 1876), lxxxvii.

74. John White, *The American Railroad Passenger Car* (Baltimore: Johns Hopkins University Press, 1978), 312–316, illustrates the Pullman Company's dining car, the "Delmonico," named for the famous New York restaurant and on the rails in 1868.

75. See *The Fort Wayne and Pennsylvania Route and the Centennial Exhibition* (Chicago: Rand, McNally: 1876), http://cprr.org/Museum/Centennial Exhibition 1876/ (accessed December 2012). This work reported, "The management of that great route has, from the origin of the International Exhibition, been zealous in advocating it as an event important to the people, and has materially assisted in establishing it on a basis so comprehensive as to reflect credit on the entire nation."

76. George H. Burgess and Miles C. Kennedy, *Centennial History of the Pennsylvania Railroad: 1846–1946* (Philadelphia: Pennsylvania Railroad, 1949), 357.

77. The roots of Disneyland in Victorian exhibitions are apparent in its planning and in its scenic railroad ride that complements the Victorian theme of Disneyland. At Disneyland the ride is powered by Locomotive #3, a narrow-gauge engine that was constructed in 1894 by Philadelphia's Baldwin Locomotive Works and is the oldest steam locomotive in operation in the nation. Two other Baldwin locomotives are still working at Disneyland as well.

78. Pettit would later join the Furness office, where he worked between 1876 and 1888. See "Henry Pettit," *Cyclopedia of American Biography*, vol. 6 (Boston: Federal Book, 1903), 232. Pettit was an in-law of Joseph M. Wilson and was selected to write his obituary: Henry Pettit, "Joseph Miller Wilson, A.M., C.E.," *Proceedings of the American Philosophical Society* 42 (May 1903): i–vi.

79. "Centennial Exhibition," *Journal of the Franklin Institute* 69, no. 5 (May 1875): 313–314. See also "Sale of the Exhibition Buildings: Two and a Half Millions' Worth of Property Sold for Less than Three Hundred Thousand Dollars; Destination and Use of the Principal Structures, Incidents of the Sale, Amounts Paid and the Purchases," *New York Times*, December 2, 1876, p. 5. The largest structures, the Main Exhibition and Machinery Halls, were retained as ongoing features of the park for several years. Despite the carping from New York, the demolition was paid for and a profit realized.

80. Domenic Vitiello, "Engineering the Metropolis," and in richer detail in his "Engineering the Metropolis: The Sellers Family and Industrial Philadelphia" (Ph.D. dissertation, University of Pennsylvania, 2004).

81. Wilson, *Masterpieces of the International Centennial Exhibition*, vol. 3, cxx.

82. For a later comment on the Philadelphia fair, see Alfred T. Goshorn, "The Effects of the Centennial Exhibition," *Engineering Magazine* 6 (October 1893–March 1894): 423–429. Goshorn had been a director for the Centennial and in his article compares the Centennial and Columbian fairs in multiple dimensions. Among the best contemporary descriptions of the Centennial just before the opening is "The Centennial Under Roof," *Lippincott's Magazine of Popular Literature and Science* 17, no. 100 (April 1876): 393–409. Furness would later design a private library room for Goshorn as a gift from the people of Philadelphia.

83. Dorsey Gardner, United States Centennial Commission, *Grounds and Buildings of the Centennial Exhibition, Philadelphia, 1876* (Philadelphia: J. B. Lippincott, 1876), 18.

84. Melvil Dewey, *A Classification and Subject Index for Cataloguing and Arranging the Books and Pamphlets of a Library* (Amherst, MA: Amherst College Library, 1876); the book was written in his junior year and used in the fair the following year.

85. Condit, *American Building Art*, 214–219.

86. Ibid., 218.

87. Wilson Brothers & Co., *Catalogue of Work Executed,* 46.

88. The building ended up at 1,880 feet because of overages in the sizes of materials but, like the recently completed One World Trade Center, a.k.a. "Freedom Tower," whose top mast reaches 1,776 feet in the air, there was no visual scale to make the number visible.

89. The selection of George Corliss's engine, made in Rhode Island, was perhaps a political act by Sellers to ensure that state's support for the Centennial Exhibition, and it marked another of William Sellers's connections to the national machine industry. His first managerial role was in the Bancroft, Nightingale & Co. steam engine plant in Providence, which later became George Corliss's operation. "William Sellers," *Cassier's Magazine* 10, no. 3 (July 1896): 231–233.

90. John Loughery, *John Sloan: Painter and Rebel* (New York: Henry Holt, 1995), 4.

91. Widely publicized, the Phoenix tower is described in the "Editor's Scientific Record," *Harper's New Monthly Magazine* 48, no. 286 (March 1874): 606. Two smaller towers of some two hundred feet in height were eventually constructed. See Clay Lancaster, "The Philadelphia Centennial Towers," *Journal of the Society of Architectural Historians* 19, no. 1 (March 1960): 11–15.

92. Kouwenhoven, *Made in America.*

93. Lluis B. Pascual, "Modernisme and the 1888 Universal Exposition of Barcelona," Historical Lab–Bruxelles–Brussels, October 22, 2005, http://www.artnouveau-net.eu/LinkClick .aspx?fileticket=iqpeBjIqymM%3D (accessed April 2015).

CHAPTER 3

1. "The Prospect for Philadelphia," *New York Daily Times*, March 10, 1852, p. 2, col. 2, outlined the reasons for Philadelphia's decline—a distant port, loss of government roles— and found no value in the city. A week earlier, the Pennsylvania Railroad had been caught trying to damage New York trade by excluding merchandise from that city on its railroad. "Philadelphia vs. New York," *New York Daily Times*, March 6, 1852, p. 2, col. 3; "Philadelphia and Her Rivalries," *New York Daily Times*, March 19, 1852, p. 2, col. 1.

2. For an overview of the early New England regional culture and its continuing influence today, see David Hackett Fischer, *Albion's Seed: Four British Folkways in America* (New York: Oxford University Press, 1989), 13–205, particularly 130–134.

3. George E. Thomas, "Mining . . . and Other Kindred Subjects," in Ann Strong and George E. Thomas, *The Book of the School: A Century of the Graduate School of Fine Arts* (Philadelphia: University of Pennsylvania, Graduate School of Fine Arts, 1990), 3–12. Columbia's architecture program in the School of Mines, founded by Furness's former atelier mate William Ware, was established in 1881.

4. Daniel D. Reiff, *Houses from Books, Treatises, Pattern Books and Catalogs in American Architecture, 1738–1950* (State College: Pennsylvania State University Press, 2000), 131ff.

5. Henry Adams, *The Education of Henry Adams* (Boston: Houghton Mifflin, 1918). See in particular chapter 25, "The Dynamo and the Virgin," written in 1900, on 379–390, which captured the conflict between the new acultural "economy of forces" and the cultured classics that he had studied.

6. Jeffrey T. Schnapp, address at the faculty opening of the Harvard Art Museums, November 13, 2014.

7. James F. O'Gorman, ed., *The Makers of Trinity Church in the City of Boston* (Amherst, MA: University of Massachusetts Press, 2004), provides a full narrative of the history of the church on which much of my comparative analysis is based.

8. Brooks was a close friend of S. Weir Mitchell, M.D., and through him was certainly connected to the Furness family and their abolitionist activities. Ernest Earnest, *S. Weir Mitchell, Novelist and Physician* (Philadelphia: University of Pennsylvania Press, 1950), 45. The connection was utilized in 1880 when Horace Howard Furness was deputized by Penn's board to visit Phillips Brooks to see if he could be persuaded to become Penn's provost after the removal of Charles Stille. See James M. Gibson, *The Philadelphia Shakespeare Story: Horace Howard Furness and the Variorum Shakespeare* (New York: AMS Press, 1990), 214.

9. Designed in 1829 by Boston architect George W. Brimmer, the old church was a rough-textured, first generation Gothic-revival building with a massive front tower. It is illustrated in Roger Reed, *Building Victorian Boston: The Architecture of Gridley J. F. Bryant* (Amherst: University of Massachusetts Press, 2007), 20.

10. The story of the Trinity Church competition is ably told by Theodore E. Stebbins, Jr., "Richardson and Trinity Church: The Evolution of a Building," *Journal of the Society of Architectural Historians* 27, no. 4 (December 1968): 281–298. This story is reprised and updated by Stebbins in O'Gorman, *Makers of Trinity Church*, 11–21.

11. Pennsylvania Academy of the Fine Arts Archives, Board of Directors Minutes (hereafter Board Minutes), vol. 1858–1876, November 14, 1864. The board first raised the question of whether it would be appropriate to enlarge the original building at Tenth and Chestnut or to build a new structure: "Resolved that a Committee be appointed to take into consideration the present condition, and future prospects of the Academy, with especial reference to the increased usefulness and prosperity of the Institution." A committee of artist John Sartain, industrialist George Whitney, and financier and future president of the board James Claghorn was appointed (185–186). Two months later the committee reported on the problems with the existing building. This resulted in its recommendation to either enlarge the present building or sell it and build a new structure that would provide "accommodations exactly adopted to our needs, and also it is hoped, in a style suited to our object and worthy of the city." Board Minutes, January 16, 1865, 193. Sartain's account is in *Reminiscences of a Very Old Man* (New York: D. Appleton, 1899), 250–253.

12. Board Minutes, August 29, 1867, 236–237.

13. Ibid., January 16, 1865, 193–196. The idea of a joint project with other institutions was first broached on February 13, 1865 (198–199). Over the next generation, the Academy of Natural Sciences and the Library Company would each build new homes and the American Philosophical Society would add a giant book storage "top-hat" designed by Wilson Brothers atop the society's building on Independence Square. Center Square was part of Philadelphia's original five squares and, in the 1680s, had been the site for the city's first Friends' Meeting House and its courthouse. The distance from the main settlement near the Delaware proved too great and the civic buildings were dismantled and moved east toward the downtown along the river bank where they were more accessible. The square was left vacant as a memorial to William Penn, but again because of its distance was underutilized. In 1799, the square became the site of Benjamin Latrobe's steam-powered engine and water tank, which powered the city's first waterworks, but that system's inefficiencies caused it to be replaced by the waterworks on the Schuylkill River and, once again, the center square was left

as a landscaped garden. Scarcely a generation later Latrobe's pump house was demolished and its columns were incorporated into William Strickland's façade for the new Unitarian church at Tenth and Locust Streets (1828), which represented the growth of the reenergized congregation under the leadership of its new minister, William Henry Furness.

14. Board Minutes, December 24, 1870, 343.

15. This idea persisted from the eighteenth-century differentiation between proper Philadelphians south of Market and Germans and others to the north. It was still alive in popular fiction into the early twentieth century. See Katharine Bingham, *The Philadelphians* (Boston: L. C. Page, 1903), 13–15, especially this passage: "In Philadelphia to live uptown is to be unknown by the kind of people whom you are accustomed to. Fashionable society—those whom you would call the 'nice people'—all live in a very small section of the city, the oldest part, and nothing would induce them to set foot in any part north of Market Street, much less live there." Quote on 15.

16. Board Minutes, Meetings, February 13, 1865–December 24, 1870, 198–343.

17. Wheaton A. Holden, "The Peabody Touch: Peabody and Stearns of Boston, 1870–1917," *Journal of the Society of Architectural Historians* 32, no. 2 (May 1973): 114–131.

18. Adams, *Education*, commented on Richardson's use of his Harvard education to build connections in Boston, in chapter 4, "Harvard College," 64: "Strangers might perhaps gain something from the college if they were hard pressed for social connections. A student like H. H. Richardson, who came from far away New Orleans, and had his career before him to chase rather than to guide, might make valuable friendships at college. Certainly Adams made no acquaintance there that he valued in after life so much as Richardson, but still more certainly the college relation had little to do with the later friendship."

19. Reed, *Building Victorian Boston*, 19–21.

20. Letters went out on May 12, 1872. Richardson's letter is preserved at the Houghton Library at Harvard University, https://blogs.law.harvard.edu/houghton/2012/12/21/youve-got-mail-h-h-richardson-sketches-trinity-church/ (accessed July 2013). See also Ann Jensen Adams, "The Birth of a Style: Henry Hobson Richardson and the Competition Drawings for Trinity Church, Boston," *Art Bulletin* 62 (September 1980): 409–433.

21. The Gambrill & Richardson scheme is illustrated in O'Gorman, *Makers of Trinity Church*, 66, 67.

22. The need for a new government center had been discussed for a generation. See *Facts in Relation to the Progressive Increase, Present Condition, and Future Prospects, of Philadelphia, as Connected with the Permanent Location of Public Buildings* (Philadelphia: J. Sharp, 1838), 19. Its author argued that it was unreasonable to locate City Hall where it had been located when the population of the city was a few thousand and instead that it should be built at Penn Square. For a contemporary account of the city, see H.C.S., "Sketches of Philadelphia," *Lippincott's Magazine of Literature, Science and Education* 9 (May 1872): 505–521.

23. During the construction of the Academy, Schussele's classes were relocated in the artist's home on the north side of Penn Square. See Henry Adams, *Eakins Revealed: The Life of an American Artist* (New York: Oxford University Press, 2005), 258.

24. Academy of Fine Arts Archives, Building Committee Minutes, February 27, 1871 (hereafter Building Committee Minutes). In attendance were W. Charles Macalister (called to the chair), Caleb Cope, [James] Claghorn, [George] Whitney, [Henry] Gibson, Fairman Rogers, Charles H. Rogers, [Henry G.] Morris, [William] Bement, [Edwin] Lewis, John Haseltine, M.[atthew] Baird, John Rothermel, [Daniel] Haddock, Jr., and John Sartain.

25. Board Minutes, June 12, 1871, 368. The initial building committee members were Sartain; James Claghorn; the Academy president, Henry C. Gibson; Henry G. Morris; and Fairman Rogers.

26. Building Committee Minutes, between June 12 and June 19, 1871; the list of architects and their advocates was cited on June 19.

27. Board Minutes, building committee appointed, June12, 1871, 367–368; "Invitation for Proposals to Erect a Building for the Pennsylvania Academy of the Fine Arts," June 20, 1871.

28. Hutton lists Windrim in his list of competitors—"Furness, Windrim, Richards, Hutton, Sims." Hutton Daybook for 1871, June 15, 1871, Quaker Collection, collection 1122, Special Collections, Haverford College Library, hereafter Hutton Daybook. The fact that he listed Furness and not Furness & Hewitt may suggest that he saw Furness as the chief opponent.

29. Hutton's career is described in Elizabeth Biddle Yarnall, *Addison Hutton: Quaker Architect, 1834–1916* (Philadelphia: Pennsylvania Art Alliance Press, 1974).

30. The 1868 building was listed in the bank records as the work of Sloan and Hutton, but the firm had dissolved prior to the submission and the design was Hutton's alone. Though it was led by Quakers, its board was ecumenical, with members spanning the diverse religious groups among its founders and later board members. See James M. Willcox, *A History of the Philadelphia Savings Fund Society* (Philadelphia: J. B. Lippincott, 1916), 62–79.

31. Hutton had studied at the Institute in 1859, taking courses in drawing, architectural design, and chemistry. Franklin Institute Archives, Drawing School.

32. For an overview of Richards's career, see George E. Thomas, "Thomas Webb Richards," in Strong and Thomas, *Book of the School*, 16–17. Richards's brother, William Trost Richards (1833–1905), was an important artist specializing in seascapes who preceded Thomas as an associate of the Academy by five years and continued to exhibit there for the rest of his career.

33. "T. W. Richards" was listed as an associate of the Academy at the meeting of March 12, 1860, along with Bass Otis. Board Minutes. Richards's brother, William, had been elected on April 9, 1855, along with William Henry Furness, Jr.

34. The first study of Sims was undertaken by Leslie L. Beller, "The Diary of Henry Augustus Sims" (MA thesis, University of Pennsylvania, 1976), on file at the Fisher Fine Arts Library, University of Pennsylvania. St. John's Anglican Church in Prescott, Ontario, is one of his designs. Sims's grandfather emigrated to Philadelphia in 1794 under the surname Simm. For a richer study, see Michael J. Lewis, "The Architectural Library of Henry A. Sims," in *American Architects and Their Books: 1840–1915*, ed. Kenneth Hafertepe and James F. O'Gorman (Amherst: University of Massachusetts Press, 2007), 173–193.

35. Fraser's letter, dated October 5, 1871, with Furness & Hewitt crossed off the letterhead remains in the Academy archives. Catalogued Building Construction box.

36. For the building committee of Trinity Church, see Thomas M. Paine, "Chairman of the Building Committee: Robert Treat Paine," in O'Gorman, *Makers of Trinity Church*, 37–59, 57 n. 19.

37. Sartain was elevated to the board when William Sellers resigned. Board Minutes March 12, 1866, 217–218.

38. For Morris, see "Obituary," *Journal of the American Society of Mechanical Engineers* 37 (April 1915): 244. Morris was an early advocate of the Bessemer process of steelmaking and promoted electrical engineering as a new professional field. He won prizes for a successful electric automobile and held numerous patents for storage batteries. His firm would provide the specialty steel for the Academy building including the pipe columns of the upper-level galleries.

39. Hutton Daybook for 1871, June 15: "Invited by Caleb Cope to present plans for new Academy of Fine Arts at SW corner of Broad & Cherry Sts." See also Yarnall, *Addison Hutton*, 69.

40. "Death of a Philanthropist," *Pittsburgh Dispatch*, December 21, 1891, p. 7, col. 4. The obituary recounts the means by which Gibson skirted the Civil War tax on alcohol but sold his product at the higher taxed price, reaping a windfall that established his fortune.

41. H.[orace] H.[oward] F.[urness], *F.[airman] R.[ogers], 1833–1900* (Philadelphia: privately published, 1903), 11–12.

42. "I never knew of but one artist, and that's Tom Eakins, who could resist the temptation to see what they think ought to be rather than what is," said Walt Whitman, in conversation with Horace Traubel on April 4, 1888; quoted by Traubel in *With Walt Whitman in Camden*, vol. 1 (Boston: Small, Maynard & Co., 1906), 41.

43. Kathleen A. Foster, *Thomas Eakins Rediscovered: Charles Bregler's Thomas Eakins Collection at the Pennsylvania Academy of the Fine Arts* (New Haven, CT: Yale University Press, 1997), 151.

44. For much new information about the collaborative relationship between Eakins and Rogers, see Sidney D. Kirkpatrick, *The Revenge of Thomas Eakins* (New Haven, CT: Yale University Press, 2006), 245–251. Michael J. Lewis was the source for much of Kirkpatrick's information about the planning of the Academy building.

45. The photozincograph from an inked perspective was published in *Lippincott's Magazine of Literature, Science, and Education* 11 (February 1872): 308.

46. Henry A. Sims, "Memorandum Which Accompanied a Design Submitted by Mr. Henry A. Sims, Architect, for the Proposed New Building for the Pennsylvania Academy of the Fine Arts, at the Southwest corner of Broad and Cherry Streets," Academy of Fine Arts, Catalogued Archives, November 2, 1871. The booklet was given to the Academy by Sims's former student Charles Burns with a reference to the tragic loss of Sims, indicating that it was given after Sims's death in 1875. The photographs of the drawings show the plan of the principal gallery floor and the ground or school floor, a section down the length of the building, a detail of the Cherry Street elevation showing a detail of the studio and gallery wall, and the elevation on Broad Street and Cherry Street.

47. Ibid., 5.

48. Ibid.

49. Michael Lewis pointed out this source, which he references in his recent article for the bicentennial of the Academy. Hutton Daybook, October 6, 1871. The most interesting feature is the beveled outline, which probably reflects interior space rather than exterior volume. This was likely sketched as Hutton returned on a train from previewing the opening of Vanderbilt's Grand Depot in New York City, where he was working on alterations to A. T. Stewart's Retail Store.

50. John Sartain to Thomas W. Richards, November 2, 1871, Richards papers, University of Pennsylvania Archives. Rogers did in fact give $2,500 to the new project, approximately 1 percent of the original estimated cost.

51. Report from the Building Committee, Board Minutes, November 13, 1871, 370–375. Hutton reported that he learned that he did not win the following day: "Rec'd intelligence of the non-adoption of my plan for the Pennsylvania Academy of the Fine Arts. Furness & Hewitt elected architects." Hutton Daybook, November 14, 1871.

52. Board Minutes, vol. April 1874–March 1883, April 22, 1876.

53. John Ruskin, *Lectures on Architecture and Painting Delivered at Edinburgh in November 1853* (New York: John Wiley & Sons, 1887), 53–54.

54. A. Hunter Dupree, *Science in the Federal Government: A History of Policies and Activities to 1940* (Cambridge, MA: Harvard University Press, 1957; reprinted New York: Arno Press, 1980), 133ff. Davis was a leading scientist in the U.S. Navy working with Alexander Bache on the U.S. Coastal Survey and formed the beginnings of the National Academy of Science. See also C. H. Davis, "Memoir of Charles Henry Davis, 1807–1877, Read Before the National Academy, April, 1896," *Proceedings of the National Academy of Sciences* 4 (1902), 23–55. It contains the full quote on 34–35. In 1853, Davis had served as superintendent of the Crystal Palace exhibition in New York City.

55. For an account of the bridge, see R. Hering and T. C. Clarke, "Girard Avenue Bridge," *Journal of the Franklin Institute* 97, no. 3 (January–June 1874): 179–185. In 1877 Sims's protégé Charles Burns used exposed iron columns and imposts at the corners of the façade of the St. Timothy's Working Men's Club at 5164 Ridge Avenue in Roxborough. Though Burns would later reject all modern materials in the construction of his Episcopal churches, in the immediate afterglow of the Centennial he too was using modern materials.

56. Strickland Kneass, "Superstructure of the Chestnut Street Bridge," *Journal of the Franklin Institute* 59, no. 2 (February 1870): 98.

57. Such comments as the engineers' instructions were common in Philadelphia. The account of the Pennsylvania Railroad's first Broad Street Station in Wilson Brothers & Co., *Catalogue of Work Executed* (Philadelphia: Lippincott, [1885]), 49, specifically noted that "iron work is all exposed to view, and decorated in colors."

58. Maria Thompson pointed out this important requirement. Vestry of the Church of the Redeemer, Minutes, Committee on Plans of the Vestry of the Church of the Redeemer, August 8, 1879, archives of the Church of the Redeemer, Bryn Mawr, PA.

59. *American Architect and Building News* 18, no. 519 (December 5, 1885): 271. The Church of the Redeemer became a repository of windows dedicated to great industrialists who lived in the immediate vicinity with windows dedicated to members of the Cassatt family as well as windows dedicated to William Henszey (1832–1909), a leader of the Baldwin Locomotive Works and a Furness client for his house on Lancaster Avenue, who himself was a birthright Quaker and a member of the local Quaker meeting.

60. Academy of Fine Arts Archives, Catalogued Archives, History of PAFA, vol. 1871–1876, "Folder PAFA 1873–4 Building Plans," MS, subscription lists. These are lists of names with dollar amounts.

61. Board Minutes, vol. 1858–1876, April 8, 1872, 398. Twenty-one of the subscribers promised $10,000 and four promised $5,000 with others making up the estimated total cost of $235,000, which with the remainder of the funds from the sale of the Chestnut Street building was to meet the cost of the project of approximately $400,000.

62. Caleb Cope, "Address of Caleb Cope," *Exercises at the Laying of the Cornerstone of the New Building of the Pennsylvania Academy of the Fine Arts, December 7, 1872* (Philadelphia: Collins, 1872), 6–8.

63. The cornerstone ceremony was reported Board Minutes, 1858–1876, December 7, 1872, 417–419, and included a transcription of "Address of Fairman Rogers" in *Exercises at the Laying of the Cornerstone*, 10–13. Rogers described the layout and the process that would occur in the further refinement of plans.

64. Academy of Fine Arts Archives, Building Construction Box, folder 1871–1872, proposal from Steward & Stevens, November 14, 1872, and specifications for wrought iron

beams, November 19, 1872. The firm's bid was lowest at $8,378 and was accepted on December 9, 1872. Board Minutes, 1858–1876, 423.

65. Hammered glass was a textured glass made by rolling it on a hammered metal plate that produced a texture that diffused light. Sizes available in Philadelphia were listed in *Sloan's Architectural Review and Builders' Journal* (November 1868): 321. Flooring glass in 1¼″ plate was available in sheets up to 24″ × 36″; hammered glass for skylighting in ½″ plate was available in sizes up to 30″ × 120″. Building Committee Minutes, Committee decision, February 12, 1873.

66. H. H. F[urness], *F.[airman] R.[ogers]*, 13. Frank Furness's brother Horace, in his obituary essay for his brother-in-law Fairman Rogers, noted his contributions to the Academy design: "In its internal design and arrangement, much that is admirable and best is owing to his careful and earnest thought."

67. During the restoration of the Academy in 1973, I found reference to the promised photographs in correspondence with the Corcoran and inquired of the Renwick whether it had such images. The staff responded that there was no record. A search of the Academy archives found the photographs by Frederick Gutekunst, in an envelope that was addressed but never sent.

68. Leland M. Williamson et al., "Jacob Myers," *Prominent and Progressive Pennsylvanians of the Nineteenth Century* (Philadelphia: Record Publishing, 1898), 349–351. Myers built several later projects for Furness including the University of Pennsylvania Veterinary Hospital, the Franklin Building, and the Lippincott, Johnson Building, as well as numerous academic projects. He served on the Architects' Plans and Contracts Committee of the Master-Builders' Exchange. A list of prominent commissions including later work with Furness is included in the *Catalogue of the T-Square Club Architectural Exhibit: 1896–7* (Philadelphia: George H. Buchanan & Co., 1897), 16. The first listed item is "the Pennsylvania Academy of the Fine Arts, the first fireproof building in Philadelphia."

69. For Norcross Brothers, builders of Trinity Church, see James F. O'Gorman, "Builder: Orlando Whitney Norcross (Norcross Brothers)," in O'Gorman, *Makers of Trinity Church*, 105 ff.

70. Some saving may have resulted from Struthers employing a new sandblast technology for cutting the ornament. See G. F. Barker, "Sand Blast," *Johnson's New Universal Cyclopedia*, vol. 4 (New York: Alvin J. Johnson & Son, 1878), 64, which cites the Pennsylvania Academy of the Fine Arts as an example of the technology.

71. Building Committee Minutes, June 8, 1874, report of Fairman Rogers, chair: "As the labor attending the drawings, plans and contracts with builders greatly exceeded their expectations, they ask that the sum of $6000 agreed on as their compensation, be increased. Increased to $7,500 to the final completion of the work." The fee was still far less than 2 percent of the final cost of the project of $400,000.

72. Academy of Fine Arts Archive, Catalogued Building Construction box, 1873–1874 folder, proposal dated May 16, 1873.

73. Board Minutes, 1858–1876, December 8, 1873, 443–444.

74. Academy of Fine Arts Archives, Atkinson & Myhlertz to John Sartain, April 10, 1874.

75. Board Minutes, 1858–1876, June 8, 1874, Fairman Rogers, reported to the board for the building committee.

76. By the fall the situation was sufficiently alleviated to enable the board to purchase the adjacent property to the south for $55,000, presumably to guarantee adequate light for the building. Board Minutes, 1858–1874, September 14, 1874, 457–459. The following spring in

May 1875, the board was investigating selling the mortgage on the former building to pay for the new building's completion.

77. Board Minutes, 1858–1876, June 14, 1875, 476–477. Godfrey Krouse provided the heating and plumbing systems and was paid for the work in August 1875.

78. Board Minutes, 1858–1876, June 14, 1875, 476–477. The problems of financing probably explain why the large stone panels on either side of the great arched window intended to contain busts of Apelles and Phidias were never carved. Similarly the metope panels on the return of the main façade along Cherry Street were left blank. In 1874, with the budget difficulties in mind, Sartain asked whether the upper-level sculptures could be cast using Frederick Ransome's cast stone process. His inquiry was in response to a paper that was read by Ransome and discussed at the Franklin Institute in a meeting on November 10, 1873. *Journal of the Franklin Institute* 97, no. 2 (February 1874): 139–140. The final details of the façade carving by Kemp are discussed in Board Minutes, 1858–1876, February 14, 1876.

79. The perspective drawing of the envisioned building was created by the architects and reproduced by the new process of photozincography and published as an illustration with Earl Shinn's "The First American Art Academy," *Lippincott's Magazine* 9 (February 1872): 143–153.

80. We have no direct account of the mechanical systems of the Academy other than the drawings and the remaining elements in the building. Contemporary interest in the subject in Philadelphia is evident in the seven lectures on the subject given between 1866 and 1868 at the Franklin Institute by Louis W. Leeds. These were published as *A Treatise on Ventilation* (New York: John Wiley & Son, 1868). See also Robert Ritchie, *A Treatise on Ventilation: Natural and Artificial* (London: Lockwood, 1862). Furness's knowledge of the subject can be gauged from the slightly later Jefferson Hospital. H.O., "The Jefferson Medical College Hospital," *Boston Medical and Surgical Journal* 96, no. 8 (February 1877): 236–241. The article describes the mechanical and ventilating systems in detail and provides hints at the original Academy systems.

81. This fusion returned to a theme that Furness and his fellow students had raised in the Hunt atelier before the war. See Thomas et al., *Frank Furness: The Complete Works,* 21–23.

82. Frequently described as Ceres, the figure had a Greek origin, which meant that she was actually Demeter, dating from the fourth century BC, and obviously was a stand-in for Greek art. In his account of his time in the office Sullivan recalled Furness saying, "Only the Greeks knew how to build." The sculpture was brought by Commodore Daniel Patterson aboard his command, the U.S.S. *Constitution* from Megara, near Athens. See Ken Finkel, "When Philadelphia's 'Earth Mother' Bit the Dust," May 2, 2012, *Philly History Blog*, http://www.phillyhistory.org/blog/index.php/2012/05/when-philadelphias-earth-mother-bit-the-dust/#sthash.fRs0BArb.dpuf (accessed May 2012).

83. The tiles are described in a piece on the Centennial National Bank, "Correspondence–the Centennial National Bank," *American Architect and Building News* 1 (December 23, 1876): 413–414.

84. Beginning in the 1840s, William Struthers, himself a member of the Franklin Institute, paid for numerous members of his firm to attend the drawing classes at the Institute, presumably to learn the representational means to take a client's idea and turn it into a stone form. Franklin Institute Archives, class lists.

85. These were noted as "sketches of two lamps, prepared by the architect to stand on stone posts right and left of the main entrance to the Academy on Broad Street." The second pair were set out at the curb and were apparently of iron. Building Committee Minutes, December 13, 1875.

86. Walter H. Cates, "History of Steel Water Pipe, Its Fabrication and Design Development," April 1971, 2, http://www.steeltank.com/LinkClick.aspx?fileticket=NndJFN-bSyE%3D&tabid=94&mid=452 (accessed January 2012).

87. Furness's numerous patents are discussed in Michael Lewis, *Frank Furness: Architecture and the Violent Mind* (New York: W. W. Norton, 2001), and in Preston Thayer, "The Railroad Designs of Frank Furness: Architecture and Corporate Imagery in the Late Nineteenth Century" (Ph.D. dissertation, University of Pennsylvania, 1993).

88. In another instance of cost savings benefiting the project, the original intention was for tile flooring on the order of the first floor stair hall, but the cost caused Rogers to propose concrete to Sartain. Academy of Fine Arts Archives, Catalogued Building Construction box, 1875 folder, Rogers to Sartain, August 12, 1875, discussing the use of "lithogen," or concrete "after we found the mosaic would be so costly."

89. The railings are discussed in a letter from the architects to Sartain, January 14, 1874: "We would respectfully urge upon you the necessity of coming to a discussion in relation to the bronze rail for the main stairway of the Academy." The architects proposed bronze instead of the cheaper iron. The actual contract for the railing was not signed until January 22, 1876, when Robert Wood signed a proposal to furnish the railing in iron for $1.25 per foot. This was apparently changed to bronze for the actual construction. Catalogued Building Construction box.

90. The present stair hall lamps remain something of a mystery, appearing in none of the group of photos taken at the time of the opening in 1876, which show clusters of storks standing back to back with oil lamps above their heads. The present lamps appeared in all of the later interior photographs but there is no mention of the replacement of the naturalistic lamps in the Academy records. Sketches for them appear in Furness's sketchbooks.

91. O'Gorman, *Makers of Trinity Church*, 19.

92. For photographs of the primitive construction at Trinity, see ibid., 114.

93. Ibid., xx. Ironically Phoenix Iron Works also made the steel that was incorporated into the structure of Richardson's Trinity Church in Boston, but where it was celebrated in Philadelphia, it was concealed in Boston to the point that Richardson may not have even known of its presence in his building. See O'Gorman, "Builder: Orlando Whitney Norcross," 116 n. 20.

94. William Henry Furness, "Address," *Inauguration of the New Building of the Pennsylvania Academy of the Fine Arts, 22 April 1876* (Philadelphia: Pennsylvania Academy of the Fine Arts, 1876), 16.

CHAPTER 4

Note to epigraph: Ralph Waldo Emerson, "Self Reliance," *Essays by Ralph Waldo Emerson, First Series* (originally published 1841; Boston: Houghton Mifflin, 1903), 45–88, quote on 46.

1. The magazine began in 1868 as *Lippincott's Magazine of Literature, Science, and Education.*

2. An illustration of some Furness ironwork was published in the *American Architect and Building News* in 1886 and others images of his work appear in advertisements. For example, illustrations of Karl Bitter's sculptural panels for Broad Street Station were published in the *American Architect and Building News* 43, no. 945 (January 1894): 34.

3. H.O., "The Jefferson Medical College Hospital," *Boston Medical and Surgical Journal* 96 (January–June 1877): 237.

4. *Philadelphia Evening Telegraph*. The Provident Life and Trust had provoked comment in the regional press. quoted in James F. O'Gorman, *The Architecture of Frank Furness* (Philadelphia: Philadelphia Museum of Art, 1973), 45.

5. "Buildings of Beauty," *Philadelphia Press*, May 24, 1885, p. 10.

6. Thompson Westcott, Scrapbook 7, 133, Historical Society of Pennsylvania, Philadelphia.

7. Montgomery Schuyler, "Architectural Aberrations: The Hale Building," *Architectural Record* 3 no. 2 (October–December 1893): 208.

8. The Indianapolis narrative is discussed in George E. Thomas, *William L. Price: Arts and Crafts to Modern Design* (New York: Princeton Architectural Press, 2000), 157–162.

9. Lewis Mumford, "The Imperial Age." *American Institute of Architects Journal* 12 (August 1924): 366–371.

10. The bank was organized by West Philadelphia businessman and developer Clarence H. Clark (1833–1906), the son of Enoch W. Clark, a Unitarian from New England who established the important Philadelphia brokerage firm of E. W. Clark & Co. and was a member of Frank's father's congregation. The elder Clark supported the construction of Furness's first significant commission, the Germantown Unitarian Church (1866) near the Clark family property in Germantown. Furness was the likely designer of portions of Clarence Clark's massive residence at Forty-Second and Locust Streets.

11. *Philadelphia Inquirer*, January 22, 1876, cited in http://www.brynmawr.edu/iconog/up hp/AABN/centbank/centbank.html (accessed May 2012).

12. The Bank of Commerce in Kansas City, a close replica of the Provident Bank, is discussed by George Ehrlich, "The Bank of Commerce by Asa Beebe Cross: A Building of the Latest Architecture," *Journal of the Society of Architectural Historians* 43, no. 2 (May 1984): 168–172. For the Salem imitation, see Lee H. Nelson, "White, Furness, McNally and the Capital National Bank of Salem, Oregon," *Journal of the Society of Architectural Historians* 19 (May 1960): 57–61.

13. Pettit wrote Wilson's obituary: "Obituary Notices of Members Deceased, Joseph Miller Wilson, A.M., C.E.," *Proceedings of the American Philosophical Society* 42, no. 173 (April 1903): i–vi.

14. In the 1880s, the engineer-led Pennsylvania Railroad began to apply the regional industrial principle of standardization to all of corporate actions, extending this process to station types that were dependent on the size and importance of the market. This led the Pennsylvania Railroad to reduce its array of building types to a few models such as those on its Chestnut Hill West line built in the early 1880s in response to Furness's work for the Reading. See Walter Berg, *Buildings and Structures of American Railroads* (New York: John Wiley & Sons, 1893), which illustrates several of the Furness schemes for the Philadelphia and Reading Railroad as well as the Pennsylvania Railroad's schemes for the Chestnut Hill branch stations on 326–328.

15. For an overview of corporate strategy by the various railroads, see Preston Thayer, "The Railroad Designs of Frank Furness: Architecture and Corporate Imagery in the Late Nineteenth Century" (Ph.D. dissertation, University of Pennsylvania, 1993).

16. See also the Wilson Brothers stations for the New York, West Shore & Buffalo Railroad, Wilson Brothers & Co., *Catalogue of Work Executed* (Philadelphia: Lippincott, 1885), n.p. It depicts symmetrical stations of larger size and wildly asymmetrical stations of smaller sizes, each highly individualized on the Furness-Reading model with some including an agent's house and station such as the station on the Pennsylvania Railroad at Hawkins. Their similarity suggests that the Pennsylvania was looking closely at Furness and his work for the Reading Railroad, a charge that Furness later made in regard to the Pennsylvania Railroad's stations on the West Chestnut Hill branch of the railroad designed by Washington Bleddyn Powell. Frank Furness to John Wooten, December 23, 1884, Historical Society of Pennsylvania.

17. Thayer, "Railroad Designs," 49–50.

18. Thayer raises the question of how much of this work was actually handled by Focht. According to a biographical sketch of Focht in Morton Montgomery, *Historical and Biographical Annals of Berks County, Pennsylvania* (Chicago: Beers Publishing, 1909), 375, "Mr. Focht has had numerous contracts from the Philadelphia & Reading Railway Company, having erected most of the stations along their line, besides many elegant and commodious residences along the line of the Pennsylvania road. He also put up the stock farm buildings on the estate of Mr. A. J. Cassatt . . . [and] an addition to the Haverford (Pa.) College buildings." All of these mentioned projects were designed by Furness.

19. Furness, quoted in George E. Thomas et al., *Frank Furness: The Complete Works* (New York: Princeton Architectural Press, 1991, revised ed., 1996), 345–356.

20. In 1979, after a 1973 Philadelphia Museum of Art exhibit on *The Architecture of Frank Furness*, renewed interest in Furness led the Chestnut Hill Historical Society to commission architects Lynch/Martinez-Conill to work from the existing photographs from the Reading Railroad files, many of which were taken immediately after the construction of the building, to re-create the missing porch toward the tracks and to make the major repairs necessary. The firm undertook paint analysis at the same time that revealed the original color scheme that corroborated the evidence of the historic images.

21. Louis Heiland, *The Undine Barge Club of Philadelphia: 1856–1924* (Philadelphia: Undine Barge Club of Philadelphia, 1925), 13–14.

22. Signed specifications dated October 20, 1875, are in the files of the club. This is one of the earliest of the independent works by Furness and marks the dissolution of Furness & Hewitt.

23. The colors were developed according to modern paint analysis and were generally followed in the 1997–1999 restoration of the building but the turned posts and front surfaces of the wood were painted green as they had been for many years instead of the original brownstone brown. Hopefully, in a future restoration, the color scheme will be fully restored.

24. Plans and photographs of the Crabtree house are in Thomas et al., *Frank Furness: The Complete Works*, catalog #320, p. 260.

25. Ibid. Photographs of Idlewild are on catalog #371, p. 295.

26. Ibid., commissions #252, p. 199 and #470, p. 319 and #483, p. 321.

27. The house eerily anticipated George Howe's High Hollow in Chestnut Hill in which a stair at the main entrance leads down to a landing at the lower hillside grade.

28. It was in this ballroom that Philadelphia capitalists led by Griscom, Cassatt, and the University of Pennsylvania's provost, Charles Harrison, ensured the presidential nomination of William Howard Taft. Charles Custis Harrison, "Memoirs," UPA 6.2H Harrison Papers, box 5, folder 17, University of Pennsylvania Archives.

29. The office renovated Edward Sayres's house in 1900; see Thomas et al., *Frank Furness: The Complete Works*, #536, p. 331.

30. J. Thomas Scharf and Thompson Westcott, *A History of Philadelphia*, vol. 2 (Philadelphia: L. H. Everts, 1884), 1350.

31. Cochran was a lawyer and financier who established the city's taxation system and in 1877 was made president of the Guarantee Trust and Safe Deposit Company, an important Furness & Hewitt commission on Bankers' Row. Ibid., vol. 3, 2104–2105.

32. Much of the background research on St. Peter's Church was developed for my article "From a Side Pew: Meditations on the Saints of St. Peter's Church," in *St. Peter's Church: Faith in Action for 250 Years*, ed. Cordelia Frances Biddle et al. (Philadelphia: Temple University Press, 2011), 118–128.

33. The Gregg house was restored in 1996 by architect Doug Seiler for the Academy of Vocal Arts. Paint analysis was conducted by J. Christopher Frey.

34. Gregg is listed at this address in 1883 in *Gopsills' Philadelphia Directory* (Philadelphia: James Gopsill, 1883), 653.

35. This building survived into the 1960s and drew a loving analysis by Robert Venturi, *Complexity and Contradiction in Architecture* (New York: Museum of Modern Art, 1966), 61. Venturi discussed it in "Contradiction Juxtaposed," as representing "an array of violent pressures within a rigid frame, . . . seemingly held up by the buildings next door; it is an almost insane short story of a castle on a city street" whose purpose is "to contradict the severe limitations associated with a façade, a street line, and contiguous row houses."

36. This was a Pennsylvania Railroad–related commission with George Roberts, son of the president of the railroad, on the board.

37. Louis Sullivan, "The Tall Building Artistically Considered," *Lippincott's Magazine* 57 (March 1896): 403–409, quote on 406.

38. Thayer cites the anger of Philadelphia industrialists when they discovered that the local railroads were excluding their competitors and thus raising rates in Philadelphia. "Railroad Designs," 23. The extent of railroad collusion is discussed at length in Henry Demarest Lloyd, "The Story of a Great Monopoly," *Atlantic Monthly* 47 (March 1881): 317–334.

39. Cornelius Nolen Weygandt, April 27, 1886, diary for 1886, Cornelius Nolen Weygandt Papers, UPT 50 W547, vol. 1887 (2): March 30, 1886–July 18, 1886, box 3, folder 4, University of Pennsylvania Archives. This source was discovered and shared by James Duffin, office manager, University of Pennsylvania Archives.

40. John Ruskin, *The Seven Lamps of Architecture* (New York: Wiley & Halsted, 1857), 100.

41. Much of the research on the history of the library was undertaken to support the restoration of the building with Venturi, Scott Brown Associates and my former consulting practice, the Clio Group, Inc. Some of this material has been previously published in George E. Thomas, "'The Happy Employment of Means to Ends': Frank Furness's Library of the University of Pennsylvania and the Industrial Culture of Philadelphia," *Pennsylvania Magazine of History and Biography* 126, no. 2 (April 2002): 249–272.

42. Moses King, *Harvard and Its Surroundings* (Cambridge, MA: Moses King, 1884), 25. Henri Labrouste's Bibliotheque Nationale similarly separated the bulk of the book storage from the reading room—but the reading room walls were lined with tiers of book shelves. For the Ware & Van Brunt stack, see *American Architect and Building News* 4, no. 152 (November 23, 1878): 172–173.

43. William Pepper, James Boswell, and Horace Howard Furness, "Letter to the Community" (n.d., c. 1886), Joseph Clarke Sims Scrapbook, University of Pennsylvania Archives. See also Talcott Williams, "Plans for the Library Building of the University of Pennsylvania," *Library Journal* 13, no. 8 (August 1888): 237–243.

44. William Pepper, *University of Pennsylvania Provost's Report* (Philadelphia: Collins Printing House,1885), 28.

45. Williams, "Plans for the Library," 238: "The subscriptions thus far secured by the Committee on Ways and Means of which Mr. Charles C. Harrison is chairman are Wm. Pepper, $10,000; Harrison Frazier & Co., $10,000; Wharton Barker, $10,000; H. H. Houston, $10,000; C. H. Clark, $10,000; A. J. Drexel, $10,000; Henry C. Gibson, $10,000; Alexander Brown, $7000; Mrs. Thomas H. Powers, $5000; Mrs. J. Campbell Harris, $5000; Mrs. Harry Ingersoll, $5000; George Bullock, $5000; Joseph D. Potts, $5000; Joseph F. Sinnott, $5000; A. M. Moore, $5000; Thomas McKean, $5000; C. B. Wright, $5000; Samuel Dickson, $5000;

Strawbridge & Clothier, $5000; the Misses Blanchard, $3000; J. Vaughan Merrick, $2500; and many smaller amounts."

46. Horace Howard Furness, "Dedicatory Address," February 17, 1891, University of Pennsylvania Archives.

47. Minutes of the Board of Trustees, Library Committee, April 5, 1887, University of Pennsylvania Archives.

48. For Winsor's bibliography, see William F. Yust, "No. 54 A Bibliography of Justin Winsor," *Library of Harvard University Bibliographic Contributions*, ed. William Coolidge Lane, vol. 4 (Cambridge, MA: Library of Harvard University, 1902). Winsor's bibliography was extensive, covering thirty pages of small-point type. Pages 31 and 32 cover biographical materials and obituary references. He apparently published nothing on his work with the University of Pennsylvania.

49. Melvil Dewey, *A Classification and Subject Index for Cataloguing and Arranging the Books and Pamphlets of a Library* (Amherst, MA: Case, Lockwood & Brainard [Hartford, CT] 1876). The decimalized system was based on the rationalization of the metric order and was first published as a reference by the Amherst Library.

50. Poole graduated from Yale College in 1849, where he organized and published a guide to periodical literature (*Poole's Index* [New York: George P. Putnam: 1848 and later]) and then worked as an assistant to the librarian of the Boston Athenaeum before becoming the librarian of the Cincinnati Public Library and then the Chicago Public Library from 1873 to 1887. Poole wrote several articles on library design and his points became the basis for the discussion of the modern library in the *Encyclopedia Britannica*. See H. R. Tedder and E. C. Thomas, "Libraries," *Encyclopedia Britannica*, vol. 14 (9th edition, 1888), 536.

51. William F[rederick] Poole, *Report on the Progress of Library Architecture* (Boston: American Library Association, 1882). Poole's *Report* was also published in preliminary form without the comments on particular libraries in *Circulars of Information of the Bureau of Education: The Construction of Library Buildings*, vol. 1 (Washington, DC: Government Printing Office, 1881).

52. W[illiam] F[rederick] Poole, "The Construction of Library Buildings," *Library Journal* 6, no. 4 (April 1881): 69–77, quote on 73. Reprinted in *American Architect and Building News* 10, no. 291 (September 17, 1881): 131.

53. Ibid.

54. Poole, *Report on the Progress of Library Architecture*, 15.

55. Poole, "The Construction of Library Buildings," 132. This is an early use of the word "modern," in the sense of progressive industrialism. His "means to ends" phrase was echoed five years later by Horace Howard Furness in his address at the cornerstone laying for the University of Pennsylvania's library. Was the phrase common or had Frank shown his brother Poole's article? Most telling is Poole's willingness to drop all historical references and instead to see libraries created following a purely industrial or mechanical logic.

56. William F. Poole, "Small Library Buildings," *Library Journal* 10, no. 10 (October 1885): 250–256.

57. Poole, *Report on the Progress of Library Architecture*. This version was published as a separate report after the meeting of the American Library Association in Cincinnati in May 1882. It is augmented with comments on several projects including the first steps toward the new Boston Public Library and a report on the University of Michigan Library, which was then under way. It met with Poole's approval.

58. The issue of control was central to the plan of the Chancellor Green Library at Princeton. It was presided over by a former assistant to the Librarian of Congress, Frederick Vin-

ton, who sat in a raised desk in the center where he copied cards for the card catalog and surveyed all of the research desks. See http://library.princeton.edu/about/history.php?iframe=true&width=100%&height=100% (accessed December 2011).

59. Richard H. Janson, "The Billings Library," unpublished manuscript, University of Vermont Special Collections, 2; quoted in David Provost, "A Gem of Architecture: The History of the Billings Library," www.uvm.edu/campus/billings/billingsprovost/billingshistoryprovost.html (accessed July 2016).

60. "Personal Notes—Richardson," *Library Journal* 11, no. 5 (May 1886): 149.

61. Edward Bosley, *The University of Pennsylvania Library* (New York: Phaidon Press, 1996), 13. Bosley misunderstood the dates of Dewey's meeting with Furness and his letter to the provost in April 1887 and thus misinterpreted the extent of their collaboration.

62. Melvil Dewey to Dr. William Pepper, April 20, 1888, University of Pennsylvania Archives, box 61, folder 1888– Library.

63. Williams, "Plans for the Library Building." Williams was a close friend of the Furness family. He is depicted as the aesthete, St. Clair, in S. Weir Mitchell's novel about Philadelphia life *Dr. North and His Friends* (New York: Century, 1901).

64. The cataloguing department was largely subsumed in the Lea Reading Room, a 1920s addition by the Furness office; its functions were removed to the basement but the skylights are still in place above the computer terminal area that supplants the old card catalog. Horace Howard Furness, "Dedicatory Address," *Proceedings of the Opening of the Library of the University of Pennsylvania* (Philadelphia, 1891), 8.

65. Ibid., 8.

66. See John T. Bailey & Co. in Thomas et al., *Frank Furness: The Complete Works*, 319. Earlier panels on the same factory with the date 1885 indicate that Furness was using this technique before the library. Furness used a similar gouge pattern to ornament sawn wood beams in the alterations to the Joshua Gregg house (called the Richard D. Wood House in Thomas et al., *Frank Furness: The Complete Works*), also in 1888.

67. Wilson Brothers encountered the same issue with its great train sheds and resolved it by skylighting only narrow strips amounting to less than 10 percent of the total roof area. When the library was restored in the 1980s Venturi, Scott Brown Associates used insulated glass panels on the eastern face to light work areas of the stacks while the remainder of the roof was covered with lead-coated copper over insulated panels. Modern lighting supplements the original daylighting.

68. According to James Duffin of the University of Pennsylvania Archives, the library's original community was roughly one thousand students in all programs; at the time that the Duhring Wing was added in 1913, the community was roughly six times larger; in 1961 when the Van Pelt Library replaced Furness's building, the university community numbered eighteen thousand.

69. For a discussion of the industrial character of the library, see Thomas, "Happy Employment of Means to Ends," 258–264. "Means to ends" characterizes industrial design principles. See Pietro Micheli, Joe Jaina, Keith Goffin, Fred Lemke, and Roberto Verganti, "Perceptions of Industrial Design: The 'Means' and the 'Ends,'" *Journal of Product Innovation Management* 29, no. 5 (September 2012): 687–704: "Managers and industrial designers use some common terms augmented by additional terms that are specific to each group: managers are commercially orientated in the 'ends' they want to achieve and designers perceive more antecedents 'means') necessary to achieve their 'ends'—iconic design" (687).

70. This as with most of the other quotes on the windows was selected by the architect's brother, the Shakespeare scholar, Horace. In this instance it is a comic line of Falstaff, himself a talker rather than a doer.

71. Francis Newton Thorpe, "New Library of University of Pennsylvania," *Harper's Weekly* 35, no. 119 (February 14, 1891): 124.

72. *Proceedings at the Opening of the Library of the University of Pennsylvania, 7th of February, 1891* (Philadelphia: University of Pennsylvania Press, 1891), 6.

73. George E. Thomas, "'The Happy Employment of Means to Ends:' Frank Furness's Library of the University of Pennsylvania and the Industrial Culture of Philadelphia," *Pennsylvania Magazine of History and Biography,* 126, no. 2 (April 2002): 249–272. The title comes from a phrase of Horace Howard Furness at the dedication; see note 64.

74. Williams, "Plans for the Library Building," 240, n.1.

75. Talcott Williams, "An Address Delivered at the Dedication of the Library of the University of Pennsylvania, February 7, 1891," *Library Journal* 16, no. 4 (April 1891): 108. In the *Proceedings at the Opening of the Library of the University of Pennsylvania,* published by the University of Pennsylvania, Williams's talk was entitled "The Memory of Man."

76. J. Thomas Scharf, *A History of Delaware*, vol. 2 (Philadelphia: L. J. Richards, 1888),879.

77. Carlo Viola, Library Committee, Trustees of New Castle Common, "History of the New Castle Library, 1810–2010," http://nc-chap.org/history/NClibrary.php (accessed May 2016). He cites an approving contemporary account that reported the "exterior colors, brick red, toffee and apple green" forming "rich earth colors in surprising combinations."

78. "Alterations at the Boston Public Library," *Library Journal* 26, no. 1 (January 1899): 20–21; the same issue reported that the Pennsylvania Library Club toured the Penn Library in its December 1898 meeting (28).

79. Charles Soule, "Modern Library Buildings," *Architectural Review* 9, no. 1 (January 1902): 1–60.

80. The interior views of the hotel were published by Bible House, New York, in the *Illustrated American* 8, no. 89 (31 October 1891): 535–536. It was not published for its architecture but as an illustration of the decorative work of Philadelphia dry goods merchants Darlington, Runk & Co., who furnished the interiors. See http://books.google.com/books?id= 3nFNAAAAYAAJ&pg=PA532&lpg=PA532&dq=the+illustrated+american++October+ 1891&source=bl&ots=ygiVpVEd_p&sig=lIpM2-qBgRrri2r_vaway34b28U&hl=en&sa= X&ei=iCwSUpK8A5LOyAH2mYAw&ved=0CDwQ6AEwAw#v=onepage&q=the%20 illustrated%20american%20%20October%201891&f=false (accessed August 2013).

81. H. H. Furness to his daughter Caroline A. Furness, July 24, 1892, *Letters of Horace Howard Furness in Two Volumes*, ed. H.[orace] H.[oward] F.[urness] J.[r.], vol. 1 (New York: Houghton Mifflin, 1922), 276–277.

82. The project is described and illustrated with a perspective of the view in *Railway International Passenger and Ticket Agents' Journal* 8, no. 6 (March 1901): 9–10. The building was commonly known as the Arcade Building for its arcade that spanned the sidewalk and formally as the Commercial Trust Building.

83. *The Pennsylvania Railroad Company Fifty-Sixth Annual Report: For the Year 1902* (Philadelphia: Broad Street Station, 1903), vii–viii. The overall project is described under "General Remarks" on 22–26.

84. For a contemporary overview of Cassatt's views and experiences, see E.D.B., "Alexander J. Cassatt," *New York Times, Illustrated Magazine Supplement,* June 18, 1899, p. SM2, col. 1. Furness commissions are detailed in Thomas et al., *Frank Furness: The Complete Works.*

85. Christopher T. Baer, Hagley Museum, e-mail message to author, May 2012.

86. "Brief Railroad Items," *New York Times*, September 8, 1900, p. 12: "A new passenger station is planned for Wilmington, Del. by the Pennsylvania Railroad. Negotiations are now under way for the acquisition of four blocks in the center of the town adjoining the terminals of the Philadelphia, Wilmington, and Baltimore, which is an important part of the Pennsylvania system." In regard to the Wilmington station complex, see Alexander J. Cassatt to Charles McKim, "Letter of Appointment," April 24, 1902, New York Historical Society, McKim Papers, quoted in Hillary Ballon et al., *New York's Pennsylvania Stations* (New York: W. W. Norton, 2002), 200. The letter includes this instruction: "The part of the work which will be placed in your charge will be all that above the waiting room level. The retaining walls up to the street levels, and the foundations up to the waiting room, and all the work below will be under the charge of the Company's engineers." Ignored by Ballon and other critics was the striking contrast between the exterior classical stonework and the exposed steel frame interior. The steel interior links the station to the Pennsylvania Railroad industrial culture. Christopher Baer of the Hagley Museum suggests that another reason for Furness's loss of the great railroad commissions was that his office had fallen behind in designs for the corporate structure of the office, which remained more a personal instrument, while Burnham in particular, and McKim, Mead & White to a lesser degree, had evolved a modern office structure that better meshed with the Pennsylvania Railroad's corporate model.

87. *First Annual Report of the Board of Directors to the Stockholders, Philadelphia, Baltimore and Washington Railroad* (Philadelphia: Broad Street Station, 1903). The 1904 annual report noted the death of Sellers after thirty-nine years of service to the board. The 1905 annual report lists nearly $1,000,000 in expenses for the track elevation in Wilmington and $39,309 in expenses toward the new passenger terminal (16). The 1906 report lists $203,681 for expenses relating to the Wilmington Terminal (16), indicating that the project was well under way. Another $108,851 of expenditure was reported in the 1907 report (17). The 1908 report lists $64,481 for the completion of the Wilmington Terminal (18), providing a beginning date of 1905 and an end date of 1907 for the project.

88. The Pennsylvania Railroad is the subject of a remarkable online chronology by year that is coordinated by Christopher Baer at the Hagley Museum. See http://www.prrths.com/Hagley/PRR1905%20Mar%2005.pdf (accessed January 2014).

89. Horace Howard Furness to W. Aldis Wright, July 29, 1912, *Letters of Horace Howard Furness*, vol. 2, 276.

EPILOGUE

1. George Howe, "What Is This Modern Architecture Trying to Express?" *American Architect* 137 (May 1930): 22–25.

2. Ibid., 24.

3. George E. Thomas, *William L. Price: Arts and Crafts to Modern Design* (New York: Princeton Architectural Press, 2000), 44–45.

4. George E. Thomas and Susan N. Snyder, "William Price's Traymore Hotel: Modernity in the Mass Resort," special issue, "The American Hotel," *Journal of Decorative and Propaganda Arts* 25 (2005): 183–211.

5. Thomas, *William L. Price*, 175 ff.

6. Ibid., especially 175–182. See also Edward Warren Edward Warren Hoak and Willis Humphrey Church, eds., *Masterpieces of Architecture in the United States* (New York: Charles Scribner Sons, 1930), 167–179. It misdates the building as 1918, three years after its actual

completion. The essay on the Traymore in the volume was written by Charles Harris Whitaker, Sullivan's acolyte, who four years later would mention Price's Chicago Freight Terminal in *The Story of Architecture: From Ramses to Rockefeller* (New York: Random House, 1934), 329. Two years before, in 1932, Henry Russell Hitchcock's exhibit of *Modern Architecture: International Exhibit* at the Museum of Modern Art had undercut American modernism by focusing only on the new European moderns. The Whitaker reference would be the last time that any of Price's masterpieces were included in a significant publication until Peter Collins's *Concrete: The Vision of a New Architecture* (New York: Horizon Press, 1959), plates 22–24, pp. 87–88. Two years later, Carl Condit rediscovered his work from the perspective of engineering in *American Building Art: The Twentieth Century* (New York: Oxford University Press, 1961).

7. *President of the United States, to Congress, Executive Document # 211, 52nd Congress* (Washington, DC: Government Printing Office, 1893), 94–97; *Message from the President of the United States Transmitting the Annual Report of the World's Columbian Commission and other Papers Relating to the Exposition* (Washington, DC: Government Printing Office, 1893), 60–61; "Report of Committee of Architects," in *Message from the President*, [signed Frank Furness, E. E. Myers, Geo. Orff], 94–96.

8. Alfred Bendiner, *Bendiner's Philadelphia* (New York: A. S. Barnes, 1964), 40–41. The "University Library" and Wright's assessment of it in an accompanying text were part of a series of columns by Bendiner published about Philadelphia landmarks in the *Philadelphia Evening Bulletin*'s Sunday magazine. Wright's comments in the 1950s began the appreciation of the library that led to its restoration thirty years later.

9. [Montgomery Schuyler], "Architectural Aberrations No. 9: The Hale Building," *Architectural Record*, 3, no. 2 (October–December 1893): 207–210.

10. Ralph Adams Cram, "The Work of Messrs. Frank Miles Day & Brother," *Architectural Record* 15, no. 5 (May 1902): 398.

11. [Schuyler], "Architectural Aberrations No. 9: The Hale Building." For Schuyler's remarks on the University of Pennsylvania see "Architecture of American Colleges: University of Pennsylvania, Girard, Haverford, Lehigh, and Bryn Mawr Colleges," *Architectural Record,* 28 (July–December 1910), 183–212; the university is treated 183–200; the library is singled out 187–189. Huger Elliott, "Architecture in Philadelphia," *Architectural Record* 23, no. 4 (April 1908): 294–309, quote on 296. Elliott's position at the time was as an instructor. The split personality of architectural criticism at the time is nowhere more evident than in this single issue. It begins with A. D. F. Hamlin's attack on the Beaux Arts method as counter to the American experience; then includes an important early publication of the design by Furness's pupil, William Price, of the Blenheim Hotel in Atlantic City as exemplifying an appropriate design sensibility in reinforced concrete; moves on to praise of the Beaux Arts campus of the University of California by John Galen Howard; and attacks Philadelphia and Furness in Elliott's article; before ending with Russell Sturgis's evisceration of Frank Lloyd Wright's Larkin Building as "an extremely ugly building," "a monster of awkwardness." "The Larkin Building," 311–321, quote on 312.

12. "FURNESS, FRANK an architect, died in Media, Pennsylvania, June 30, 1912. He was a member of the firm of Furness, Evans & Company and was Captain of the Sixth Pennsylvania Cavalry during the Civil War, receiving a Congressional medal for courage." Obituary, *American Art Annual* 10 (1913): 77. For a telling comparison with Furness's obituary in the same *American Art Annual*, see the report of the death of Daniel Burnham, who was described as "A prominent Chicago architect, chief of construction and director of works of

the World's Fair in Chicago in 1893. He designed many prominent buildings in New York and Chicago, and when San Francisco was devastated by the earthquake he was called to direct the laying out of the new city" (ibid., 75–76).

13. Cram, "Work of Messrs. Frank Miles Day & Brother," 399; Lewis Mumford, *The Brown Decades: A Study of the Arts in America, 1865–1895* (New York: Harcourt, Brace, 1931), 65. Similar comments were made by William Jordy in his essay on "Montgomery Schuyler," *American Architecture and Other Writings by Montgomery Schuyler*, vol. 1 (Cambridge, MA: Harvard University Press, 1961), 22, which refers to Furness's "fearlessness" and "daring."

14. Thomas Carlyle, "Signs of the Times," *Edinburgh Review* 98 (1829), reprinted in *The Complete Works of Thomas Carlyle,* vol. 1 (New York: P. F. Collier & Sons, 1901), 462–487, quote on 465.

15. Thorsten Veblen, *The Theory of Business Enterprise* (New York: Charles Scribner's Sons, 1904), 311.

16. Ibid., 317–318.

17. Leonard K. Eaton, *Two Chicago Architects and Their Clients: Frank Lloyd Wright and Howard Van Doren Shaw* (Cambridge, MA: MIT Press, 1969), 49.

18. Ibid., 49–50.

19. George E. Thomas et al., *Frank Furness: The Complete Works*, commission 32, p. 169. The known photographs of the exterior of the house date from after its sale and subsequent redesign by Charles Burns. An insurance survey describes the main façade as a combination of stone and brick. Louis Sullivan, *Autobiography of an Idea* (1924; reprint, New York: Dover, 1956), 191.

20. The paneling was moved from the city house to Walter Rogers Furness's suburban house near Media that was built when the family residence at 222 Washington Square was sold and demolished. At one point the decorative paneling was painted black; it was restored by the then owner in the 1990s.

21. The table is now in Atlanta's High Museum. Theodore Roosevelt, Jr., would have been an impressionable fourteen when Furness designed furnishings and interior fittings for his father's house in 1873. Most of the Furness-designed furniture of the Roosevelt house was removed by Theodore Roosevelt to his summer house on Long Island, attesting to his affection for his childhood hero. Pieces are illustrated in Thomas et al., *Frank Furness: The Complete Works*, 182–183. Furness retained a relationship with Roosevelt. In 1887, the then-twenty-nine-year-old Theodore Roosevelt, fresh from his loss as a candidate for mayor of New York and just returned from two years ranching on the Little Missouri River in the Badlands of North Dakota, was elected president of a new conservation organization, the Boone and Crockett Club. Theodore Roosevelt and George Bird Grinnell, eds., *Hunting in Many Lands: The Book of the Boone and Crockett Club* (New York: Forest and Stream, 1895). A list of the founding members on 444 includes Frank Furness and his nephew, Walter Rogers Furness; Furness's in-law-by marriage and future western novelist Owen Wister; and several future Furness clients including Frank Thomson, later president of the Pennsylvania Railroad. See also Theodore Roosevelt and George Bird Grinnell, eds., *American Big Game Hunting* (New York: Forest and Stream, 1901). Furness is again listed as a member on 342. Membership was attained by having killed three of the American big game animals—buffalo, elk, mountain goat, sheep, bear, etc. For an account of the club and its members, see Christine Bold, *The Frontier Club: Popular Westerns and Cultural Power, 1880–1924* (New York: Oxford University Press, 2013).

22. Paul Sprague, *The Drawings of Louis Henry Sullivan: A Catalog of the Frank Lloyd Wright Collection in the Avery Architectural Library* (Princeton, NJ: Princeton University

Press, 1979). Some of these are on tracing paper and may well have been direct tracings of Furness drawings—or possibly may have been by Furness himself. In the collection of Furness drawings remaining with Charles Savage are similar ornamental drawings, at least one of which was pinholed for transfer to a stencil.

23. Early Sullivan buildings are surveyed in Robert Twombly, *Louis Sullivan: His Life and Work* (New York: Viking, Penguin, 1986), 77–136.

24. Reverend William H. Furness to Miller McKim, spring 1867, McKim Collection, Library of Congress, quoted in Thomas et al., *Frank Furness: The Complete Works*, 18.

25. Sullivan, *Autobiography* 194. This is obviously a strong counter to Henry Russell Hitchcock's dismissive comment that "it is hardly correct to call the latter his 'master': nor for that matter, should one say he was 'inspired,' but merely 'encouraged' by Furness's bold stylistic innovations—if indeed, even that is not too definite a conclusion." Henry Russell Hitchcock, *The Architecture of H. H. Richardson and His Times* (1936; revised, Cambridge, MA: MIT Press, 1966), 293.

26. Sullivan returned from Liverpool to New York on the S.S. *Britannic* on May 25, 1875. Ancestry.com, 1875 Arrivals, New York; microfilm serial: M237; microfilm roll: 398; line: 26; list number: 425 (accessed January 2014).

27 For Sullivan's banks, see Lauren S. Weingarten, *Louis H. Sullivan: The Banks* (Cambridge, MA: MIT Press, 1987).

28. The day-to-day operations of that project were recorded in a receipt book that survived as an actor's prop in a local theater before being rescued and acquired by the Architectural Archives at the University of Pennsylvania. It recounts the fees to be paid and marks the regular job meetings that were first attended by Furness and then, as the job proceeded toward its conclusion, by Frank Price, who signed the purchase orders. William Price's early life and background are discussed in Thomas, *William L. Price*.

29. Another young member of the office at the time was William Masters Camac, a graduate of the University of Pennsylvania in 1872. He was mentioned as architect of "one of the first buildings erected by the Order [of the Holy Cross] nearly forty years ago—the Chapel of the summer home at Farmingdale Long Island." See *An American Cloister: An Account of the Life and Work of the Order of the Holy Cross*, 2nd edition (West Park, NY: Holy Cross, 1922), 139. This would be c. 1878 when Camac was in the Furness office and implies another office work. See also "William Masters Camac," *Pennsylvania Gazette* 16, no. 29 (April 18, 1918): 817.

30. See Thomas, *William L. Price*, 98. The quote comes from a Price lecture, "A Philadelphia Architect's Views on Architecture," *American Architect* 87 (October 17, 1903): 27.

31. In the *Secretary's Fourth Report: Harvard College Class of 1908; Quindecennial Report, 1923* (Cambridge, MA: Harvard College, 1923), quoted by Robert A. M. Stern, *George Howe: Toward a Modern Architecture* (New Haven, CT: Yale University Press, 1975), 24.

32. The Lutheran Church of the Holy Communion, by Fraser, Furness & Hewitt in 1870, which stood at Broad and Arch Streets, had already been demolished c. 1903, beginning the long line of demolitions that marked the Beaux Arts' and the modernists' rejection of Furness's break with tradition.

33. *Secretary's Second Report: Harvard College Class of 1908* (Cambridge, MA: Harvard College, 1914), 162, entry for "George Howe": "In August 1907 shortly after my graduation and marriage, I sailed for Europe and spent the remainder of the year traveling in Italy. In the spring of 1908 I went to Paris to study architecture and entered the Beaux Arts in December of the same year. Here I remained until my graduation and returned to Philadelphia in June

1913. In November, 1913 I became a partner in the firm of Furness, Evans and Company architects and now appeal to all good and true men of 1908 to give me a job. Member: Philadelphia Club, Racquet Club of Philadelphia, University Barge Club, Philadelphia Chapter of the American Institute of Architects, Societe des Architectes diplomes par le gouvernement." In the *Secretary's Third Report: Harvard College Class of 1908* (Cambridge, MA: Harvard College, 1920), 244–246, Howe reported that he left the Furness office for Mellor & Meigs.

34. Stern, *George Howe*, 24–25.

35. John Harbeson, "Philadelphia's Victorian Architecture, 1860–1890," *Pennsylvania Magazine of History and Biography* 67, no. 3 (July 1943): 271; cited in Stern, *George Howe*, 126–127.

36. Helen Howe West, *George Howe: Architect* (Philadelphia: Helen Howe West, 1973), 34–40.

37. Carl Boggs and Tom Pollard, *A World in Chaos: Social Crisis and the Rise of Post-Modern Cinema* (Lanham, MD: Roman & Littlefield, 2003), 64–65.

38. The notion of a fixed hierarchy of taste and knowledge marked social theory for a century from John Ruskin's *Seven Lamps of Architecture* and *The Stones of Venice* to Pierre Bourdieu, *Distinction: A Social Critique of the Judgment of Taste*, trans. Richard Nice (Cambridge, MA: Harvard University Press, 1984).

39. For a chronology of Museum of Modern Art exhibits, see http://www.moma.org /learn/resources/archives/archives_exhibition_history_list (accessed January 2014).

40. This narrative still continues although at least one of Richardson's chief advocates, James F. O'Gorman, author of the first comprehensive look at Furness in 1973, has recanted to the extent of acknowledging that Furness was more about the future than Richardson. See James F. O'Gorman, "Then and Now: A Note on the Contrasting Architecture of H. H. Richardson and Frank Furness," in *H. H. Richardson: The Architect, His Peers, and Their Era*, ed. Maureen Meister (Cambridge, MA: MIT Press, 1999), 76–101. O'Gorman compares Richardson's "architecture of memory" with Furness's "architecture of the machine," the former looking to the "proven past" and the other to "the industrial present" (85).

41. Sigfried Giedion, *Mechanization Takes Command* (New York: Oxford University Press, 1948), v.

42. Henry Russell Hitchcock, *Architecture: Nineteenth and Twentieth Centuries* (New York: Pelican, 1958, and later editions) remains the standard text.

43. K. G. Pontus Hultén, *The Machine: As Seen at the End of the Mechanical Age* (New York: MoMA, 1968).

44. Walter Gropius, *The New Architecture and the Bauhaus*, trans. P. Morton Shand (Boston: Charles T. Branford, n.d.), 48. Walter Gropius concluded that modernism was an outgrowth of the consequences of World War I, which required "an intellectual change of front" to bridge "the disastrous gulf between reality and idealism."

45. This cultural difference accounts for difference between the white planes of early Le Corbusier, made of stucco over rubble, and the problems that so many modern buildings have had in the physical world as dirt and weather undid their abstract planarity. Howe's stone and brick modern did not suffer from being in the world.

46. Lewis Mumford, preface to *American Architecture of the Twentieth Century*, ed. Oliver Reagan (New York: Architectural Book, 1929; reprint, *American Architectural Masterpieces*, ed. George E. Thomas (New York: Princeton Architectural Press, 1992), 233.

47. Lewis Mumford, *Roots of Contemporary American Architecture* (1952; revised, New York: Grove Press, 1959), 29. Mumford assembled the texts for his course at the University of Pennsylvania that introduced historical themes into G. Holmes Perkins's design curriculum with the purpose of enabling American students to understand the role of their culture in the creation of the modern world.

48. Lewis Mumford, "The Skyline Philadelphia—1," *New Yorker* (April 28, 1956): 106.

49. Reyner Banham, *Los Angeles: The Architecture of Four Ecologies* (London: Allen Lane; Penguin, 1971), 23.

50. Three Philadelphians were notably missing from the standard historical narrative—Frank Furness, Joseph Wilson, and William L. Price and his successor office, who together would have formed the basis for understanding the rise of the vertical style later called Art Deco as well as the architecture of George Howe and the later Philadelphia School. See Thomas, *William L. Price*, especially 174–182. The Traymore design was widely exhibited in Europe immediately after World War I in an exhibition organized by the American Institute of Architects. Its vertical motifs, lightened hue, and rich color palette led to the American 1920s while its location in the American playground of Atlantic City gave it an international presence.

51. Joseph M. Wilson, discussion of Edward Shankland's "Steel Construction in Chicago," in the British *Minutes of Proceedings of the Institution of Civil Engineers*, vol. 128 (London, by the Institution or Institution of Civil Engineers 1897), 54–55.

52. See David B. Brownlee, David De Long, and Grant Mudford, *Louis I. Kahn: In the Realm of Architecture* (Los Angeles: Museum of Contemporary Art, 1991).

53. Kenneth Frampton, "Towards a Critical Regionalism: Six Points for an Architecture of Regionalism," in *Postmodern Culture*, ed. Hal Foster (London: Pluto Press, 1985), 16–30, quotes on 20.

54. Vincent J. Scully, introduction to Brownlee, DeLong, and Mudford, *Louis I. Kahn*, 12.

55. See Michael Lewis, "Louis I. Kahn and His Lenin Memorial," *Journal of the Society of Architectural Historians* 69, no. 1 (March 2010): 7–11.

56. Robert Venturi, "The Preservation Game at Penn," in *Iconography and Electronics upon a Generic Architecture: A View from the Drafting Room* (Cambridge, MA: MIT Press, 1996), 145–148.

57. Frampton, "Towards a Critical Regionalism," 20.

58. Anne Shaw Faulkner, "Does Jazz Put the Sin in Syncopation?" *Ladies Home Journal*, August 1921, 16,34, quote on 34. Faulkner was the head of the Music Department of the General Federation of Women's Clubs.

59. David Gebhard, "The Moderne in the U.S. 1920–1941," *Architecture Association Quarterly* 2, no. 3 (July 1970): 4–20.

60. Paul Rudolph, "Regionalism in Architecture," *Perspecta* 4 (1957): 13.

61. Ralph Waldo Emerson, *Prose Works of Ralph Waldo Emerson,* "Prospects," 1 (Boston: James R. Osgood, 1875), 41.

SELECTED BIBLIOGRAPHY

This list includes principal works on Frank Furness and his milieu since 1988.

FRANK FURNESS

Architecture

Aichele, Richard O. "The Furness Restoration: The Library of the University of Pennsylvania." *Classic America* 3, no. 3 (Autumn 1988): 24–30.

Bosley, Edward. *The University of Pennsylvania Library.* New York: Phaidon Press, 1996.

Bryant, George B. "Frank Furness and Henry Holiday: A Study of Patronage, Architecture and Art." *Architectural History* 56 (January 2013): 169–211.

Caron, Barbara Ann. "James Hill House, Symbol of Status and Security." *Minnesota History* 55, no. 6 (Summer 1997): 234–249.

Goldberger, Paul. "Architecture View: In Philadelphia, a Victorian Extravaganza Lives." *New York Times,* June 2, 1991.

Hain, Mark, et al. *Pennsylvania Academy of the Fine Arts: Two Hundred Years of Excellence.* Philadelphia: Pennsylvania Academy of the Fine Arts, 2005.

Lewis, Michael. *Frank Furness: Architecture and the Violent Mind.* New York: W. W. Norton, 2001.

———. "Frank Furness, Rational Rogue." *New Criterion* 35, no. 6 (February 2013).

O'Gorman, James F. "Then and Now: A Note on the Contrasting Architecture of H. H. Richardson and Frank Furness." In *H. H. Richardson: The Architect, His Peers, and Their Era.* Edited by Maureen Meister. 76–101. Cambridge, MA: MIT Press, 1999.

Thayer, Preston. "The Railroad Designs of Frank Furness: Architecture and Corporate Imagery in the Late Nineteenth Century." Ph.D. dissertation, University of Pennsylvania, 1993.

Thomas, George E. "Frank Furness." In *Grove Encyclopedia of American Art*. Edited by Joan Marter. Vol. 1, 293–297. New York: Oxford University Press, 2011.

———. "From a Side Pew: Meditations on the Saints of St. Peter's Church." In *St. Peter's Church: Faith in Action for 250 Years*. Edited by Cordelia Frances Biddle et al. 118–127. Philadelphia: Temple University Press, 2011.

———. " 'The Happy Employment of Means to Ends': Frank Furness's Library of the University of Pennsylvania and the Industrial Culture of Philadelphia." *Pennsylvania Magazine of History and Biography* 126, no. 2 (April 2002): 249–272.

———. *First Modern: The Pennsylvania Academy of the Fine Arts*. Philadelphia: Pennsylvania Academy of the Fine Arts, 2017.

Uechi, Naomi, "Emersonian Transcendentalism in Frank Furness's Pennsylvania Academy of the Fine Arts." *Soundings* 94, nos. 3–4 (Fall–Winter 2011): 229–255.

———. *Evolving Transcendentalism in Literature and Architecture: Frank Furness, Louis Sullivan, and Frank Lloyd Wright*. Cambridge: Cambridge Scholars Publishing, 2014.

Webster, Sally. "A Mural Carved in Stone." *Museum History Journal* 5, no. 2 (2012): 283–302.

Wills, Eric. "Frank Furness, Philadelphia's Architect and Mentor to Louis Sullivan," *Architect* (October 5, 2012) http://www.architectmagazine.com/design/culture/frank-furness -philadelphias-architect-and-mentor-to-louis-sullivan_o

Family

Dearinger, David B. "William Henry Furness, Jr." In *Paintings and Sculpture in the Collection of the National Academy of Design*. 219. Manchester, VT: Hudson Hills Press, 2004.

Gibson, James M. *The Philadelphia Shakespeare Story: Horace Howard Furness and the Variorum Shakespeare*. New York: AMS Press, 1990.

Gougeon, Len, *Virtue's Hero: Emerson, Antislavery, and Reform*. Athens: University of Georgia Press, 1990.

Tatlock, Lynne. *German Writing, American Reading: Women and the Import of Fiction, 1866–1917*. Columbus: Ohio State University Press, 2012.

Tatlock, Lynne, and Matt Erlin, eds. *German Culture in Nineteenth Century America: Reception, Adaptation, Transformation*. Rochester, NY: Camden House, 2005.

Contemporaries, Rivals, and Students

Ballon, Hillary, et al. *New York's Pennsylvania Stations*. New York: W. W. Norton, 2002.

Janson, Richard H. "The Billings Library." Unpublished manuscript, University of Vermont Special Collections, 2. Quoted in David Provost, "A Gem of Architecture: The History of the Billings Library." Accessed December 2014. www.uvm.edu/campus/billings/billings provost/billingshistoryprovost.html.

Lewis, Michael J. "The Architectural Library of Henry A. Sims." In *American Architects and Their Books: 1840–1915*. Edited by Kenneth Hafertepe and James F. O'Gorman. 173–193. Amherst: University of Massachusetts Press, 2007.

O'Gorman, James F., ed. *The Makers of Trinity Church in the City of Boston*. Amherst: University of Massachusetts Press, 2004.

Thomas, George E. *William L. Price: Arts and Crafts to Modern Design*. New York: Princeton Architectural Press, 2000.

Thomas, George E., and Susan N. Snyder. "William Price's Traymore Hotel: Modernity in the Mass Resort." Special issue, "The American Hotel." *Journal of Decorative and Propaganda Arts* 25 (2005): 183–211.

Preservation

Venturi, Robert. "The Preservation Game at Penn." In *Iconography and Electronics upon a Generic Architecture: A View from the Drafting Room.* 145–148. Cambridge, MA: MIT Press, 1996.

Websites and Exhibits

"Frank Furness: Inventing Modern." Accessed April 2013, http://www. frankfurness.org.

"Furnesque: The Designs of Frank Furness." Accessed March 2016, http://furnesque.tumblr .com/.

Wojtowicz, Robert. "Review: Learning from Frank Furness: Louis Sullivan in 1873; Furness in Space: The Architect and Design Dialogues on the Late Nineteenth-Century Country House; Frank Furness: Making a Modern Library—from Gentleman's Library to Machine for Learning: Frank Furness: Working on the Railroads; Building a Masterpiece: Frank Furness's Factory for Art; Face and Form: The Art and Caricature of Frank Furness." *Journal of the Society of Architectural Historians* 72, no. 4 (December 2013): 606–609.

CULTURAL REGIONALISM AND ARTISTIC AND INDUSTRIAL CULTURE

Adams, Henry. *Eakins Revealed: The Life of an American Artist.* New York: Oxford University Press, 2005.

Baer, Christopher. "Timeline of the Pennsylvania Railroad." Accessed January 2014, http:// www.prrths.com/Hagley/PRR1905%20Mar%2005.pdf.

Brown, John K. *Baldwin Locomotive Works, 1831–1915: A Study in American Industrial Practice.* Baltimore: Johns Hopkins University Press, 1995.

Foster, Kathleen A. *Thomas Eakins Rediscovered: Charles Bregler's Thomas Eakins Collection at the Pennsylvania Academy of the Fine Arts.* New Haven, CT: Yale University Press, 1997.

Kanigel, Robert. *The One Best Way: Frederick Winslow Taylor and the Enigma of Efficiency.* New York: Viking, 1997.

Kirkpatrick, Sidney D. *The Revenge of Thomas Eakins.* New Haven, CT: Yale University Press, 2006.

Scranton, Philip. *Endless Novelty: Specialty Production and American Industrialization, 1865–1925.* Princeton, NJ: Princeton University Press, 1997.

Surowiecki, James. "Turn of the Century." *Wired* 10, no. 1 (January 2002). Accessed February 2012, http://www.wired.com/wired/archive/10.01/standards_pr.html.

Thomas, George E. "Building Penn's Brand." *Pennsylvania Gazette* 101, no. 1 (September–October 2002).

Thomas, George E., and David B. Brownlee. *Building America's First University: An Historical and Architectural Guide to the University of Pennsylvania.* Philadelphia: University of Pennsylvania Press, 2000.

Thomas, George E., et al. *Buildings of the United States: Philadelphia and Eastern Pennsylvania.* Charlottesville: University of Virginia Press, 2010.

Thomas, George E., et al. *Frank Furness: The Complete Works.* New York: Princeton Architectural Press, 1991, revised 1996.

———. "Philadelphia." In *Grove Encyclopedia of American Art.* Edited by Joan Marter. Vol. 2, 97–101. New York: Oxford University Press, 2011.

Vitiello, Domenic. "Engineering the Metropolis: The Sellers Family and Industrial Philadel-
    phia." Ph.D. dissertation, University of Pennsylvania, 2004.
———. "Engineering the Metropolis: William Sellers, Joseph M. Wilson and Industrial Phila-
    delphia." *Pennsylvania Magazine of History and Biography* 126, no. 2 (April 2002): 272–303.
———. *Engineering Philadelphia: The Sellers Family and the Industrial Metropolis.* Ithaca:
    Cornell University Press, 2013.
———. *The Philadelphia Stock Exchange and the City It Made.* Philadelphia: University of
    Pennsylvania Press, 2010.

INDEX

Adams, Henry: 81–82, 116

Anshutz, Thomas: 43

Architectural innovation centers. *See individual cities*

Armét & Davis: x

Armstrong, Thomas: 293

"Ashcan School," Philadelphia origins: 43

Atlantic City: ix, x, xi, 7, 72, 192, 217, 257 n. 11, 261 n. 50

Banham, Reyner: 13, 217, 218, 220

Baudelaire, Charles: 43

Behrens, Peter: 7, 21, 188–189 Figure 75

Bellamy, Edward: 6

Berlin: 7, 50, 60, 188

Bernal, J. F.: 46

Bierstadt, Albert: 33, 231 n. 34

Boston/Cambridge city culture: 12, 17, 31, 37, 50, 65, 81, 79–82; *American Architect and Building News*: 81; European sources for design: 81; Fogg Museum redesign: 82; Massachusetts Institute of Technology: 81; modern architectural history narrative: 215; Museum of Fine Arts: 81

Bourdieu, Pierre: cultural conservation: 214, 218, 260 n. 38

Boyle, Richard: 293

Brimmer, George W.: 92, 242 n. 9

Brimmer, Martin: 92–93

Brooks, Phillips: rector of Holy Trinity Church, Philadelphia: 82; rector of Trinity Church, Boston: 82, 86

Bryant, Gridley J. F.: 85

Burnham, Daniel H.: Chicago Plan: 226 n.9, 232 n. 45; comparison of Burnham's Rookery with Furness's Baltimore & Ohio Railroad Station: 155; Furness rival for Pennsylvania Railroad commissions: 122, 183, 256 n. 86; obituary compared to Furness: 257–258 n.12

Burns, Charles M.: iron expression in designs: 101–102, 245 n. 46, 246 n. 55, 258 n. 19

Button, Stephen Decatur: 52, 90

Cassatt, Alexander J.: Furness client (*see under* Furness—suburban and urban houses); Pennsylvania Railroad leadership: 58, 80, 136, 178, 182–185

Chaplin, Charlie: 216

Chicago: x, xi, 4, 7, 9, 10, 16, 20–23, 41, 65, 67–68, 74, 77, 118, 121–122, 155, 176, 192, 194, 196–200, 202–203, 215, 220, 226 n. 9, 222 n. 45, 256–257 n. 6

Cincinnati: 8, 16, 227 n. 21

Claghorn, James: 92, 242 n. 11, 243 n. 24

Cochran, Thomas (nineteenth-century banker): 143, 251 n. 31

267

ACKNOWLEDGMENTS

Every book is a journey but this venture has lasted longer than most. Its genesis began in 1971 when Evan Turner, director of the Philadelphia Museum of Art, asked me to undertake the research for the museum's proposed exhibit on Frank Furness that was to be held in the spring of 1973. The prime author of the catalog would be the University of Pennsylvania's brilliant young historian James F. O'Gorman and the photography would be undertaken by Cervin Robinson, the master of perfect light and the telling architectural view. I was at the time a graduate student in art history at Penn, combining documentary sources with old-fashioned connoisseurship methods to better understand Philadelphia. No better team could have been assembled. O'Gorman, with his previous focus on Henry Hobson Richardson, brought passion and knowledge about post–Civil War American architecture and a critical frame into which Furness could be situated, not as a freak, but rather as an innovative American architect. Cervin created the iconic images of existing Furness buildings that in turn led to restoration for many. Working from newspaper and journal sources, I found in my research that far from being a rogue architect responsible for a handful of bizarre designs, Furness had been remarkably prolific, receiving hundreds of commissions across the principal building types of the Victorian age that spanned the eastern third of the United States from Maine, where his clients vacationed, west to Minnesota and south to Washington, D.C.

As a direct outgrowth of the museum exhibit, in 1973 architect Hyman Myers asked me to serve as the historian for the restoration of the Pennsylvania Academy of the Fine Arts. A decade later, in 1985, Robert Venturi approached me to partner with his firm to research the history and evolution of the University of Pennsylvania Library, which would become the basis for its restoration. Venturi, Scott Brown and Associates were the Philadelphia architects most in touch with the broad cultural issues of contemporary life, applying their insights gained in multiple fields ranging from anthropology and pop culture to transform the culture of architecture. Instead of embalming the library they intended to breathe new life into it. Our collaboration returned me to thinking about Furness and the culture of Philadelphia. This resulted in an exhibition on Furness at the time of the reopening of the library and the ill-named but aspirational publication, *Frank Furness: The Complete Works* (Princeton Architectural Press, 1991, revised edition 1996). That book gave me a chance to work with two of my former students at the University of Pennsylvania, Jeffrey Cohen and Michael Lewis, who brought their remarkable talents as sleuths and analysts to our task of situating Furness in his time and finding images for the roughly 675 buildings that we had by then identified. My own essay began to look at Furness's city and his clientele, linking the idea of political and cultural reform to the architect's career.

When James O'Gorman read the draft of the *Complete Works*, he asked whether political or social reform would truly energize a career. O'Gorman remains a great teacher. This book represents my agreement with him but continues the thesis that architecture is a profoundly cultural activity. This research has led me to a different but related question, how an architect who was supposed to be so far from the norms of his time received so many commissions, and from such important clients. Furness was clearly an original thinker—but he also ran a remarkably successful practice. By my situating Furness in the cultural ecology of Philadelphia, answers to the question of why he was hired and what he intended to create become clear and begin to explain his career.

In the ensuing twenty years, just when I would think I was finished with him, Furness would pull me back in. In 1997 the Undine Barge Club involved me in the fund-raising for and restoration of its main boathouse. That project, accomplished with the assistance of a generous grant from the William B. Dietrich Foundation, brought to me a new appreciation of Furness as a colorist as he riffed on the cocoa brown of the stone with hot red-orange accents for the pointing, the chimneys, the roof crestings, and the window frames. That Furness was as careful about interior colors became evident when I was asked by

Doug Seiler to work with him on the restoration of the interior of the Academy of Vocal Arts, a former residence that had been renovated by Furness. There, Furness's wall colors picked up the hues of the woodwork, attesting again to the totality of his art.

To thank all of those who have made this journey possible would take many pages. Evan Turner, Cervin Robinson, and James O'Gorman began my journey; Jim has continued with me to the present, graciously reading, commenting, prodding. Furness family members, first Frank's grandson George Wood Furness, then direct descendant Charles Savage and by marriage the admirable addition to the family, Maria Thompson, have provided information, access to family treasures, and support. Hyman Myers, Thomas Armstrong, and Richard Boyle at the Pennsylvania Academy of the Fine Arts gave me my first opportunity to delve deeply into a single institution; Hy Myers has continued as a colleague as well. Robert Venturi, Denise Scott Brown, and the team at VSBA were the next catalysts in the opportunity both to dig into the University of Pennsylvania's culture and the history and evolution of the library and also to learn from their intense focus on making a building that would work for the digital age and beyond; Bob graciously wrote the introduction to *The Complete Works*; Denise has been a generous friend and a lamp of wisdom.

Other students have come my way to broaden my understanding of Furness's world. Domenic Vitiello began as my student, became a colleague, and has become the master of industrial Philadelphia, broadening my understanding of the systems and culture that engaged Furness and his peers. For this project, Williamena Granger from my University of Pennsylvania urban studies class tackled the questions about the Franklin Institute and the Pennsylvania Academy of the Fine Arts. In 2012 Jeffrey Cohen and Michael Lewis joined in the creation of the Frank Furness festival of exhibits, lectures, tours, and talks that reintroduced him to his native city. Jeremy Nowak, who brought his vision of Philadelphia as a center of innovation to the William Penn Foundation, thought enough of our idea of Philadelphia as a city of creativity to provide a grant in 2012 in support of the exhibits across the city that explored multiple aspects of Furness's career. David Barquist at the Philadelphia Museum of Art, Sarah Weatherwax and John Van Horne at the Library Company of Philadelphia, William Whitaker at the Architectural Archives of the University of Pennsylvania, Greg Montanaro at Drexel University, Harry Philbrick, David Brigham, and Anna Marley at the Pennsylvania Academy of the Fine Arts, Sandra Tatman and Bruce Laverty at the Athenaeum, and Steven Grasse and the Art in the Age of Mechanical Reproduction crew all brought their institutions to the celebration of Frank Furness. The symposium on libraries held in Furness's University of Pennsylvania Library was made possible by William Keller's active support and was enlivened by William Whitaker's introduction and enriched by James O'Gorman's reprise of his Ph.D. dissertation on early libraries and architect Henry Myerberg's astute commentary on the future of libraries. Michael Lewis's efforts produced a remarkable exhibit on Furness's drawings and led to an international conference on Furness at the Athenaeum to close the year of Frank Furness.

Archivists William Whitaker of the University of Pennsylvania's Architectural Archives, Mark Lloyd and James Duffin at the University of Pennsylvania Archives, Gail Rawson at the Pennsylvania Academy of the Fine Arts, John Alviti and Virginia Ward at the Franklin Institute, Sarah Weatherwax at the Library Company of Philadelphia, Bruce Laverty and Sandra Tatman at the Athenaeum of Philadelphia, Diana Peterson at the Haverford College Quaker Collection, the Historical Society of Pennsylvania, over many years have provided images and information that undergirds forty years of work, and the Ryerson and Burnham Archives at the Art Institute of Chicago have all given freely of their time and knowledge, helped with images and made possible the visual richness of this volume.

The editors at Penn Press, especially Jerome Singerman, Hannah Blake, Noreen O'Connor-Abel, and copyeditor Robert Milks have immeasurably improved the book, by both slowing it down for a more critical evaluation and hammering rough-hewn phrases into readable text.

The photography of this book is largely the work of my longtime colleague Lewis Tanner, who made the effort to photograph Furness without the limits of classical photography, using oblique angles and views to capture the inherent dynamism while using light to bring the restored Furness buildings to their original intensity. We were fortunate that much of the recent restoration work of Furness's architecture has resulted in first-rate photographs by top photographers that were made available to us for this project. Special thanks are due to Venturi, Scott Brown & Associates and their present incarnation as VSBA Architects and Planners for permission to use Matt Wargo's photographs of the restored Fisher Fine Arts Library. We are also grateful to Bernardon Haber Holloway for permission to use Don Pearse's splendid photographs of the restored Joseph Biden Station in Wilmington, Delaware, and to Amtrak's Sally Rich, who gained permission for Lewis Tanner's photographs. Lewis Tanner's photographs for the Furness Centennial of 2012 were funded by the William Penn Foundation.

Alan Hess, the guru of automobile-based West Coast modernism, read the manuscript and pushed me to look at the great gaps in the standard historical narrative that exclude Furness and much of American design. With his focus on the architecture of the highway strip and the masters of florid modernism from Oscar Niemeyer to Frank Lloyd Wright, Alan, as architect, critic, and historian, keeps our eye on the present and the future and ties Furness to the energy of now. Historians should learn from Alan Hess.

Finally and most important this study draws on the research into aesthetic and cultural meaning as an expression of contemporary life that has been the focus of study of my partner in work and life, Susan Snyder. As an architect she is resolutely focused on the world of the present, which she sees through multiple lenses from philosophy and anthropology to consumption theory. This background leads her to ask questions about the reciprocity of modern lifestyle and urban form and to understand modern places on their own terms instead of what we think they should be. Susan makes the point that historical researches and narratives, however accurate and detailed, are irrelevant unless they can be connected to now. She is of course correct. Architecture as a cultural act represents choices made within an ecological niche of a place and the values, interests, institutional narratives, and possibilities that make each region unique. Frank Furness's works, like the later works of Robert Venturi and Denise Scott Brown, designed buildings that expressed the poetry of their time and therefore were modern. This means more than simply being different or adopting a "modern" stance. To be a great architect making buildings that are expressive of their time requires understanding what it is to be alive and in the moment, engaging in the cultural issues that shape the future. More than any architect of his time Frank Furness was in the moment, making architecture that reflected the remarkable currents of innovation that swirled around him in Philadelphia in the middle of the nineteenth century.

To Jim, and Mike, and Jeff, and Bob and Denise, and above all to Susan, I couldn't have done it without you—thanks!

To Frank—enough already!